Lecture Notes
in Business Information Processing 272

Series Editors

Wil M.P. van der Aalst
  Eindhoven Technical University, Eindhoven, The Netherlands
John Mylopoulos
  University of Trento, Trento, Italy
Michael Rosemann
  Queensland University of Technology, Brisbane, QLD, Australia
Michael J. Shaw
  University of Illinois, Urbana-Champaign, IL, USA
Clemens Szyperski
  Microsoft Research, Redmond, WA, USA

More information about this series at http://www.springer.com/series/7911

Robert Pergl · Martin Molhanec
Eduard Babkin · Samuel Fosso Wamba (Eds.)

Enterprise and Organizational Modeling and Simulation

12th International Workshop, EOMAS 2016, Held at CAiSE 2016
Ljubljana, Slovenia, June 13, 2016
Selected Papers

 Springer

Editors
Robert Pergl
Czech Technical University in Prague
Prague
Czech Republic

Martin Molhanec
Czech Technical University in Prague
Prague
Czech Republic

Eduard Babkin
National Research University Higher School
 of Economics
Nizhny Novgorod
Russia

Samuel Fosso Wamba
Toulouse Business School
Toulouse University
Toulouse
France

ISSN 1865-1348   ISSN 1865-1356 (electronic)
Lecture Notes in Business Information Processing
ISBN 978-3-319-49453-1   ISBN 978-3-319-49454-8 (eBook)
DOI 10.1007/978-3-319-49454-8

Library of Congress Control Number: 2016957640

Printed on acid-free paper

This Springer imprint is published by Springer Nature
The registered company is Springer International Publishing AG
The registered company address is: Gewerbestrasse 11, 6330 Cham, Switzerland

Preface

Modern enterprises are complex living organisms. They comprise people, technologies, and human interactions intertwined in complex patterns. In analyzing these patterns, researchers face primarily two challenges: ontology and design. At the ontological level, we try to capture the status quo and understand it. In the design, we try to engineer new artifacts with some purpose. Ontology and design need to work together in the newly emerging discipline of enterprise engineering. In both ontology and design, modeling and simulation not only have prevailing role as methods of scientific inquiry, but have proven to be a viable approach.

With this research objective in mind, the Enterprise and Organizational Modeling and Simulation Workshop was founded and in the past 12 years has contributed with research results to the body of knowledge in the field. During this period, both the scope and depth have increased in accordance with the field and technological advancements. Building on strong scientific foundations, researchers have been bringing new insights into various aspects of enterprise study using modeling and simulation methods.

In recent years, we have witnessed a shifting focus, or, more precisely, a broadening of the discipline of enterprise engineering toward the human-centered view, where coordination and value co-creation play a pivotal role. Communication and coordination have always been the greatest asset that enabled the human race to progress rapidly and enterprises are not exempt to this. Leveraging communication and coordination in enterprise study thus brings us to a new mindset after the technology-focused era. However, the role of technologies is not diminished in enterprises, on the contrary, as they are the carrier of today's massive social media march, as well as the heart of other communication and coordination platforms that permeate our personal and professional lives, they carry on being an integral part of modern enterprises.

We embraced this idea in the 12th edition of EOMAS, which was held in Ljubljana, Slovenia, on June 13, 2016, in conjunction with CAiSE, sharing the topic "Information Systems for Connecting People." Out of 26 submitted papers, 12 were accepted for publication as full papers and for oral presentation. Each paper was carefully selected, reviewed, and revised, so that you, dear reader, may enjoy reading and may benefit from the proceedings as much as we enjoyed preparing the event.

June 2016   Robert Pergl

Organization

EOMAS 2016 was organized by the Department of Software Engineering, Czech Technical University in Prague in cooperation with CAISE 2016 and CIAO! Enterprise Engineering Network.

Executive Committee

General Chair

Robert Pergl — Czech Technical University in Prague, Czech Republic

Program Chairs

Eduard Babkin — National Research University – Higher School of Economics, Russia

Martin Molhanec — Czech Technical University in Prague, Czech Republic

Samuel Fosso Wamba — Toulouse Business School, France

Reviewers

E. Babkin	F. Hunka	G. Rabadi
J. Barjis	P. Kroha	P.R. Krishna
Y. Bendavid	R. Lock	S. Ramaswamy
A. Bobkowska	P. Malyzhenkov	G. Ramsey
M. Boufaida	V. Merunka	V. Romanov
M.I. Capel Tuñón	M. Molhanec	A. Rutle
S. Fosso Wamba	N. Mustafee	M. Soares
J.L. Garrido	M. Ntaliani	D. Sundaram
S. Guerreiro	R. Pergl	S. van Kervel

Sponsoring Institutions

Czech Technical University in Prague, Czech Republic
AIS-SIGMAS
CIAO! Enterprise Engineering Network

Contents

Formal Approaches

Towards Simulation- and Mining-Based Translation of Process Models

Lars Ackermann[1]([✉]), Stefan Schönig[1,2], and Stefan Jablonski[1]

[1] University of Bayreuth, Bayreuth, Germany
{lars.ackermann,stefan.schoenig,stefan.jablonski}@uni-bayreuth.de
[2] Vienna University of Economics and Business, Vienna, Austria

Abstract. Process modeling is usually done using imperative modeling languages like BPMN or EPCs. In order to cope with the complexity of human-centric and flexible business processes several declarative process modeling languages (DPMLs) have been developed during the last years. DPMLs allow for the specification of constraints that restrict execution flows. They differ widely in terms of their level of expressiveness and tool support. Furthermore, research has shown that the understandability of declarative process models is rather low. Since there are applications for both classes of process modeling languages, there arises a need for an automatic translation of process models from one language into another. Our approach is based upon well-established methodologies in process management for process model simulation and process mining without requiring the specification of model transformation rules. In this paper, we present the technique in principle and evaluate it by transforming process models between two exemplary process modeling languages.

Keywords: Process model translation · Simulation · Process mining

1 Introduction

Two different types of processes can be distinguished [1]: well-structured routine processes with exactly predescribed control flow and flexible processes whose control flow evolves at run time without being fully predefined a priori. In a similar way, two different representational paradigms can be distinguished: imperative process models like BPMN[1] models describe which activities can be executed next and declarative models define execution constraints that the process has to satisfy. The more constraints we add to the model, the less eligible execution alternatives remain. As flexible processes may not be completely known a priori, they can often be captured more easily using a declarative rather than an imperative modelling approach [2–4]. Due to the rapidly increasing interest several declarative languages like *Declare* [5], *Dynamic Condition Response* (DCR) Graphs [6] or *DPIL* [7] have been developed in parallel and can be used to represent these models. Consequently, flexible processes in organizations are

---

[1] The BPMN 2.0 standard is available at http://www.omg.org/spec/BPMN/2.0/.

© Springer International Publishing AG 2016
R. Pergl et al. (Eds.): EOMAS 2016, LNBIP 272, pp. 3–21, 2016.
DOI: 10.1007/978-3-319-49454-8_1

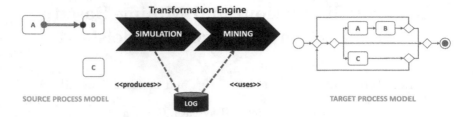

Fig. 1. Overview of the model transformation approach

frequently modeled in several different notations. Due to several reasons in many cases a translation of process models to a different language is desired: *(i)* since declarative languages are difficult to learn and understand [3], users and analysts prefer the representation of a process in an imperative notation, *(ii)* even if the user is familiar with a particular notation neither imperative nor declarative languages are superior for all use cases [8], *(iii)* adopted process execution systems as well as analysis tools are tailored to a specific language and *(iv)* since process modeling is an iterative task, the most appropriate representation for the evolving process model may switch from a declarative to an imperative nature and vice versa. To facilitate these scenarios, a cross-paradigm process model transformation technique is needed. While contemporary research mainly focuses on transforming process models between different imperative modeling languages, approaches that comprise declarative languages are still rare [8].

We fill this research gap by introducing a two-phase, bi-directional process model transformation approach that is based upon existing process simulation and mining techniques. Model-to-model transformation (M2MT) techniques usually involve the creation of transformation rules which is a cumbersome task [9,10]. Even if one is familiar with the involved process modeling languages, the particular model transformation language and the corresponding technologies built around them, there is always a manual effort. Hence, our approach, summarized in Fig. 1, avoids the definition of transformation rules completely. First, a set of valid execution traces of the process is automatically generated by simulating the source model. Second, the resulting event log is analyzed with a process mining approach that uses the target language to represent the discovered model. Once an appropiate configuration is found, the transformation can be automized completely. However, our approach does not claim to produce perfect process models, e.g. in terms of the well-known seven modeling guidelines (7PMG) [11]. Instead the approach provides a fast preview of the source process model in a different language and can be used as a starting point for model re-engineering using the target language. For the work at hand we use Declare and BPMN. We have chosen this pair of languages according to the fact that their interoperability tend to be desired [12]. Furthermore, they are preferable since they are well-known representatives of the two frequently discussed modeling paradigms. Declare is a declarative and BPMN is an imperative process modeling language. However, note that the approach works in principle with every language framework that provides model simulation and mining function-ality. The reason is its decoupling of language-dependent tools via the event log. Yet, the configuration and the result quality always depends on the particular language pair. In the context of the paper at hand we evaluate functionality and performance by transforming four simple examples and two real-life process models between BPMN and Declare.

The remainder of this paper is structured as follows: Sect. 2 describes the fundamentals of declarative process modeling at the example of Declare as well declarative and imperative simulation and mining. In Sect. 4 we introduce our approach to transform declarative process models. The approach is evaluated in Sect. 5. We discuss related work in Sect. 6 and Sect. 7 concludes the paper.

2 Background and Preliminaries

In this section we introduce declarative process modeling as well as the simula-tion and mining of declarative process models.

2.1 Declarative Process Modeling

Research has shown that DPMLs are able to cope with a high degree of flexibil-ity [13]. The basic idea is that, without modeling anything, everything is allowed. To restrict this maximum flexibility, DPMLs like Declare allow for formulating rules, i.e., constraints which form a forbidden region. An example is given with the single constraint $ChainSuccession(A, B)$ in Fig. 1, which means that task B must be executed directly after performing task A. Task C can be performed anytime. The corresponding BPMN model mainly consists of a combination of exclusive gateways. Declare focuses almost completely on control flow and, thus equivalent BPMN models may only consist of control flow elements as well. A brief discussion of issues related to differences in the expressiveness of the two languages is given in Sect. 4.1. Declarative and imperative models are in a man-ner opposed. If one adds an additional constraint to a declarative model, this usually results in removing elements in the imperative model and vice versa. If, for instance, we add the two constraints $Existence(A)$ and $Existence(C)$ to the source process model in Fig. 1, the edge directly leading to the process termina-tion event must be removed. For a transformation approach this means that the identification of appropriate transformation rules would be even more compli-cated, because a control-flow element in the source language does not necessarily relate to the same set of control-flow elements in the target language in all cases.

2.2 Process Simulation and Process Mining

In this section, we briefly describe the two methods our transformation approach is based on. Simulating process models is well-known as a cost-reducing alterna-tive to analyzing real-world behavior and properties of business processes [14]. Though, there are different simulation types, for our purpose, we exclusively refer to the principle of *Discrete-event Simulation (DES)* [15]. DES is based upon the assumption that all relevant system state changes can be expressed using discrete sequences of events. By implication this means that there is no invisible state change between two immediately consecutive events. This assumption is valid since we use a simulation technique for the purpose of model translation. This means that, in our case, a source process model fully describes the universe of system state changes. For the application in our approach we use simulation techniques to generate exemplary snapshots of process executions allowed by an underlying process model. The produced simulation results are the already mentioned event logs, containing sets of exemplary process execution traces. These logs are then consumed by process mining techniques.

Process Mining aims at discovering processes by extracting knowledge from event logs, e.g., by generating a process model reflecting the behaviour recorded in the logs [16]. There are plenty of process mining algorithms available that focus on discovering imperative process models, e.g., the simplistic *Alpha miner* [16] or the *Heuristics Miner* [17]. Recently, tools to discover declarative process models like DeclareMiner [18], MINERful [19] or SQLMiner [20] have been developed as well. In the approach at hand, we use process mining techniques to automatically model the simulated behaviour in the chosen target language.

3   Challenges and Preconditions

Our approach at hand requires some prior analysis and raises some challenges we have to deal with. Probably the most important as well as the most trivial challenge is to prevent the transformation approach from causing information loss *(CP1)*. This means that source and target model must be behaviorally equivalent. This challenge was already identified in [8]. Consequently, an equivalent representation postulates that source and target language have the same expressiveness. However, our approach itself is robust in the case of differing expressiveness. We provide a limited comparative analysis of the expressiveness of Declare and BPMN in Sect. 4.1. *(CP2)* complements the issue of expressiveness. It must be examined whether a process log *can be* expressive enough to be able to cover the behavioral semantics of a process model. Some details related to this issue are discussed in [16, pp. 114–123]. While *(CP2)* discusses the general *ability* of log data to preserve the behavioral semantics of a process model, we now have to make sure that it *actually contains* the required execution traces [17]. Therefore both transformation steps, simulation as well as process mining, require appropriate parameterizations *(CP3)*. Many process mining approaches suggest that the best parametrization is data-dependent and can therefore be determined in particular only. Hence, it is necessary to provide a strategy for the determination of well-fitting parameter values.

4   Contribution

The translation of a model specified in one language to another is usually done using *mapping rules* [9]. A translation system of n languages that uses this *direct*, mapping-rule-based translation principle requires $O(n(n-1)) = O(n^2)$ rule sets in order to be able to translate any model into any of those languages. Finding all rule sets for a system of modeling languages is, therefore, a time-consuming and cumbersome task [9]. On the contrary, our transformation approach is based on the following two core techniques: *(i)* Process Model Simulation and *(ii)* Process Mining. Therefore, our approach does not require the creation of transformation rules but uses the core idea to extract the *meaning* of a particular model by generating and analyzing valid instances of the model through simulation. The resulting event logs are the usual input for process mining techniques such as [17, 18, 21]. This means that our transformation approach is based on the assumption that we are able to find appropriate simulation and mining technologies for the individual language pair. In the case of our continuously used BPMN-Declare language pair several simulation and mining techniques are ready to use. Since process mining is an inductive discipline and simulation is not necessarily complete, our approach in general is *lossy*. However, in order to reduce the information loss, we discuss appropriate configurations of the used technologies and evaluate them using exemplary process models.

4.1 Language and Log Expressiveness

We have to discuss two key factors for our translation approach: *(i)* Differences in the expressiveness of the particular source and target language and *(ii)* potentially insufficient expressiveness of event logs. Equal *Language Expressiveness* (*CP1*) means, in our context, that two languages, e.g. BPMN and Declare, are able to model the same semantics, no matter if the resulting model is imperative or declarative. Considering our two exemplary process modeling languages, we can easily find significant differences. Even though Declare is extendable, it's expressiveness is currently limited to concepts that describe tasks and temporal or existence constraints. In contrast, BPMN allows for modeling organizational associations as well as data flow and other elements. In order to provide a profound catalog that describes model patterns which can be translated successfully, an extensive comparison of the two particular process modeling languages is required. Due to the fact that such a deep analysis is currently not available and because this topic would go beyond the scope of this paper we choose example processes for our evaluation that can be represented in both languages.

The second issue is the question of *Sufficient Log Expressiveness* (*CP2*). An event log "contains historical information about 'When, How, and by Whome?' " [22]. An event log describes examples of process executions and, hence, possible traces through the source process model. Process mining techniques are built based upon the following assumptions regarding the log contents and structure: *(i)* a process consists of cases that are represented by traces, *(ii)* traces consist of events and *(iii)* events can have attributes like the activity name, a timestamp, associated resources and a transaction type [16]. An event can, therefore, unequivocally be associated with the corresponding activity, resources and the type of the system state change. All of these information describe a single state change but not dependencies between state changes. Thus, process

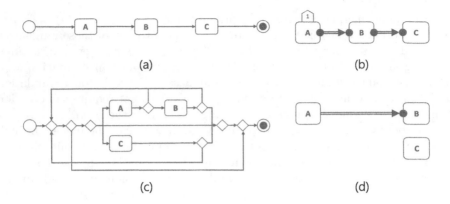

Fig. 2. Continuous example

mining techniques are limited to the information that can be encoded in sequential, discrete event logs. However, let us consider model *(d)* shown in Fig. 2. In order to extract this $chainPrecedence(A, B)$ rule from a process event log, the following condition must be valid for all traces: Whenever an event occurs that refers to activity B then the event occurring immediately before[2] must refer to activity A. This suggests that temporal relationships can be extracted from the log if the latter's quality and length is sufficient. However, the activity labeled with C in the same model is not restricted by any constraint. This means, by implication, that it can be executed arbitrarily often. Because a log has a finite length, we cannot encode this knowledge. Instead the mining technique could use some threshold following the assumption, that, if a particular task has been executed n times, the number of possible executions is theoretically unlimited.

Like in the case of language expressiveness, a much deeper dive into the limitations of information encoding in discrete-event logs is required but would go beyond the scope of this paper. So far we briefly discussed, what information an event log is *able* to provide. The following three subsections focus on *if* and *how* we can make sure that the desired information are contained in the log.

4.2   General Simulation Parameters

There are two general properties which influence the transformation quality as well as the performance of the whole approach, i.e. *(i) the Number of Traces (N)* and *(ii) the Maximum Trace Length (L)*.

Setting the value for N appropriately is the basis for including all relevant paths in the log. Considering the example BPMN model in Fig. 2(c), there are several gateways whereby each unique decision leads to a new unique execution trace. Hence, we need a strategy for determining the minimum number of traces to include in the log. However, this number depends on the second parameter L. Without providing a value for L the simulation of a process model that allows for

---

[2] Declare does not distinguish between different transaction types.

loops could hypothetically produce traces of infinite length. Thus, the potential number of different traces is also infinite. We therefore need an upper bound for L. The lower bound is governed by the process model itself.

The appropriate setting ($CP3$) of the introduced parameters depends on the source process model. In the case of the BPMN model in Fig. 2(a) the trace $<ABC>$ describes the model's behavioral semantics exhaustively. Obviously this single trace does not represent the semantics of Fig. 2(c) appropriately, because of several decision points and loops. A simple formula to calculate the minimum number is shown in Eq. 1. This formula considers the size of the set of tasks ($|T|$) and is further based on the knowledge that the length of the longest possible sequence of tasks without repetition is given by L. The formula also factors in arbitrary task orderings (the ith power) and shorter paths (the sum). The formula for L is based on the idea that all tasks of the longest trace without repetition ($|T|$) could be repeated (Eq. 2). Using these formulae we do not need any information about the structure of the process model.

$$N \geq \sum_{i \leq L}^{i=0} |T|^i \tag{1}$$

$$L \geq 2|T| \tag{2}$$

Though both formulae describe just the lower bound for both dimensions, in practice, the process model reduces the number of allowed task combinations and it is therefore not necessary to choose higher values for both parameters. Quite the contrary, research has shown that it is not necessary to provide a *complete* log in order to discover a well-fitting process model [23]. For many approaches it is sufficient to include all *directly-follows examples*, i.e. each ordered pair of consecutive tasks. Since N increases exponentially with L, using the presented formula makes the approach expensive very fast and we therefore suggest even significantly lower values. Hence, our evaluation has the twofold purpose to test our approach in general and to serve as a guideline for checking the quality of the transformation for a particular configuration in practice.

Even if we calculate an appropriate number of traces there is no guarantee that all relevant paths are considered. Hence, the particular simulation engine is supposed to ensure that all possible or at least the desired traces are contained in the log. However, since this cannot be configured directly in the chosen tools, we provide a simplified configuration, which is discussed in the next two subsections. This issue is also summarized in Sect. 5.1. Fortunately, in Sect. 5 it shows that this configuration is sufficient but yet will be improved in future.

4.3   Simulating Imperative Process Models

To be suitable for our purposes, the simulation technique has to be able to produce a certain number of traces of appropriate length. In contrast, simulation tools built for measuring KPIs[3] usually use different configurable

---

[3] KPI = Key Performance Indicator (used in performance measurement to rate success regarding a particular ambition).

parameters [22,24]: *(i)* the Case-Arrival Process *(CAP)*, *(ii)* the service times *(st)* for tasks as well as *(iii)* the probabilities for choices. Since our intent is to reuse existing techniques and technologies we have to map our desired simulation parameters from Sect. 2.2 to the implemented parameters of the particular simulation technique.

The CAP influences the number of traces that can be generated and usually is described by an the inter-arrival time (t_a) and a simulation duration d. In order to ensure that the desired amount of traces N is generated, t_a must be set to a constant value. Finally d can be calculated according to the formula $d = \frac{N}{t_a}$.

Another influencing factor is the task *service time*, i.e. the usual duration. For our purposes these service times have to be equal and constant for all tasks. Executing two tasks A and B in parallel with $st_B > st_A$ would always produce the same sequence during simulation: $<...AB...>$. Otherwise, the subsequent Declare mining algorithm would falsely introduce a *chainsuccession(A, B)* instead of a correct *coexistence(A, B)* rule. With constant and equal values the ordering is completely random which actually is one intuition of a parallel gateway. However, this *randomness* must also be supported by the particular simulation tool.

Probability distributions are used to simulate human decisions [22] at modeled gateways, which means that the outgoing edges are chosen according to a probability that follows this distribution. The probabilities for all outgoing edges of one gateway must sum up to one and, thus, the uniform-distributed probability can be calculated according to the formula $\frac{1}{n_{O,G}}$ with $n_{O,G}$ denoting the number of outgoing edges for gateway G. Determining these probabilities only locally leads to significantly lower probabilities for traces on highly branched paths. However, since we assume a completely unstructured process when developing Formula 1, in many cases we will generate far too much traces. Thus, we suggest this as an initial solution which is proved in our evaluation.

Configuring the maximum trace length L is slightly more complicated. The reason is that imperative processes are very strict in terms of valid endings of instances. This involves some kind of *look ahead* mechanism which is able to check whether the currently chosen step for a trace does still allow for finishing the whole process validly *and* within a length $\leq L$. Our approach restricts the trace length in a post-processing step based on a simulation of arbitrary length which is only restricted by the simulation duration. Afterwards we select only those traces which do not exceed the configured maximum trace length.

4.4 Simulating Declarative Process Models

The main difference between imperative and declarative process modeling languages is that the former means modeling allowed paths through the process explicitly utilizing directed-graph representations while the latter means modeling them implicitly based on rules. In [25] the authors presented an approach for simulating Declare models based on a six-step transformation technique. First, each activity name is mapped to one alphabetic character. Afterwards, the Declare model is transformed into a set of regular expressions. For each regular expression there exists an equivalent *Finite State Automaton (FSA)* which is derived in the third step. Each regular expression and, therefore, each FSA corresponds to one Declare constraint. To make sure that the produced traces respect all constraints the product of all automatons is calculated in step four. During the next step, the traces are generated by choosing a random path along the FSA product and by concatenating the characters for all passed transitions. In the sixth and last step the characters are mapped to the original activity names and the traces are written to a log file. Similar to the simulation of imperative process models, it is necessary to configure the parameters N and L. In [25] both parameters can be configured directly. In contrast, we have no influence on the probability distribution for the traces since the algorithm internally assigns equal probabilities to all outgoing edges of each state in the FSA. Hence, again, there is a mismatch regarding the probability for highly branched paths as in the simulation for imperative models. Though the approach transforms Declare models to FSAs in a rather complex manner we prefer it over the approach presented in [26] since the former has been designed explicitly for the purpose of log generation and due to our personal positive experiences with the approach.

4.5 Mining Imperative BPMN Process Models

In order to complete our tool chain for translating Declare models to BPMN we selected the Flexible Heuristics Miner (FHM) [17]. Though this mining algorithm first produces a so called *Causal Net* that must be later converted to BPMN, the advantages outweigh the disadvantages: *(i)* The algorithm is able to overcome the drawbacks of simpler approaches (e.g. Alpha algorithm [16]). *(ii)* It is specialized for dealing with complex constructs. This is very important since a Declare model with not too many constraints usually leads to a comparatively complex BPMN model. *(iii)* Finally, the algorithm is able to handle low-structured domains (LSDs), which is important since the source language is Declare - which was designed *especially* for modeling LSDs.

After choosing an appropriate algorithm a robust and domain-driven configuration is needed. A suggestion is shown in Table 1 (left). The *Dependency* parameter should be set to a value < 50.0 because the simulation step produces noise-free logs. It is therefore valid to assume that, according to this configuration, a path only observed once was also allowed in the source model and is therefore not negligible. The dependency value for such a single occurrence is 50.

Table 1. Miner configurations: FHM (l), DMM (r)

Param	Value		Param	Value
Relative-to-best	0.0		Ignore Event Types	false
Dependency	49.0		Minimum Support	100.0
Length-one/two loop	0.0		Alpha	0.0
Long distance	100.0			
All tasks connected	true			
Long distance dep.	true			
Ignore loop dep. thresh.	false			

Consequently, there is no need for setting a *Relative-to-best* threshold higher than zero. If a dependency already has been accepted and the difference between the corresponding dependency value and a different dependency is lower than this threshold, this second dependency is also accepted. *All tasks connected* means that all non-initial tasks must have a predecessor and all non-final tasks must have a successor. The *Long distance dependencies* threshold is an additional threshold for identifying pairs of immediately or distant consecutive tasks. Setting this value to 100.0 means, at the example of tasks A and B, that A and B must be always consecutive and must have equal frequencies. The FHM requires some special attention for short loops like $<...AA...>$ or $<...ABA...>$. Setting both parameters to 0 means that if a task has been repeated at least once in one trace, we want to cover this behavior in the target model. Consequently we have set *Ignore loop dependency thresholds* to false. This configuration completes our tool chain for translating a Declare model to a trace-equivalent BPMN model.

4.6   Mining Declarative Process Models

Choosing an appropriate mining technique for discovering Declare models is much easier. The reason is that there are only three major approaches, one of them is called *MINERful* [19]. The second, which is more a compilation of a mining technique and several pre- and post-processing steps, is called *Declare Maps Miner* (DMM) [27,28]. Finally, there is the *UnconstrainedMiner* [29] but since its current implementation does not produce a Declare model but a report that describes the identified constraints along with quality measurements we discarded it. Hence, we selected the second bundle of techniques, where the decision this time is driven by a slight difference regarding quality tests [19] and our own experiences pertaining the tool integration. Though both approaches are comparable in terms of the result quality MINERful is a bit more sensitive to the configuration of two leading parameters, namely *confidence* and *interest factor*. However, MINERful outperforms the DMM in terms of computation time. But according to the experiences of the authors in [19], the latter is more appropriate in case of offline execution and is therefore also more appropriate for a highly automated tool chain. Finally the question of a target-aimed configuration is answered in Table 1 (right). Setting *Ignoring Event Types* to *false* is necessary since our source model is a BPMN model and therefore may allow for parallel execution of activities. A log is based on the linear time dimension, which means that we have to distinguish between the *start* and the *completion* of an activity, in order to represent a parallel execution. Since Declare does not allow for parallelism explicitly, we have to interpolate this behavior through consideration of the event types. Of course, this leads to a duplication of the tasks, compared to the original model. The threshold for the *Minimum Support* can be set to 100.0 because the log does not contain noise. The last parameter, called *Alpha* avoids that some considered rules are trivially true. This can be the case, for instance, with the *chainprecedence*(A, B) rule in Fig. 2(d). If B is never executed this rule would be falsely consolidated because it is never violated.

5   Evaluation

Within this section, we evaluate our approach in two stages, starting in Sect. 5.4 with a translation of the continuous simple examples from Fig. 2. The second stage considers more complex real-life models in Sect. 5.5. We also describe a chain of well-established tools which are equipped with the desired functionalities as well as meet the assumptions and requirements we identified in the course of the paper at hand. The latter are summarized within the immediately following subsection.

5.1   Assumptions and Restrictions

There is a lack of appropriate translation techniques for process models, which by implication is one justification to provide such a technique. Consequently, our approach is based on a couple of assumptions and restrictions which are summarized within this subsection.

Log Contents. An event log is a snapshot of the reality and, therefore, is and must be finite. A process model that allows for arbitrarily repeating activities could theoretically produce an infinite number of traces and traces of infinite length. However, this issue and others that are related to the log's expressiveness are not limited to our approach. Instead they are already known from the process mining domain [16].

Simulation Configuration. In order to translate Declare models or BPMN models appropriately into the opposite language, it is necessary to preserve their behavioral semantics in the event log. This means that the simulation accounts for an exhaustive traversal of all possible execution paths. In graph-based simulation tools like those, we used in the paper at hand, this means that for all branching points the outgoing edges must be chosen in all possible combinations. Both of the discussed simulation techniques make the decision locally, i.e. the outgoing edges are chosen according to a locally specified probability. Due to the nature of stochastic experiments, there is no guarantee that all possible paths through the model are traversed.

Tool Availability. Our approach is based upon two techniques, process simulation and process mining. One of the major advantages is the opportunity to reuse existing implementations - as long as they are available for the particular pair of languages. Otherwise the approach cannot be applied without accepting the manual effort of implementing one or even both required tools.

Choice of Example Models. As already mentioned, the quality of the results of a translation system is heavily dependent on the equality of the expressiveness of the involved languages. Due to the fact that there is no corresponding comparison between Declare and BPMN, we decided to choose exemplary models that can be represented in both languages. This restricts BPMN models to the control-flow perspective since Declare does not consider the other perspectives, yet.

5.2 Implementation

Many BPMN modeling tools provide simulation features, however, not all of them allow for the export of simulated traces. IYOPRO [30] allows for importing existing BPMN models. In order to run the simulation appropriately it is possible to influence the following basic parameters: *(i)* Inter-arrival times for *Start Events*, *(ii)* the duration of activities and *(iii)* probability distributions for the simulation of decisions at gateways. Additionally it is possible to modify the overall simulated execution time. These parameters influence the number and contents of generated traces. In order to model the preferred trace length we have to run multiple simulations with different probability distributions for gateways. Paths through the process are computed randomly.

For simulating Declare models, we use the implementation of [25]. Since its primary application was the quality measurement of declarative process mining tools it is possible to specify the number of traces to generate and the maximum trace length explicitly. The Declare models are transformed into *Finite State Automata* and paths along them are chosen randomly. We export the traces in the XES standard format. For mining processes we use the well-known *ProM 6* toolkit [31]. For BPMN it provides the *BPMN Miner* extension [32], that contains the FHM and for Declare we use the *DMM* plugin [18]. Additionally, we use ProM's conformance checking features for transformation quality measurement.

5.3 Used Evaluation Metrics

Since the final result is generated by process mining techniques we can reuse the corresponding well-known evaluation metrics. For reasons of comprehensibility we first give a small, fuzzy introduction to these metrics [16]:

(1) *Fitness*: Proportion of logged traces *parsable* by discovered model,
(2) *Appropriateness*: Prop. of behavior allowed by model but not seen in log,
(3) *Generalization*: Discovered models should be able to parse unseen logs, too,
(4) *Simplicity*: Several criteria, e.g. model size (number of nodes/edges).

It would be more appropriate to directly measure the equality of source and target model but unfortunately there are no solid metrics, yet. We consider only fitness and appropriateness. The resulting simplicity of a model completely depends on the used process mining algorithm and cannot be controlled by the available simulation parameters. Furthermore, measuring this dimension independently from the source model does not give any clue whether the model complexity is caused by inappropriate mining configuration or by the complexity of the source model.

Generalization metrics are used to assess the degree of *overfitting* a process mining approach causes. Overfitting is a well-known issue in machine learning and is, in our case, caused by process mining techniques that assume the completeness of a log regarding the allowed behavior. The discovered model is tailored to the log data used for training but may be not able to explain an unseen log of a second process execution if the log *is not* complete. Though, our simulation engines should be configured to produce all traces necessary to explain the source model's behavior, this cannot be guaranteed, yet. To the current state of research, the generalization ability of the approach is hard to measure since process mining techniques currently lack appropriate methods. It is therefore strictly planned to develop a method for measuring the generalization ability based on cross validation through splitting the log data into training and testing sets.

Since there are no comparable approaches so far, this paper focuses on checking the principal capability of the presented translation system in terms of correctness - which can be measured through the two metrics for fitness and appropriateness. For our calculations in the following subsection we use the formulae for fitness and appropriateness provided in [33] but do not reuse the log files for measuring the appropriateness that already have been used in the mining step. Instead we generate new log files for the evaluation in order to compensate our missing generalization evaluation to a certain degree.

5.4   Transformation Result Quality: Simple Models

In order to start measuring the transformation quality we first apply the introduced metrics to our small continuous examples shown in Fig. 2. The corresponding simulation configurations and measurement results are shown in Table 2. All measurements have been produced using the corresponding ProM replay plugins with anew generated and completely random 10000 sample traces for each of the four resulting models. The experiments have been repeated ten times and the results have been averaged. Though the used source model for this first evaluation are very simplistic, it is possible to discern four important facts. First, the two simplest models (cf. Fig. 2(a) and (b)) can be transformed correctly, as expected, with a very low amount of traces of short length. Secondly, the appropriateness is almost always 100 %. The reason is that, the less traces are passed to the relevant process miner, the more restrictive is the resulting model. Both miners treat the traces as the only allowed behavior and, therefore, produce models that are as strict as the traces themselves. The third insight is that in the case of the more complex models (cf. Fig. 2(c) and (d)) the fitness decreases. This means that for translating from BPMN to Declare more traces are required to raise the fitness, which is expected due to more execution alternatives. Finally, we have to point out that we are able to achieve 100 % fitness and appropriateness because our simulation components generate noise-free logs.

5.5   Transformation Result Quality: Complex Models

Our second evaluation state is based on two more complex models than used in the previous subsection. The Declare source model is a model mined from real-life log data which was provided in the context of the *BPI Challenge 2014*[4]

---

[4] Log available at: http://www.win.tue.nl/bpi/doku.php?id=2014:challenge.

Table 2. Quality: models (a)–(d) shown in Fig. 2

N	L	Fitness				Appropriateness			
		(a)	(b)	(c)	(d)	(a)	(b)	(c)	(d)
10	3	1.0	1.0	0.7110	0.4932	1.0	1.0	0.9917	1.0
100	3	1.0	1.0	0.8911	0.6295	1.0	1.0	1.0	1.0
1000	3	1.0	1.0	1.0	0.7286	1.0	1.0	1.0	1.0
10000	3	1.0	1.0	1.0	0.7286	1.0	1.0	1.0	1.0
10	6	1.0	1.0	0.713	0.6111	1.0	1.0	0.9929	1.0
100	6	1.0	1.0	0.9874	0.7257	1.0	1.0	1.0	1.0
1000	6	1.0	1.0	1.0	0.9975	1.0	1.0	1.0	1.0
10000	6	1.0	1.0	1.0	1.0	1.0	1.0	1.0	1.0
10	9	1.0	1.0	0.713	0.6420	1.0	1.0	0.9929	1.0
100	9	1.0	1.0	1.0	0.7844	1.0	1.0	1.0	1.0
1000	9	1.0	1.0	1.0	1.0	1.0	1.0	1.0	1.0
10000	9	1.0	1.0	1.0	1.0	1.0	1.0	1.0	1.0

and is shown in Fig. 3. Furthermore, the mined model has been used in [25] as evaluation data, too. The logs have been produced in the context of customer-service-desk interactions regarding disruptions of ICT[5] services. Consequently, the model has been mined with the Declare Maps Miner extension for ProM. Our more complex BPMN model has already been used in [34] in order to prove the understandability of BPMN models supported by human-readable textual work instructions. The model, shown in Fig. 4 allows for 48 different paths through a bread-delivery process. Again, we evaluated the translation quality with ten log

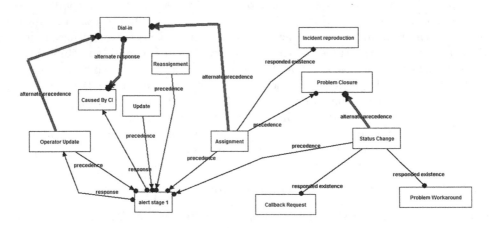

Fig. 3. Process model discovered from BPI challenge 2014 Log

---

[5] ICT = Information and Communication Technology.

Table 3. Model translation quality BPI Ch. 2014 (l), bread deliv. process (r)

N	L	Fitness	App.
100	24	0.6371	1.0
1000	24	0.8181	1.0
10000	24	0.9992	1.0
100000	24	1.0	1.0
100	36	0.6554	1.0
1000	36	0,8988	1.0
10000	36	0.9998	1.0
100000	36	1.0	1.0

N	L	Fitness	App.
10	15	0.5	1.0
100	15	0.6253	1.0
1000	15	0.7462	1.0
10000	15	0.8784	1.0
100000	36	0.9335	1.0

files containing 10000 random traces, respectively. The averaged quality measurements are shown in Table 3. Both tables show that we are able to translate the models to a very high degree and confirm the findings of the previous evaluation step, which means that the quality is only a matter of fitness and, thus, target models produced with too few traces tend to be unable to generate the behavior seen in the evaluation log, which is an expected and well-known issue in machine learning. For these two example a significant higher amount of traces is required.

Additionally, we analyzed the performance of our approach only slightly, since it is based upon techniques that have already been analyzed regarding the computation time. Our evaluation has been performed on the following hardware:

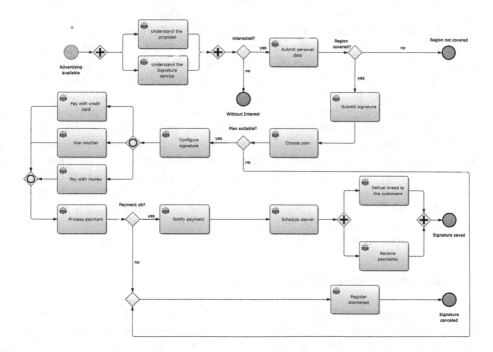

Fig. 4. Bread delivery process (source: [34])

Dell Latitude E6430, intel Core i7 3720QM (4 × 2.6 GHz), 16 GB DDR3 internal memory, SSD, Windows 8 (64 bit). Translating models like our small continuous examples in Fig. 2 require only few traces and, therefore can be performed in an average time of one second. Translating our two more complex models require far more traces which leads to an average computation time of 8 (BPI Ch.) or 10 (Bread del.) seconds. For more precise and broader performance analysis, please consider the corresponding literature for the four used components [17, 25, 28, 30].

6   Related Work

This paper relates to different streams of research: process modelling approaches and process model transformation. In general, the differences between declarative and imperative process modeling approaches have been discussed in [3] where both imperative and declarative languages are investigated with respect to process model understanding. One of the most relevant papers in the context of process model transformation between these different paradigms is [8]. The paper describes an approach to derive imperative process models from declarative models. It utilizes a sequence of steps, leading from declarative constraints to regular expressions, then to a finite state automaton and finally to a Petri net. Secondly there is an approach [35] which translates declarative workflow models, specified in the DecSerFlow language, into an equivalent operational model based on the Petri net notation. The transformation approach maps each Dec-SerFlow construct to a Petri net pattern that achieves the same behavioral effect and merges the partial nets for conjoining constraints. The former approach does not provide the bi-directionality feature of a translation system and the latter focuses a different declarative language than our approach and requires the definition of new mapping rules in case of new language patterns. To the best of our knowledge there is no other specific approach for the translation of declarative process models. There are, however, different approaches that translate process models from one imperative language to another one, e.g., BPMN to BPEL [36]. Furthermore our work is related to the approach presented in [9] which avoids writing cumbersome model transformation rules and instead generates them based on examples. Our approach also works on exemplary models, however, these are composed using simulation techniques which means that we prevent the user from any overhead. For our transformation approach we make use of process model simulation [25] and process mining techniques [17, 28] that have already been mentioned and described throughout the paper.

7   Conclusion and Future Work

The process model translation approach presented in this paper provides an alternative to classical M2MT-based systems. It is based on the assumption that a representative event log can be used as a transfer medium for model translation systems. In order to ensure suitability in practice we evaluated our approach on real-life data. Our evaluation showed that with a certain amount of simulated traces it is possible to cover the behavioral semantics of our exemplary source models in the logs. Since there are only few process model translation approaches we decided to discuss our generic solution in principle first and we therefore focused on a very strict selection of technologies. This should be complemented by a comparative analysis of technology compilations and precisely tailored configurations. Hence, the evaluation serves the two-fold purpose to prove the approach in principle as well as to check the translation result quality for a reasonable tool configuration. Furthermore, we are currently working on an extensive study on the applicability of our approach compared to traditional M2MT-based techniques. The result can be used as a guideline for the decision whether the process model translation should be implemented based on M2MT or via simulation and mining techniques.

Additionally, in order to use the approach in real-life applications, the general log and language expressiveness must be investigated in advance. Furthermore there are pairs of languages where both provide a certain support for modeling relations beyond plain control-flow dependencies. In order to generate all relevant traces from large and highly branched BPMN models, it is necessary to find a more suitable algorithm to define appropriate probability distributions for decisions at gateways. This could be achieved, for instance, if the algorithm considers not only the number of outgoing edges of each gateway but also the branching factor of all subsequent gateways. These two improvements lead to a more accurate calculation of the maximum number of traces and, hence, of the number of required simulated traces.

We based our evaluation in the paper at hand on a selection of quality metrics well-known in the domain of process mining. However, for general M2MT approaches another common quality measurement are property tests. There the equivalence of source and target model is measured based on the *proportion of properties* that are equivalent. In the context of process models, an example is a particular order or co-existence property of a pair of activities. Furthermore, we are currently waiting for the results of a survey regarding the understandability of the translation results.

References

1. Jablonski, S.: MOBILE: a modular workflow model and architecture. In: Working Conference on Dynamic Modelling and Information Systems (1994)
2. van der Aalst, W., Pesic, M., Schonenberg, H.: Declarative workflows: balancing between flexibility and support. CSRD **23**(2), 99–113 (2009)
3. Pichler, P., Weber, B., Zugal, S., Pinggera, J., Mendling, J., Reijers, H.A.: Imperative versus declarative process modeling languages: an empirical investigation. In: Daniel, F., Barkaoui, K., Dustdar, S. (eds.) BPM 2011. LNBIP, vol. 99, pp. 383–394. Springer, Heidelberg (2012). doi:10.1007/978-3-642-28108-2_37
4. Vaculín, R., Hull, R., Heath, T., Cochran, C., Nigam, A., Sukaviriya, P.: Declarative business artifact centric modeling of decision and knowledge intensive business processes. In: EDOC, pp. 151–160 (2011)

5. Pesic, M., Aalst, W.M.P.: A declarative approach for flexible business processes management. In: Reichert, M., Reijers, H.A. (eds.) BPM 2015. LNCS, vol. 256, pp. 169–180. Springer, Heidelberg (2006). doi:10.1007/11837862_18

6. Hildebrandt, T., Mukkamala, R.R., Slaats, T., Zanitti, F.: Contracts for cross-organizational workflows as timed dynamic condition response graphs. J. Logic Algebraic Program. **82**(5), 164–185 (2013)

7. Zeising, M., Schönig, S., Jablonski, S.: Towards a common platform for the support of routine and agile business processes. In: CollaborateCom (2014)

8. Prescher, J., Di Ciccio, C., Mendling, J.: From declarative processes to imperative models. In: SIMPDA, pp. 162–173 (2014)

9. Wimmer, M., Strommer, M., Kargl, H., Kramler, G.: Towards model transformation generation by-example. In: HICSS, pp. 285–294 (2007)

10. Sun, Y., White, J., Gray, J.: Model transformation by demonstration. In: Schürr, A., Selic, B. (eds.) MODELS 2009. LNCS, vol. 5795, pp. 712–726. Springer, Heidelberg (2009). doi:10.1007/978-3-642-04425-0_58

11. Mendling, J., Reijers, H.A., van der Aalst, W.M.: Seven process modeling guidelines (7PMG). Inf. Softw. Technol. **52**(2), 127–136 (2010)

12. Giacomo, G., Dumas, M., Maggi, F.M., Montali, M.: Declarative process modeling in BPMN. In: Zdravkovic, J., Kirikova, M., Johannesson, P. (eds.) CAiSE 2015. LNCS, vol. 9097, pp. 84–100. Springer, Heidelberg (2015). doi:10.1007/978-3-319-19069-3_6

13. Fahland, D., Lübke, D., Mendling, J., Reijers, H., Weber, B., Weidlich, M., Zugal, S.: Declarative versus imperative process modeling languages: the issue of understandability. In: Halpin, T., Krogstie, J., Nurcan, S., Proper, E., Schmidt, R., Soffer, P., Ukor, R. (eds.) BPMDS/EMMSAD -2009. LNBIP, vol. 29, pp. 353–366. Springer, Heidelberg (2009). doi:10.1007/978-3-642-01862-6_29

14. Aalst, W.M.P.: Business process simulation revisited. In: Barjis, J., Pergl, R., Babkin, E. (eds.) EOMAS 2015. LNBIP, vol. 231, pp. 1–14. Springer, Heidelberg (2010). doi:10.1007/978-3-642-15723-3_1

15. Stewart, R.: Simulation: The Practice of Model Development and Use. Wiley, Hoboken (2004)

16. van der Aalst, W.: Process Mining: Discovery, Conformance and Enhancement of Business Processes, vol. 2. Springer, Heidelberg (2011)

17. Weijters, A., Ribeiro, J.: Flexible heuristics miner (FHM). In: CIDM, pp. 310–317 (2011)

18. Maggi, F., Mooij, A., van der Aalst, W.: User-guided discovery of declarative process models. In: CIDM (2011)

19. Di Ciccio, C., Mecella, M.: On the discovery of declarative control flows for artful processes. TMIS **5**(4), 24:1–24:37 (2015)

20. Schönig, S., Rogge-Solti, A., Cabanillas, C., Jablonski, S., Mendling, J.: Proceedings of the 27th International Conference on Advanced Information Systems Engineering, CAiSE 2015, Stockholm, Sweden, 8–12 June 2015 (2015, in press)

21. Schönig, S., Cabanillas, C., Jablonski, S., Mendling, J.: Mining the organisational perspective in agile business processes. In: Schmidt, R., Guédria, W., Bider, I., Guerreiro, S. (eds.) BPMDS/EMMSAD 2016. LNBIP, vol. 248, pp. 37–52. Springer, Heidelberg (2015). doi:10.1007/978-3-319-19237-6_3

22. Aalst, W.M.P.: Handbook on Business Process Management: Introduction, Methods, and Information Systems. Springer, Heidelberg (2015)

23. Leemans, S.J.J., Fahland, D., Aalst, W.M.P.: Discovering block-structured process models from incomplete event logs. In: Ciardo, G., Kindler, E. (eds.) PETRI NETS 2014. LNCS, vol. 8489, pp. 91–110. Springer, Heidelberg (2014). doi:10. 1007/978-3-319-07734-5_6
24. Nakatumba, J., Rozinat, A., Russell, N.: Business process simulation: how to get it right. In: International Handbook on BPM (2008)
25. Ciccio, C., Bernardi, M.L., Cimitile, M., Maggi, F.M.: Generating event logs through the simulation of declare models. In: Barjis, J., Pergl, R., Babkin, E. (eds.) EOMAS 2015. LNBIP, vol. 231, pp. 20–36. Springer, Heidelberg (2015). doi:10.1007/978-3-319-24626-0_2
26. Westergaard, M.: Better algorithms for analyzing and enacting declarative work-flow languages using LTL. In: Rinderle-Ma, S., Toumani, F., Wolf, K. (eds.) BPM 2011. LNCS, vol. 6896, pp. 83–98. Springer, Heidelberg (2011). doi:10.1007/978-3-642-23059-2_10
27. Maggi, F.M., Bose, R.P.J.C., Aalst, W.M.P.: Efficient discovery of understand-able declarative process models from event logs. In: Ralyté, J., Franch, X., Brinkkemper, S., Wrycza, S. (eds.) CAiSE 2012. LNCS, vol. 7328, pp. 270–285. Springer, Heidelberg (2012). doi:10.1007/978-3-642-31095-9_18
28. Maggi, F.M.: Declarative process mining with the declare component of ProM. In: BPM (Demos) (2013)
29. Westergaard, M., Stahl, C.: Leveraging super-scalarity and parallelism to provide fast declare mining without restrictions. Theor. Math. Phys. **181**(2), 1418–1427 (2014)
30. Uhlmann, E., Gabriel, C., Raue, N.: An automation approach based on work-flows and software agents for industrial product-service systems. CIRP **30**, 341–346 (2015)
31. Dongen, B.F., Medeiros, A.K.A., Verbeek, H.M.W., Weijters, A.J.M.M., Aalst, W.M.P.: The ProM framework: a new era in process mining tool support. In: Ciardo, G., Darondeau, P. (eds.) ICATPN 2005. LNCS, vol. 3536, pp. 444–454. Springer, Heidelberg (2005). doi:10.1007/11494744_25
32. Conforti, R., Dumas, M., García-Bañuelos, L., La Rosa, M.: BPMN miner: auto-mated discovery of BPMN process models with hierarchical structure. Inf. Syst. **56**, 284–303 (2016)
33. Van der Aalst, W., Adriansyah, A., van Dongen, B.: Replaying history on process models for conformance checking and performance analysis. Wiley Interdisc. Rev. DM KD **2**(2), 182–192 (2012)
34. Rodrigues, R., Azevedo, L.G., Revoredo, K., Barros, M.O., Leopold, H.: BPME: an experiment on process model understandability using textual work instructions and BPMN Models. In: SBES (2015)
35. Fahland, D.: Towards analyzing declarative workflows. In: Autonomous and Adap-tive Web Services. Dagstuhl Seminar Proceed, vol. 07061. IBFI, Germany (2007)
36. Recker, J.C., Mendling, J.: On the translation between BPMN AND BPEL: con-ceptual mismatch between process modeling languages. In: CAISE Workshops, pp. 521–532 (2006)

Complementing the BPMN to Enable Data-Driven Simulations of Business Processes

Vincenzo Cartelli, Giuseppe Di Modica$^{(\boxtimes)}$, and Orazio Tomarchio

Department of Electrical, Electronic and Computer Engineering,
University of Catania, Viale A. Doria, 6, Catania, Italy
{vincenzo.cartelli,giuseppe.dimodica,orazio.tomarchio}@dieei.unict.it

Abstract. Business Process Simulation is a useful and widely adopted technique that fits process analysts with the ability to estimate the performance impact of important business decisions before the actions are actually deployed. In order for the simulation to provide accurate and reliable results, process models need to consider not just the workflow dynamics, but also many important factors that may impact on the overall process performance, which constitute what we refer to as the *Process Context*. In this paper we formalize a new Business Process Simulation Model which strictly integrates to the BPMN 2.0 standard and encompasses all the features of a business process in terms of Process Workflow and Process Context respectively. It allows designers to build a resource-based perspective of a business process that enables the simulation of complex data-driven behaviors. To prove the viability of the proposed approach, a case study is finally discussed. The results obtained from the case simulation are also reported.

Keywords: BPMN · Business process management · Activity based costing · Data-driven simulation

1 Introduction

Business Process Simulation (BPS) is one of the most powerful techniques adopted to enforce re-design of processes. Through simulation, the impact that design choices are likely to have on the overall process performance may be quantitatively estimated. BPS involves steps such as the identification of sub-processes and activities and the definition of the process control flow. But one of the most interesting aspects that simulation should not neglect is the *process context*, i.e., all factors that during the process execution may consistently impact on the process dynamics, and thus, on the process KPIs. The accuracy of the final estimate produced by the simulation depends, among others, on how accurate the process context model is.

The purpose of the work presented in this paper is to define a novel *Business Process Simulation Model*, capable of representing all the main aspects of business processes under a *cost-sensitive* perspective. In order to build that view,

© Springer International Publishing AG 2016
R. Pergl et al. (Eds.): EOMAS 2016, LNBIP 272, pp. 22–36, 2016.
DOI: 10.1007/978-3-319-49454-8_2

our approach leverages and integrates the BPMN specification and the Activity Based Costing methodology. The work specifically focuses on the need of considering the process' context data as a crucial element capable of influencing the process dynamics and, as a consequence, the process KPIs.

Further, we developed a business process simulator to simulate business processes defined according to the proposed model. A well structured business process model was also designed and used to test the simulator. Process' incurred costs and execution times are gathered from the simulation run and presented to the process analyst.

The paper is structured in the following way. In Sect. 2 the work motivation is explained and the related literature is reviewed along. In Sect. 3 the proposal of a Business Process Simulation Model is detailed. A case study is presented in Sect. 4, while Sect. 5 concludes the work.

2   Motivation and Related Works

By the term *Process Context* we refer to the collection of factors that may potentially affect the dynamics of a business process at execution time. These factors include, among others, the timing of the process activities, the availability and the quality of the *resources* consumed by the process and the way the resources themselves are consumed by the process. The majority of commercial Business Process Simulators [1–3] offer simulation models which cover factors like the statistical behavior of the tasks duration and the consumption of both human and non human resources. From a thorough review of such tools we realized that there is low or no support for the representation and modeling of the **Process Data**, i.e., the information that is consumed, updated and dynamically generated by the process tasks. Put in a simple way, Business Processes (BPs) interact to each other's and involve multiple activities, which have to be fed with many data in order to complete successfully. Those data have the power to influence the process dynamics as well as the resources do.

In the literature many have stressed the need of looking beyond the process workflows, and propose to define business process models capable of representing all the crucial aspects of the process dynamics. In the study conducted in [4] authors point out that the classic BP modeling tools are not able to elicit all the functional requirements required to integrate the process workflow with the enterprise's information system. According to that study, a single BP is characterized, among others, by some pre/post conditions (conditions which must be fulfilled before/after the process is executed), the *data object* consumed/produced by the process flows, the business rules to be enforced in strategic points of the process branches, and the set of actions that both human beings and the system carry out during the normal execution of the process. In [5] authors discuss the limitations of traditional simulation approaches and identify three specific perspectives that need to be defined in order to simulate BPs in a structured and effective manner: the control flow, the data/rules and the resource/organization. Focus is put on modeling at the right abstraction level the business data influencing the process dynamics and the resources to be allocated to process activities.

Similarly, authors in [6] argue that a BP simulator can not disregard the *environment* where processes are executed and the *resources* required to carry on the process activities. They also propose to use an ad-hoc workflow language (YAWL [7]) to model resources involved in the process dynamics. In [8] authors propose the definition of a conceptual resource model which covers all the types of resource classes and categories that may be involved in the process execution. The resulting model is expressed in the Object Relation model (ORM) notation as they believe it fits the need to define resources and their mutual relationships in an way that can be easily understood by a non-technical audience. In that paper, a concrete example of resource modeling through ORM is provided and integrated to a workflow model which, in turn, is expressed in the YAWL.

The Business Process Modeling and Notation (BPMN 2.0) [9] is the most famous and widely adopted standard notation to model BPs. The BPMN was conceived to support process designers to model the process' *workflow* and *data flow*. It provides little support for the *resource* representation and no support at all to model the timing of activities. The Business Process Simulation BPSim [10] is a standardization effort to augment BP models (defined in either BPMN or XPDL) with information useful for the simulation and analysis of the structure and the capacity of BPs. Though many fundamental context features may be specified through the BPSim notation (resources, statistical distributions of activities' duration), data specification is left out of the scope.

The objective of our work is to overcome the limitations shown by both the commercial BP simulation tools and the most prominent standardization efforts. The gap we aim to fill specifically concerns the lack of support for the representation of BP data as a factor capable of actively influencing the dynamics of the BP execution. The remainder of the paper will discuss the design of a meta-model to define the *context* of a BP; emphasis is put on the novel approach to the *BP data representation*.

3   Business Process Simulation Model

In this section we propose the definition of a novel Business Process Simulation (BPS) Model. The model will have to cover both the structural features of BPs and all external entities and factors that may potentially affect the dynamics of BPs at execution time.

For what concerns the structure of a BP, the model will have to support:

- the representation of process' activities and tasks and their control flow, i.e., the representation of the *process workflow*;
- the representation of the high-level information that is consumed/produced by the process tasks and that evolves along the process itself, or briefly, the *data flow*.

We will refer to the *Context* of a BP as the collection of factors, external to the process logic, yet capable of influencing the process behavior and performance at execution time. This set includes, for instance, human resources responsible

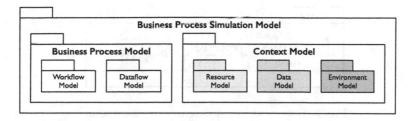

Fig. 1. Package view of the business process simulation model

for carrying out process tasks, non-human resources consumed by process tasks, business rules enforced on decisor elements, any impromptu event occurring at process execution time, and the concrete data set that the process tasks interact with. In the Fig. 1 we depicted a package view of the proposed BPS model. The *Business Process Model* encloses the Workflow and the Dataflow sub-models. The former in intended to model the dynamic flow of (sub)activities carried out within the process to attain a specific goal; the latter represents the flow of data (artifacts, documents, database records, etc.) accompanying the process activities. The *Context Model*, in its turn, is broken down into the Resource, Environment and Data sub-models respectively, whose details are going to be thoroughly discussed throughout the paper.

The business process model specified in the BPMN 2.0 standard perfectly fit into the *Business Process Model* depicted in the Fig. 1. In fact, the process workflow is fully supported by elements such as Tasks, Sequence Flows, Gateways, Message Flows, and so on. The data flow representation is realized by means of the Data Object element, which is a generic data container with a well defined lifecycle, that follows the process flow and that may undergo changes whenever is "worked" by the process tasks it traverses. That said, in the remainder of the paper we will replace the Business Process part of our BPS Model with the BPMN.

The focus of this work, then, shifts to the design of the Context Model, which instead is the novelty of our proposal. In our design, the overall *Context Model* is defined to be the union of a *Resource Model*, a *Data Model* and an *Environment Model*. In the following we will discuss in details each of the those models.

3.1   Data Model

One of the aim of this work is to define a model to represent all the process data that affect the execution of the process and thus the performance of the process' KPIs. Such a model will have to help process designers to define a "container" of process information to which process elements (tasks, activities) may access in order to (a) consume existing information, (b) make updates of existing information or (c) create new information.

In the Fig. 2 a class diagram representation of the proposed *Data Model* is shown. To keep the approach to the data as much generic as possible, the single

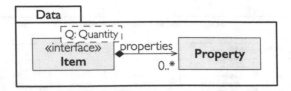

Fig. 2. Data model class diagram representation

datum is represented by the *Item* concept to which zero ore more *properties* may be associated. If on the one hand this simple representation may look too basic, on the other it ensures maximum flexibility for the characterization of complex data structures. The *Data Model* has of course a strong relationship with the *Dataflow* Model of the Business Process package depicted in the Fig. 1: the former specifies how data are structured, while the latter defines how data flow from activity to activity. Further, as better described in the Sect. 3.3, the *Data Model* is strongly coupled with the *Environment Model* as well.

3.2 Resource Model

In this section we propose the definition of a cost-oriented *Resource Model* capable of capturing the resource categories that BPs may need. The *Resource Model* aims at capturing and representing costs and other process related information regarding any kind of resource that need to be "consumed" by a process task, be it a *human* or a *non-human* resource, and more specifically puts the basis for an Activity Based Costing (ABC) [11] analysis of processes.

ABC is a costing methodology that assigns the cost of each activity that consumes resources to all products/services according to the actual consumption of resources made by each activity. The basic assumption of ABC is that any enterprise cost is generated whenever an activity consumes a resource. The strength of ABC is that all costs generated in the system from the consumption of resources by activities may be directly allocated to these activities by means of appropriate *resource drivers*; in other words, all costs – including overhead costs produced by enterprise's support activities [12] – are treated as *direct costs* when allocated to activities that are indeed precise *costs carriers*.

Given the full activity cost configuration, it is afterward possible to allocate these costs to the *final cost-objects* through their *activity drivers* that define how each activity is "consumed" by the final cost-object. By "final cost-object" we refer to every business entity whose cost has to be computed for the analysis, such as products, customers or channels.

The ABC model depicted in Fig. 3 defines the *CostObject* as the base entity for all subsequent cost-oriented concepts. Each *CostObject* has an unit of measure and can be "driven" by a set of *Drivers* that defines its requirements as the amounts of different cost-objects demanded for one unit of it. In addition, every *CostObject* can target in the run a set of other cost-objects through *Allocations* of its quantities to them over different dimensions such as cost, units and time.

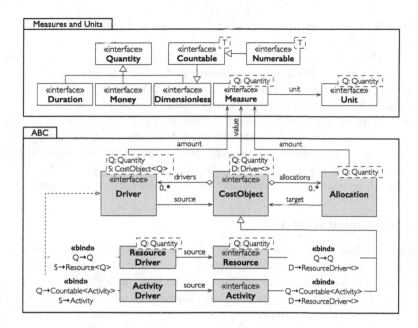

Fig. 3. Cost model. Class diagram representation

An implementation of the Java Units of Measurement API[1], namely the JSR-363, was used as measures and units framework (package *Measures and Units* in Fig. 3).

The *Resource Model* defines the resource concept as a cost-object extension itself. Figure 4 presents its relevant classes and their relationships in the UML notation [13]. A Resource, no matter the kind, produces a cost whenever it is allocated and actually consumed by some business operation. The CostObject concept depicted in the diagram represents the element that, in our proposed

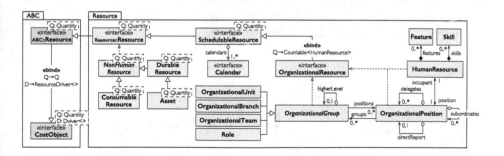

Fig. 4. Resource model. Class diagram representation

---

[1] http://www.unitsofmeasurement.org.

view, bridges the domain of resources and the domain of all the business operations that actually make use of resources.

The *NonHumanResource* class may be used to define resources such as goods and services. *ConsumableResource* extends it by introducing the concept of "residual amount" and it is suited for available-if-in-stock resources. *SchedulableResource* represents a generic resource whose availability is defined by one or more calendars where each *Calendar* represents a set of time intervals in which the resource is available to the whole system; the most common calendar based resource is the *HumanResource* (HR) which represents the physical person who, in turn, occupies an *OrganizationalPosition* within an *OrganizationalGroup* structure such as an *OrganizationalUnit* structure (organizational chart).

3.3   Environment Model

We discuss the factors that are external to the process logic but that are anyway capable of affecting the process execution. In the literature, researchers [5] have identified numerous aspects that designers either tend to neglect or are not able to account for at design time, and that have a negative impact when the process executes. Some of those are the employment of oversimplified (or even incorrect) models, the discontinuous availability of data and resources, the inhomogeneous skill of the employed human resources (which leads to non deterministic human tasks' duration), the lack of knowledge about the exact arrival time of process' external stimuli, and so on.

Our objective is to provide the process designers with a tool to simulate the effects that external factors may have on the process dynamics and performance. Basically, we introduce a model which provides for the representation of non-deterministic behaviors of the process elements. The proposed model is an extension of the one proposed in an earlier work [14]. Figure 5 shows the BPMN elements which have been associated a statistical behaviour, and the categories of statistical behaviors that have been modeled.

StatisticalBehavior is the root class representing a generic behavior which is affected by non-deterministic deviations. It includes several probability distribution models (uniform, normal, binomial to cite a few) that can be used and adequately combined to build specific behaviors.

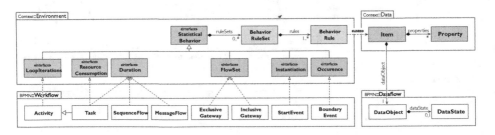

Fig. 5. Environment model class diagram representation and relationships to the BPMN and the data models

Duration models the temporal length a certain event is expected to last. This concept will be used to specify the expected duration of the following BPMN elements: *tasks, sequence flows* and *message flows.* Tasks, in fact, may have a variable duration in respect, for instance, to the skills of the specific person in charge of it or, in the case of a non-human task, to the capability of a machine to work it out. A sequence flow may have a variable duration too. It is not rare, in fact, that time may pass since the end of a preceding task to the beginning of the next one (think about a very simple case when documents need to be moved from one desk to another desk in a different room). Finally, message flows fall in this category too since they are not "instant" messages, and the time to reach the destination may vary from case to case.

ResourceConsumption models the uncertainty regarding the unpredictability of the consumption of a *Resource* by a given *Task.*

The implemented statistical behavior concerns the *amount* of a given resource type that can be consumed by a task. For instance, in the case of human type of resource, it is possible to model a task consuming a discrete number of resource units which is computed by a statistical function; whereas in the case of a non-human resource type, it will be possible to specify the statistical amount of the resource expressed in its unit of measure (kilowatts, kilograms, meters, liters, etc.). *LoopIteration* models the uncertainty of the number of iterations for a specific looped activity. This is the case of both BPMN's *standard loop* and *multi-instance loop activities,* i.e., tasks or sub-processes that have to be executed a certain number of times which either is prefixed or depends on a condition. *ConditionalFlowSet* models the uncertainty introduced by the conditional gateways (both inclusive and exclusive). It will be used to select which of the gateway's available output flow(s) are to be taken. The *Instantiation* concept models the rate at which a specific event responsible for instantiating a process may occur. In particular, it will be used to model the behavior of the BPMN's *Start Event* elements that are not triggered by the flow. The *Occurrence* models the delay after which an event attached to an activity may occur. The event is triggered exactly when the activity work-time exceeds the delay.

The novelty introduced with respect to our former proposal and to other solutions proposed in the literature is the influence of the *Data* (whose model depicted on the right end of the Fig. 5) on the *Environment.* At runtime, the *StatisticalBehavior* associated to the BPMN elements is not statically defined; rather, it may change depending on the values of the Data that are flowing along the BPMN Element itself. This feature is modeled through rules. A rule states which are the conditions under which a *StatisticalBehavior* will have to dynamically change. The conditions are expressed through combinations of data values that trigger the behavior change. In the figure, the rules are represented by the *BehaviorRuleset* and *BehaviorRule* concepts respectively. The introduced feature enables the process designers to design more refined process models. They are now able to get the Data involved in the process dynamics by simply defining the rules by which Data affect the process workflow.

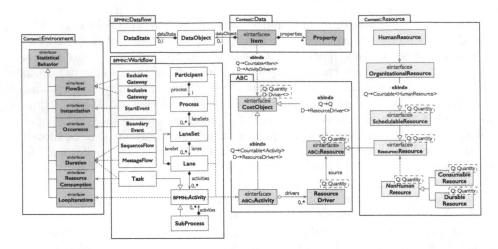

Fig. 6. Overall business process simulation model. Class diagram representation

To make a simple example of what a typical use of this feature may be, think about the duration of a task. Suppose that the task is performed by a human person who has to work an item (a document, for instance). Suppose also that there are two types of document that can be worked. Depending on the type of document, the duration of the task may sensibly vary. In this case, the process modeler would just have to define a rule which, depending on the document's type that is being worked, output the one or the other configuration of parameters for the duration's *StatisticalBehavior*. The reader will a more concrete example of rule definition in the Sect. 4.

Finally, the Fig. 6 depicts the class diagram of the overall Business Process Simulation Model. The reader may notice that the sub-models are perfectly integrated and that the ABC package plays a pivotal role in such integration.

3.4   Context Model's Serialized Notation

So far, we have given a conceptual description of all the entities that populate the Context Model. We have used the UML's class diagram notation in order to describe the concepts and explain how concepts are related to each other. The next effort was to devise a notation which can be used to serialize the presented Context model and use the serialized model to feed a Business Process Simulator. We therefore devised an XML-based notation that process designers can use as a language to define process models. For space reason it was not possible to show the serialized form of all concepts. In Listing 1 we reported a schema excerpt describing the Durable Resource element and the Usage that a Task makes of a Resource. The statistical behavior rules are defined by rule tables and applied at simulation time. An excerpt of the rule definitions for ResourceConsumption and FlowSet can be seen in the next section.

Listing 1. XSD excerpt of the (Durable) Resource element and its Usage in Task

```xml
<xsd:schema xmlns="http://www.unict.it/bpmn/2.0/sim" ...>

<xsd:complexType name="Resource" abstract="true">
    <xsd:complexContent>
        <xsd:extension base="SimItem" />
    </xsd:complexContent>
</xsd:complexType>

<xsd:complexType name="ResourceUsage" abstract="true">
    <xsd:complexContent>
        <xsd:extension base="Usage">
            <xsd:sequence>
                <xsd:choice>
                    <xsd:element ref="integerAmount" />
                    <xsd:element ref="realAmount" />
                </xsd:choice>
                <xsd:element name="unitCost" type="RealAmount" />
            </xsd:sequence>
            <xsd:attribute name="unit" type="Unit" use="required" />
            <xsd:attribute name="moneyUnit" type="MoneyUnit"
                use="required" />
        </xsd:extension>
    </xsd:complexContent>
</xsd:complexType>

<xsd:element name="durable" type="Durable" />
<xsd:complexType name="Durable">
    <xsd:complexContent>
        <xsd:extension base="Resource">
            <xsd:sequence>
                <xsd:element name="usage" type="DurableUsage"
                    maxOccurs="unbounded" />
            </xsd:sequence>
        </xsd:extension>
    </xsd:complexContent>
</xsd:complexType>

<xsd:complexType name="DurableUsage">
    <xsd:complexContent>
        <xsd:extension base="ResourceUsage">
            <xsd:attribute name="timeUnit" type="TimeUnit"
                use="required" />
        </xsd:extension>
    </xsd:complexContent>
</xsd:complexType>

<xsd:complexType name="TaskUsage">
    <xsd:complexContent>
        <xsd:extension base="ActivityUsage">
            <xsd:sequence>
                <xsd:element ref="timeSpan" minOccurs="0" />
                <xsd:element ref="resourceConsumption" minOccurs="0"
                    maxOccurs="unbounded" />
            </xsd:sequence>
        </xsd:extension>
    </xsd:complexContent>
</xsd:complexType>
```

To ease the work of process designers, we implemented a web modeler[2] that lets designers draw process models in the BPMN, define all the features of the process Context and finally serialize it in the just mentioned notation.

---

[2] http://business-engineering.it/sim-editor.

4   Case Study

The objective of this work was to devise a business process meta-model that process designers may use to define process models and characterize its context features; next step was to implement a simulator capable of running long-term, context-aware simulations of those processes and producing cost-sensitive results useful for ABC analysis. In an earlier work [14] the design and implementation of a preliminary version of the simulator was presented. It was compatible with an earlier version of the business process model. The reader may refer to that work for details on the simulator design.

A BPMN description of the investigated case study process is shown in Fig. 7. It represents the process of release of a construction permit run by the Building Authority of a Municipality. The whole process involves different actors who interacts to each other exchanging information and/or documents (represented in the model as specific messages). The involved actors are: *Applicant*, the private citizen/company who applies to obtain the building permit; *Clerk*, the front-office employee of the Building Authority who receives the Application and is in charge of (a) checking the documentation of the application, (b) interacting with the applicant in order to obtain required documents and (c) sending back the result of the application; *Senior Clerk*, the back-office employee of the Building Authority who evaluates and decides on the application; *Expert*, an external expert who may be called upon by the Senior Clerk whenever specific technical issues arise and the final decision may not be autonomously taken.

The business process spans four swimlanes, one for each actor. Both the Applicant and the Expert are external entities, i.e., are not part of the enterprise's business process dynamics. While there was no reason to represent the Applicant in the resource model, the Expert was modeled as a *DurableResource* (paid by the hour). The Clerk and the Senior Clerk were modeled as *OrganizationalPosition*. Other considered resources in the scenario are energy, modeled as *DurableResource*, paper and stamps, both modeled as *ConsumableResource*.

We defined a context scenario (say *scenario1*) where we employed all the above mentioned resources. Also, we set up a calendar (*official-calendar*) to state that for human resources the working days are Monday through Friday and the working hours follow the pattern [8:00AM to 12:00AM, 1:00PM to 5:00PM]. We then specified four different types of application ("cost object", in the ABC terminology) that potential applicants may submit: Maintenance, building and renovation, preservation and restoration and urban restructuring. Further, in the specific scenario we required 1 unit of the Clerk resource type and 2 units of Senior Clerk resource type, whose hourly costs are 10€ and 20€ respectively.

The process context was populated with data capable of influencing the process workflow. The *autonomous decision?* Gateway is associated a FlowSet statistical behavior, while the *decide on application* Task is associated the ResourceConsumption and Duration statistical behaviors. Such BPMN elements are bound to the statistical behaviors by means of rule tables, where each table row represents a specific rule that applies when a condition on data holds true. Excerpts of these rule tables (with priorities and activation groups hidden for

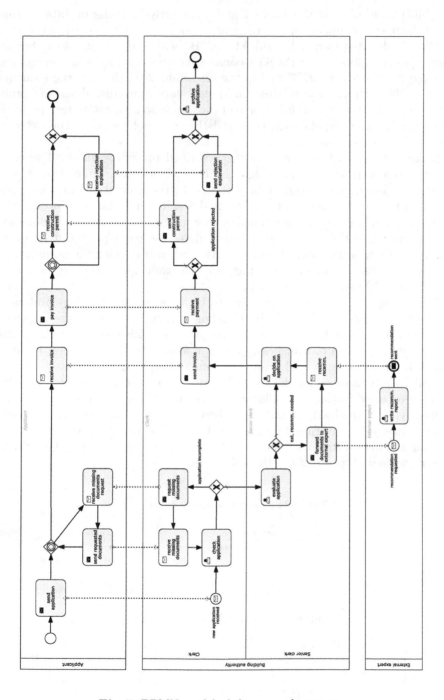

Fig. 7. BPMN model of the example process

readability) are shown in the Tables 1 and 2 respectively. Rules in Table 1 state that if the user has applied for a "preservation-and-restoration" permit, then the workflow is diverted to flow-id "sid-A1F...92B" with 100 % probability. For all other types of application, in the 80 % of cases the workflow proceeds through the sequence flow "sid-A1F...92B" and in the remaining 20 % through the sequence flow "sid-595...1E1". Similarly, Rules in Table 2 state which distribution of probability has to be chosen for the duration of the *decide on application* task depending on (a) the user's application type and (b) the involvement of the external expert in the process instance.

A simulation was finally run on the described process scenario. The cost-sensitive approach adopted to design the Business Process Simulation Model eventually allowed us to gather data produced by the simulation and easily put them in a form that facilitates the ABC analysis. In particular, the focus is put on the user application. As mentioned earlier, each submitted user application is a *cost-object*, in the sense that it accumulates the costs produced by every activity that works the application itself. Also, when traversing the activities an application is also capable of recording both the time spent in every activity's queue and the time for being processed.

Three simple process KPIs are going to be assessed through the simulation: the *monetary costs* incurred by the Building Authority to serve the requests, the *work times* spent by the activities to process applications and the *queue times* applications had to wait before being processed by the activities. Figure 8 depicts a report of analytical costs and times computed for the scenario. In particular, costs incurred for the allocation of resources to activities and activity costs are reported in the "cost allocations" section; the unit times absorbed by the four types of application are instead shown in the section "time allocations". The resource pools are spliced into internal resources (Building Authority) and external resources (External Expert) and further classified by type; the activity pools coincide with those of the BPMN model.

Table 1. FlowSet behavior excerpt

Name	Element.id	Item.name	Item.type	Flow.id	Probability
Autonomous decision?	sid-4A2...1D4	Application	Preservation-and-restoration	sid-A1F...92B	1.0
				sid-595...1E1	0.0
		Application		sid-A1F...92B	0.8
				sid-595...1E1	0.2

Table 2. Duration behavior excerpt

Name	Element.id	Item.name	Item.type	Item.ext-expert	Duration
Decide on application	sid-461...732	Application	Maintenance		h, norm, 24, 1
		Application	Building-renovation	False	h, norm, 48, 2
				True	h, norm, 24, 1.15
		Application	Preservation-and-restoration		h, pert, 0.8, 1, 1.33
		Application	Urban-restructuring		h, norm, 24, 2

Cost object		check application	send invoice	receive payment	send construction permit	archive application	request missing documents	receive missing documents	send rejection explanation	Clerk total	evaluate application	decide on application	forward documents to external expert	receive recommendation	Senior Clerk total	Building Authority total	write recommendation report	External Expert total	grand total
Organizational	Clerk	2,892.24	670.44	316.96	605.80	1,060.31	419.95	83.51	121.11	6,170.33						6,170.33			6,170.33
	Senior Clerk										271,167.48	706.67	43.94	30.77	271,948.85	271,948.85			271,948.85
	(total)	2,892.24	670.44	316.96	605.80	1,060.31	419.95	83.51	121.11	6,170.32	271,167.48	706.67	43.94	30.77	271,948.85	278,119.18			278,119.18
Durable	Energy	26.03	6.03		5.45		3.78		1.09	42.39	488.10		0.20	0.14	488.44	530.82			530.82
	External Expert																56,308.91	56,308.91	56,308.91
	(total)	26.03	6.03		5.45		3.78		1.09	42.39	488.10		0.20	0.14	488.44	530.82	56,308.91	56,308.91	56,839.74
Consumable	Paper		2.12		3.80		1.12		0.44	7.48						7.48			7.48
	Stamp		339.20		1,520.00		179.20		70.40	2,108.80						2,108.80			2,108.80
	(total)		341.32		1,523.80		180.32		70.84	2,116.28						2,116.28			2,116.28
	(cost total)	2,918.28	1,017.79	316.96	2,135.05	1,060.31	604.05	83.51	193.04	8,328.99	271,655.58	706.67	44.14	30.90	272,437.29	280,766.28	56,308.91	56,308.91	337,075.20
Application Unit Costs [€/unit]	Maintenance	10.80	4.81	1.50	11.26	5.00	10.84	1.48	8.64	54.33	1,288.19	3.33	0.72	0.50	1,292.74	1,347.07	902.41	902.41	2,249.48
	Building Renovation	11.02	4.74	1.47	11.11	4.99	10.55	1.51	8.80	54.19	1,221.76	3.33	0.67	0.50	1,226.26	1,280.45	913.49	913.49	2,193.95
	Preservation & Restoration	13.27	4.88	1.60	11.41	5.10	11.40	1.58	11.14	60.38	1,260.51	3.33	0.75	0.49	1,265.08	1,325.46	920.05	920.05	2,245.51
	Urban Restructuring	9.91	4.92	1.48	11.09	4.90				32.30	1,484.32	3.33	0.81	0.51	1,487.99	1,520.29	1,011.92	1,011.92	1,773.27
	(total)	10.89	4.80	1.50	11.24	5.00	10.79	1.49	8.77	39.29	1,281.39	3.33	0.71	0.50	1,285.08	1,324.37	908.21	908.21	1,589.98
Application Time Unit Costs [€/h]	Maintenance	10.09	15.17	10.00	35.07	10.00	14.35	10.00	16.09	13.53	20.04	20.00	20.09	20.09	20.04	19.76	30.00	30.00	20.77
	Building Renovation	10.09	15.28	10.00	36.31	10.00	14.52	10.00	15.91	13.35	20.04	20.00	20.09	20.09	20.04	18.70	30.00	30.00	21.41
	Preservation & Restoration	10.09	15.05	10.00	33.95	10.00	14.06	10.00	14.19	13.09	20.04	20.00	20.09	20.09	20.04	18.71	30.00	30.00	22.97
	Urban Restructuring	10.09	15.00	10.00	36.44	10.00				14.34	20.04	20.00	20.09	20.09	20.04	19.87	30.00	30.00	20.87
	(total)	10.09	15.18	10.00	35.24	10.00	14.38	10.00	15.94	13.50	20.04	20.00	20.09	20.09	20.04	19.75	30.00	30.00	20.95
Application Unit Work Times [h/unit]	Maintenance	1.070	0.317	0.150	0.321	0.500	0.756	0.148	0.537	2.866	64.294	0.167	0.036	0.025	64.475	67.341	30.080	30.080	74.729
	Building Renovation	1.093	0.310	0.147	0.306	0.499	0.727	0.151	0.553	3.205	60.978	0.167	0.033	0.025	61.199	64.374	30.450	30.450	77.143
	Preservation & Restoration	1.315	0.324	0.160	0.336	0.510	0.811	0.158	0.785	3.100	62.912	0.167	0.038	0.024	63.141	66.841	30.668	30.668	96.909
	Urban Restructuring	0.982	0.328	0.148	0.304	0.490				2.753	74.083	0.167	0.040	0.025	74.266	76.519	33.731	33.731	84.951
	(total)	1.079	0.316	0.150	0.310	0.500	0.750	0.149	0.550	2.811	63.955	0.167	0.035	0.025	64.139	67.049	30.274	30.274	75.903
Application Unit Queue Times [h/unit]	Maintenance	0.035	0.110	16.739	0.030	0.027	316.267	0.015		94.626	35.164	0.166	0.036	0.025	35.345	129.971			129.971
	Building Renovation	0.036	0.108	27.358	0.028	0.026	173.966	0.015		100.524	33.350	0.166	0.033	0.025	33.541	134.064			134.064
	Preservation & Restoration	0.043	0.113	11.083	0.031	0.027	434.567	0.021		83.730	34.408	0.166	0.037	0.024	34.636	118.366			118.366
	Urban Restructuring	0.032	0.114		0.028	0.026				77.675	40.517	0.166	0.040	0.025	40.700	118.375			118.375
	(total)	0.035	0.110	17.816	0.029	0.027	290.879	0.015		94.860	34.978	0.166	0.035	0.025	35.162	130.022			130.022

Fig. 8. Simulator generated report of costs and times allocation

The obtained data provide a picture of the performance of the process in terms of costs and times. Process designers may use those data to ground their analysis, and guess which part of the process (workflow, resource assignments) should undergo further improvement. If we focus on the "activities" grand total column, we can observe the unit cost and the time unit cost of each application type (*Maintenance, Building Renovation, ...*) in correspondence with the intersection of the cost object's "Application Unit Costs [€/unit]" and "Application Time Unit Costs [€/h]" row. So, for instance, the unit cost of the *Maintenance* application is 2,249.48 €/#application, i.e., every *Maintenance* application has an average cost of 2,249.48 €. Similarly, if we look at the time unit cost, the hourly cost of the *Maintenance* application is 20.77€/h, i.e., every work hour on the *Maintenance* application has an average cost of 20.77€.

5   Conclusion

Field experts agree that one of the most critical step in the business processes management is process analysis and modeling. Good models are the base for governing enterprise processes and getting them to quickly adapt to new business goals. The design of business process models is a complex activity that requires, on the one hand, the identification and the modeling of all the tasks that, adequately sequenced, lead to the attainment of the business goal, and on the other hand the characterization of the context where the process executes and that strongly influences the process dynamics. This work proposed a conceptual representation of the business process from both the workflow and the data flow perspectives. The conceptual model was translated into a machine-readable form, and may be used by process designers as a language to craft concrete business process models. We also designed and implemented a business process simulator that is compliant with the introduced notation. In the paper we discussed a case study example that showed how to practically model and simulate business processes. In the future, the "cost" concept will be further abstracted to also cover non-monetary aspects. The objective will be to study a design framework where process stakeholders get involved too.

References

1. ARIS: Aris Acrhitecture Suite (2016). www.softwareag.com
2. iGraphx: iGraphx Process (2016). www.igrafx.com/products/process-modeling-ana lysis/process
3. Oracle: Oracle BPM Suite (2016). www.oracle.com/us/technologies/bpm
4. Vara, J.L., Sánchez, J.: BPMN-based specification of task descriptions: approach and lessons learnt. In: Glinz, M., Heymans, P. (eds.) REFSQ 2009. LNCS, vol. 5512, pp. 124–138. Springer, Heidelberg (2009). doi:10.1007/978-3-642-02050-6_11
5. Van der Aalst, W.M.P.: Business process simulation revisited. In: Barjis, J. (ed.) EOMAS 2010. LNBIP, vol. 63, pp. 1–14. Springer, Heidelberg (2010). doi:10.1007/978-3-642-15723-3_1
6. Van der Aalst, W.M.P., Nakatumba, J., Rozinat, A., Russell, N.: Business process simulation: how to get it right? In: vom Brocke, J., Rosemann, M. (eds.) International Handbooks on Information Systems, pp. 317–342. Springer, Berlin (2010)
7. Van der Aalst, W.M.P., Hofstede, A.H.M.: YAWL: yet another workflow language. Inf. Syst. 30(4), 245–275 (2005)
8. Ouyang, C., Wynn, M., Fidge, C., ter Hofstede, A., Kuhr, J.C.: Modelling complex resource requirements in business process management systems. In: Proceedings of the 21st Australasian Conference on Information Systems, ACIS 2010 (2010)
9. OMG: Business Process Model and Notation (BPMN 2.0), January 2011. http://www.omg.org/spec/BPMN/2.0/
10. Coalition, W.M.: Business Process Simulation Standard (Version 1.0), February 2013. http://www.bpsim.org
11. Cooper, R., Kaplan, R.S.: Activity-based systems: measuring the costs of resource usage. Account. Horiz. 6, 1–12 (1992)
12. Porter, M.E.: Competitive Advantage: Creating and Sustaining Superior Performance. Free Press, New York (1985)
13. OMG: The UML Specification, July 2005. http://www.omg.org/spec/UML/2.0/
14. Cartelli, V., Di Modica, G., Tomarchio, O.: A resource-aware simulation tool for business processes. In: Proceedings of the 11th International Conference on e-Business, ICE-B 2014 - Part of 11th International Joint Conference on e-Business and Telecommunications, ICETE 2014, pp. 123–133 (2014). doi:10.5220/0005067001230133

Analysis of Enterprise Architecture Evolution Using Markov Decision Processes

Sérgio Guerreiro[1,2(✉)], Khaled Gaaloul[3], and Ulrik Franke[4]

[1] Lusófona University, Campo Grande 376, 1749-024 Lisbon, Portugal
sergio.guerreiro@ulusofona.pt
[2] Formetis, Hemelrijk 12c, 5281 PS Boxtel, Netherlands
sergio.guerreiro@formetis.nl
[3] Luxembourg Institute of Science and Technology (LIST),
Esch-sur-Alzette, Luxembourg
khaled.gaaloul@list.lu
[4] Swedish Institute of Computer Science (SICS),
Isafjordsgatan 22, 164 29 Kista, Sweden
ulrik.franke@sics.se

Abstract. Enterprise architecture (EA) offers steering instruments to aid architects in their decision-making process. However, the management of such a process is a challenging task for enterprise architects, due to the complex dependencies amongst EA models when evolving from an initial to a subsequent state. In this paper, we design, present and analyze an approach supporting EA model evolution. In doing so, we define EA artifacts dependencies and model their corresponding evolutions during change. Then, this model is processed using a feedback control schema to fully inform the EA design decisions. An access control model for an inventory case study is introduced to reason on issues connected to this evolution. The results obtained by a stochastic solution (Markov Decision Processes) are used to argue about the usefulness and applicability of our proposal.

Keywords: Enterprise Architecture · Evolution · Markov Decision Processes

1 Introduction

Enterprise architecture (EA) is a discipline driving change within organizations. EA provides a mechanism for cohesive steering and provides management with appropriate indicators and controls to steer the transformation of an enterprise into the desired direction [1, 2]. In the past, EA practice had focused primarily on the technological aspects of change, but the practice is quickly evolving to use a rigorous business architecture approach to address the organizational and motivational aspects of change as well [3].

The need for enterprises to constantly adapt to ever changing requirements of the environment is a continuing field of research in enterprise engineering. The notion of engineering focuses on applying a systematic approach to enterprise transformation. The transformation of enterprises is engineered by the means of appropriate models and

© Springer International Publishing AG 2016
R. Pergl et al. (Eds.): EOMAS 2016, LNBIP 272, pp. 37–51, 2016.
DOI: 10.1007/978-3-319-49454-8_3

methods [4]. Enterprise modeling provides adequate means for the description of As-is and To-be states of enterprises. Thus, enterprise models integrate the conceptual models of information systems with models representing organizational and technical structures [5].

However, current EA frameworks do not support this transformation appropriately due to inflexible EA models and missing integration of stakeholders in the modeling process [6]. In practice, organizations struggle with transformational change being demanded by the ever-increasing speed of business. In this context, enterprise architects rely on architecture modeling languages to support responsibility and alignment for the new EA models [7], but lack guidelines during EA evolution [3].

The evolution of an EA model itself is just a set of changes to the artifacts contained in this EA model. Architectural artifacts are created in order to describe a system, solution, or state of the enterprise [8]. Thus, EA artifacts document EA components from the business to the IT level. EA provides pragmatic artifacts such as requirements, specifications, and conceptual models; thereby providing information for enterprise architect when dealing with models change and decision-making.

In this paper, we define a model-driven approach to support EA evolution. The main idea is to build an intuitive and powerful paradigm that can help the architect analyze the effects of artifact changes. Such changes trigger events that can be reasoned on, viz. model transitions from As-is to To-be states. As the architect faces several possible, mutually exclusive, To-be design decisions, we offer the prospect of *evaluation* of these decisions in order to identify the best EA model alternatives. These valuations of alternatives are based on observational data and calculations using Markov decision processes. The paper extends our own previous work [18] as detailed in the next section.

This research is based on a simplification of the design-science research (DSR) as proposed by [9, 10]. The methodology applied is divided according to the two processes of design science research in information system: Build and Evaluate. The build process is composed of two stages: model definition and model construction. The first stage encompasses the evolution model based on artifact dependencies in Sect. 1 based on existing research contributions (see Sect. 2). The second stage constructs an organizational dynamics in EA context (inventory case study) to support their evolution process (see Sect. 3). The evaluation process includes a calculation using a linear programming algorithm (Markov decision processes – MDP) in Sect. 4. Finally, we conclude and present future work in Sect. 5.

2   Related Work

One influential strand of research on uncertainty in EA work is that initiated by Johnson *et al.* [11]. Here, the authors introduce three kinds of uncertainties – definitional, causal, and empirical – and propose an extension of influence diagrams to manage them in the EA context. In later work, the same research group has used probabilistic relational models (*e.g.* [12, 13]) and a probabilistic version of the OCL language [14] as tools to describe and manage uncertainty in EA. The same research group has also explored utility theory as a theoretical framework for trading different goods against each other in the EA decision-making context, viz. cost vs. availability.

While our paper is closely related to the work by Johnson *et al.* in the sense that we use probabilities to model EA activities, we differ importantly in our use of the MDP formalism, which explicitly allows us to address problems where the outcomes are only partially under the control of the decision-maker, and, in the partially observable MDP (POMDP) where the outcomes are only partially observable.

Another method proposed in the literature for addressing uncertainty in EA is real options analysis [15]. However, while Mikaelian *et al.* [15] address the problem of using real options holistically, to avoid sub-optimization in organizational silos, we address inherent uncertainties in EA work by means of MDP valuation to choose the best option.

It should also be noted that EA frameworks most often contain mechanisms for dealing with uncertainty, albeit not in a formal and quantitative manner. On the one hand, Quartel *et al.* [16] describe the well-known TOGAF Architecture Development Method (ADM) precisely as a means to address uncertainty and change, in particular the kind of uncertainty inherent in bridging requirements and actual solution. On the other hand, the Information Technology Infrastructure Library (ITIL) describes processes supporting change management to be applied by an organization during service transition [17]. However, such qualitative approaches remain generic using best practices, and thus, differ from our quantitative approach.

To summarize, we address an important problem in a novel way. This paper extends our own previous work [18] in the following aspects *(i)* enforcement of an informed decision-making solution applied for access control governance and *(ii)* evaluation of the rigor of the delivered MDP calculation results using DSR methodology.

3   Modeling Enterprise Architecture Evolution

Why is EA decision-making and evolution such a hard problem? One reason is the complex organizational setting. Almost by definition, EA decision-making takes place at the highest organization level, and aims to align and synchronize a variety of separate processes and organizational entities, each with their own expertise and their own agendas. As noted by [15], this entails a substantial risk of sub-optimization in organizational silos. Another reason is that the problems of EA evolution do not exist a priori, well defined and waiting to be solved, but rather have to be constructed and structured into well-defined problems before they can be solved [19]. A third reason, as alluded to above, is the prevalence of uncertainty. Uncertainty being the rationale for our choice of the MDP formalism, it is worth expanding on: Causal uncertainty [11] is about the effects of actions taken: Even if EA decisions and actions are guided by proper theory, there is always some degree of causal uncertainty involved. If a company switches to a more reliable IT service, what will their resulting availability be? 99.998 %? 99.999 %? Theories addressing such questions typically include uncertainty (*e.g.* [20]). Empirical uncertainty [11] is about the data used. The information used for enterprise decision-making is uncertain, *e.g.* because it is obsolete [21], measured with an imperfect instrument, or subject to some unknown bias. This kind of uncertainty is an important reason for extending the MDP into the POMDP, where the environment is only partially observable. Event uncertainty outside the enterprise is essentially the kind of uncertainty, which is at the core of standard decision theory: Will supplier A go bust, will product X form a working software ecosystem, and will there be a need to retract thousands of deployed embedded systems for security upgrades? The uncertainty of being successful in changing an EA (from As-Is to To-Be) is a classical problem that is shown in the case study (*cf.* next Sect.), and could occur because of bad implementation, bad interpretation or even a malicious action, or deception, taken by an organization actor. For instance, implementing a non-secure EA model could lead to substantial financial losses.

It is against the background of causal, empirical and event uncertainty that we find the MDP methodology useful as a means for uncertainty management in EA.

The rest of this section follows the DSR methodology. We define the first stage of the build process where the relevant concepts and relations are identified, in order to build a model describing EA evolution and their corresponding operations. Here, we introduce our concrete running example, intended to illustrate the uncertainties described, more generally, above.

We assume that the overarching EA is composed of a multitude of EA models, each being concurrently edited by different modelers (*i.e.* enterprise architects). These architects have different responsibilities and may not be fully aware of the dependencies between the models and their artifacts. (In this sense, the problem addressed is one of separation of concern, which is an important rationale for EA work, *cf.* [22]) This may lead to creating flaws and inconsistencies in EA models, when changes made on given EA models indirectly impact other EA models (see Fig. 1). A typical example of this is when a modeler X modifies the credentials or permissions assigned to a given role, in order to update a business process model Y, but is unaware that this has an impact on another business process model Z where some security requirement is broken by this change (*e.g.* a conflict of interest violation).

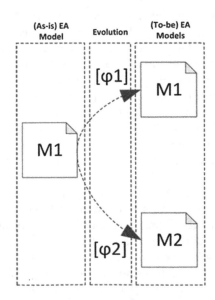

Fig. 1. Model-driven EA evolution

Describing EA evolution will enable us to reason on different alternatives for EA evolutions and thus decide upon alternatives or analyze potential evolutions from a given EA state in an informed manner. Our objective is to assist enterprise architects in deciding which EA evolutions are fully compliant and which ones are not compliant or should be considered as suspicious and need be more thoroughly analyzed by an EA expert. This expert will then have the responsibility of taking a final decision whether the EA evolution should be committed to or reverted.

4   EA Evolution Decision: A Case Study Using Models

In this section, the DSR methodology is applied to the second stage of the build process. Here we use organizational dynamics in EA to process the evolution model as introduced in Sect. 3.

In order to illustrate the need and the benefits to support the EA evolution decision, we present a case study in the field of access control models, in specific, the role-based access control (RBAC) model [23]). RBAC relies on user authentication, which in turn relies on identity management and defines relationships between the main concepts of Users, Roles and Permissions. RBAC's constraints restrict permissions depending on contextual information such as segregation of duties (*SoD*) [24].

To represent the models, DEMO[1] (Design and Engineering Methodology for Organizations) is used. DEMO is a methodology and a theory founded in language action perspective (LAP), and aims at the design, engineering, and implementation of organizations [5]. On the one hand DEMO is compatible with the communication and production, acts and facts that occur between actors in business processes. A DEMO business transaction model has two distinct worlds: *(i)* transition space and *(ii)* state space. On the one hand, the DEMO transition space is grounded in a theory named as Ψ-theory (PSI), where the standard pattern of a transaction includes two distinct actor roles: the Initiator and the Executor. Figure 2 depicts this basic transaction pattern.

The transactional pattern is performed by a sequence of coordination and production acts that leads to the production of the new fact. In detail, it encompasses: *(i)* order phase that involves the acts of request (rq), promise (pm), decline (dc) and quit (qt), *(ii)* execution phase that includes the production act of the new fact itself (depicted by the diamond) and *(iii)* result phase that includes the acts of state (st), reject (rj), stop (st) and accept (ac). Firstly, when a Customer desires a new product, he requests it. After the request for the production, a promise to produce the production is delivered by the Producer. Then, after the production, the Producer states that the product is available. Finally, the Customer accepts the new fact produced. DEMO basic transaction pattern aims at specifying the transition space of a process that is given by the set of allowable sequences of transitions. Every state transition is only dependent on the current states of all surrounding transactions.

The usage of a business transaction oriented methodology has the benefit of narrowing the domain of EA models to a single and self-contained set of models.

---

[1] http://www.demo.nl/.

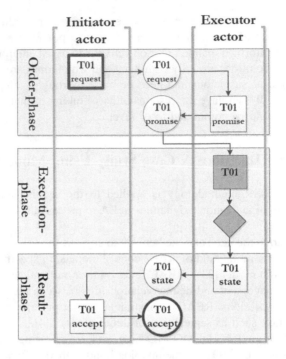

Fig. 2. The DEMO standard pattern of a transaction between two actors with separation between communication and production acts (Adapted from [5]).

4.1 Case Study Explanation

For explanation, the evolvable EA proposal is exemplified using an inventory case study. One person orders goods from suppliers, and another person logs the received goods in the accounting system. This keeps the purchasing person from diverting incoming goods for his own use. To that end, a segregation of duties (SoD^2) between both users' roles is enforced.

Figure 3 depicts a DEMO Process Model (PM) [5], where each business transaction is an abstraction represented graphically by the cylinders. The goal of performing such a transaction pattern is to obtain a new fact.

As depicted by the PM in Fig. 3-(Model 1), the user U1 (Client) who order the goods (T1) is assigned with role 1 (R1). R1 inherits read/write permissions. The user U2 (Accounter) of the accounting system is assigned with role 2 (R2) to perform log account (T2). R2 inherits read permission. The aforementioned permissions define operations on the accounting system database. Roles and responsibilities definition are dependent on organizational dynamics during EA change.

---

[2] *SoD* concept prohibits the assignment of role/responsibility to a single person for the acquisition of assets, their custody, and the related record keeping.

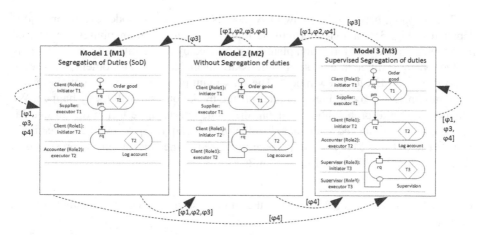

Fig. 3. Mapping the set of possible evolutions (φ) from/to Models 1, 2 and 3: a non-deterministic finite automaton representation.

However, because of the occurrence of non-expected situations, *e.g.* fraud, deception, misunderstanding or misinterpretation, there is a risk of malicious or wrongful change in the inventory scenario.

4.2   EA Evolution Options

We explain how to anticipate the impacts of each decision and consequently to avoid security failures using ex ante calculation. Two possible model transformations (M2 and M3) starting from an initial M1 (see Fig. 3-(Model 1)) are considered. Figure 3-(Model 2) represents one the one hand, a first model design. There exists a risk in changing role's hierarchy when evolving RBAC model in EA. For instance, the inventory unit may be extended with additional tasks (*e.g.* audit). The architect needs to model this change and may misinterpret the role R2 as a responsibility to supervise role R1 orders. In this case, role R2 will go up in the hierarchy and be senior to role R1. In RBAC, this means role R2 will inherit role R1's permissions. This situation may present a fraud risk and is represented in Fig. 3-(Model 2) when U1 is empowered with T1 and T2 concomitantly.

On the other hand, Fig. 3-(Model 3) represents a second model. Here, a new role 3 (R3) is added to the model in order to supervise the orders and the logging transactions that have been executed. M3 is the response to a previous deception successfully attempted, guaranteeing for some time an extra level of operational control. In this context, the role R3 is assigned with the responsibility of initiating and performing the Supervision transaction (T3).

An EA model transformation is triggered whenever the enterprise architect decides to evolve the organization with a known purpose. In this context, the following set of evolutions (φ) decisions is considered: φ1 - do not take any action; φ2 – remove *SoD*; φ3 – add *SoD*; and φ4 – add extra transaction with supervised *SoD*.

The mapping between the known EA models (M) and EA model evolutions (φ) is depicted in Fig. 3 as a non-deterministic finite automaton. The mappings are derived from the enterprise transformation planning produced by the architect. Each model may evolve, whereas different evolution options are available at each moment. Each evolution drives the EA to a new model. The maximum number of possible evolutions is given multiplying φ by M. Figure 3 presents the evolutions that will likely happen. We remark that due to probabilities division, the same φ may drive to more than one M, e.g., $\varphi 1$ will be simulated with shared probability p and $1 - p$ to evolve respectively from M1 to M1 and M2. The full probabilities used in the calculation are presented in Table 1 and will be discussed in Sect. 4.2.

Table 1. Transition matrix (P_{ij}^a) containing the set of possible evolutions (φ) from/to Models 1, 2 and 3.

$\varphi 1$	From	To			$\varphi 3$	From	To		
		Model 1	Model 2	Model 3			Model 1	Model 2	Model 3
	Model 1	p	$1 - p$	0		Model 1	p	$1 - p$	0
	Model 2	0	1	0		Model 2	p	$1 - p$	0
	Model 3	0	$1 - p$	p		Model 3	p	0	$1 - p$
$\varphi 2$	From	To			$\varphi 4$	From	To		
		Model 1	Model 2	Model 3			Model 1	Model 2	Model 3
	Model 1	0	1	0		Model 1	$1 - p$	0	p
	Model 2	0	1	0		Model 2	0	$1 - p$	p
	Model 3	0	1	0		Model 3	0	$1 - p$	p

4.3   Experimenting Enterprise Architecture Evolution Decision

This section is about the experimental design in DSR. The approach is evaluated and simulated using a linear programming algorithm (Markov Decision Process) to instantiate the theoretical conceptualization introduced in Sects. 3 and 4. The MDP is simulated and the achieved results are argued. Markov Decision Process (MDP) are used make informed design decisions by computing the best EA model alternatives. Alternatives are evolvable models and depend on roles' transformation as depicted in the inventory case study of Fig. 3. This corresponds to the execution of a given type of change operation. Moreover, the decision depends on the dependency between the model and the set of possible evolutions available for checking whether the fulfillment of segregation of duty (*SoD*) constraint is being endangered by the evolution or not.

From the probabilities theory literature, a Markov process is a stochastic process that satisfies the Markov property [25]: if the transition probabilities from any given state depend only on the actual state and not on previous history. Four classes of Markov models are usually distinguished. A Markov chain refers to a process, which has a countable and discrete set of state spaces, but is not controllable. A Markov decision process (MDP) is able to solve the problem of calculating an optimal policy in an accessible and stochastic environment with a known transition model [26].

However, in only partially accessible environments, or whenever the observation does not provide enough information to determine the states or the associated transition probabilities, then the hidden Markov model (HMM) or the partially observable Markov decision process (POMDP) solutions should be considered. The difference is that HMM is applied to uncontrolled systems and POMDP to controlled systems.

In our case study, the models and evolutions are considered as observable, and when an evolution is taken it will be successful. By other words, the system in Fig. 3 is observable and controllable, and therefore, a MDP is chosen to solve the problem of defining the optimal evolutions that maximizes value for the organization.

4.4   Enterprise Architecture Evolution Decision

The goal is to decide if the evolution contains any change that will influence adversely the model. In a real operational environment, many (and concurrent) evolutions are attempted; therefore the enforcement of a continuous process to steer the EA evolutions is demanded. Considering α as the artifact to be the aforementioned roles, then the evolution process is instantiated by the following five steps, and the challenge posed to the architect is to choose the evolution that maximizes the value to the organization:

1. *Observation*: the set of α that are being attempted at operation are observed and collected;
2. *Intelligence*: this step is equal to (1) if a full observation is considered. However, if *(i)* uncertainty about the α exists, or if *(ii)* due to manual task-based environments is not possible to automatically collect α, or if *(iii)* different perceptions coexist within the organization in regard to α; then a partial observation solution should be considered. In the EA context, the different kinds of uncertainty described by Johnson et al. merit further research into Partially observable Markov decision processes (POMDP) [26–28], to estimate the belief α.

   In this case study, however, we merely assume that all the artifacts are observable and employ a Markov decision processes (MDP). MDP evaluates a given EA transformation process maximizing the expected value *(v)* after discounting the decay throughout time. A MDP usually defined by the tuple *(S,A,P,R,γ)* where:
   $S = \{S_1,...,S_n\}$ is a set of states, representing all the possible underlying states the process can be in (our case study, the states of S are the models *M1–M3*);
   $A = \{A_1,...,A_n\}$ is a set of actions, representing all the available control choices at each point in time (our case study represents A by the evolutions φ);

$$
P_{ij}^a = \begin{array}{c} \\ i_0 \\ i_1 \\ ... \\ i_k \end{array}
\begin{array}{cccc} j_0 & j_1 & \cdots & j_k \end{array}
\left[\begin{array}{cccc}
p_{00} & p_{01} & \cdots & p_{0k} \\
p_{10} & p_{11} & \cdots & p_{1k} \\
... & ... & ... & ... \\
p_{k0} & p_{k1} & \cdots & p_{kk}
\end{array} \right]
$$

is a transition matrix that contains the probability of a state transition, whereas i is the actual state and j is the final state if a given action a that is being used;[3]
$R = \{R_1, ..., R_n\}$ is an immediate reward function, giving the immediate utility for performing an action that drives the system towards each state[4];
Finally, γ is a discounted factor of future rewards, meaning the decay that a given achieved state suffers throughout time.

3. *EA re-design*: in regard to a possible *SoD* violation, the enterprise architect need to re-design a new set of evolution (α, α') pairs, *e.g.*, adding an auditing task such as an extra supervision task. If partial observations are occurring, then the new (α, α') pair depends on the belief α obtained in step (2);

4. *Choose best EA re-design*: a qualitative and/or quantitative valuation of the best evolution to take. This step is the responsibility of enterprise architect. To support the architect the MDP is solved. There are many solutions available to solve the MDP. Our goal is to use MDP using a well-known solution with stable results. Therefore, to obtain the maximized V, we solve the MDP as specified by the following recursive Eq. 1:

$$V(s) := \sum_{s'} P_{\pi(s)}(s, s') \left(R_{\pi(s)}(s, s') + \gamma V(s') \right) \tag{1}$$

where:

$$\pi(s) := arg \max_{a} \left\{ \sum_{s'} P_a(s, s')(R_a(s, s') + \gamma V(s')) \right\};$$

5. *Enforce new EA model*: it is equal to result in (4) if a full actuation is considered. Whether operational environment is not completely controllable then α' will be only partial enforced.

Next, the results of an exemplification of this MDP approach is presented to foresee the support that could be delivered to the architect while choosing the best EA evolution.

4.5   Evolvable Enterprise Architecture Results

The obtained results emphasize the rationale behind our approach to deliver valuation when the architect faces different EA model evolution options. In fact, this rationale is

---

[3] Clearly, how to elicit these probabilities is a key issue for applying the method. Having developed the formalism in this paper, probability elicitation is an important future work to be addressed in industrial case studies. Here, let us just note that it will probably involve a combination of manual analytical methods such as identifying forbidden transitions and setting their probabilities to 0, data-driven methods such as using historical data to find probabilities and expert methods such as surveys (cf. [29] for an example in the EA context) and interviews (cf. [30] for an example in the EA context).

[4] The need to estimate rewards could also be found in literature, e.g., [31] proposes an EA support tool where the score of a given architecture solution should be indicated by the architect. See also [32] for a discussion of utility in EA evaluation.

more important than the particular results obtained for the case study at hand. More-over, this approach is to be used recursively: observing the reality, simulating different options, enforcing new models and then restarting the loop.

The MDP is computed by a *Matlab*© toolbox[5] using a linear programming algo-rithm. The transition matrix with the probabilistic estimation between the evolutions (φ) required to transit from a model (M_{actual}) to other (M_{final}) is presented in Table 1. Each cell of Table 1 accounts the previous defined $P^{\varphi}_{M_{actual}M_{final}}$. Let p be the probability of φ be succeed, and for calculation purposes, p is tested in the range [0.1,...,1.0] with small steps of 0.1 each. A positive value is attributed to a cell if and only if an evolution exists in Fig. 3.

Moreover, the reward matrix R, when achieving the desired M_{final}, is defined in Table 2. For all φ, Model 1 and 3 contain an access control model; therefore they have an higher reward. In the specific situation of Model 3, the sum of rewards for all φ is higher because it has a more sophisticated access control model (supervised SoD). Model 2 has zero reward because it should be avoided. Moreover, using the same previous rationale, $\varphi1$ (*do not take any action*) has a positive reward, because achieving an access control model without effort is valuable; $\varphi2$ (*removing SoD*) has a zero reward because it is not desirable; $\varphi3$ (*add SoD*) is the considered as the best com-mitment cost/benefit for this organization; and finally, $\varphi4$ (*add extra transaction with supervised SoD*) is valuable, but, because of implementation effort to enforce a new transaction the reward is less than $\varphi3$.

Table 2. Reward matrix (R) containing the set of rewards when achieving a model through each evolution (φ).

Achieved model	Evolution			
	$\varphi1$	$\varphi2$	$\varphi3$	$\varphi4$
Model 1	2	0	4	0
Model 2	0	0	0	0
Model 3	2	0	3	3

For example, the probability to be in state *M3* at time $t + 1$, starting in state *M3* and choosing $\varphi1$ at time t, is $P(3,3,1) = p$ and the associated reward is $R(3,1) = 2$. Translating for the case study language, this denotes that keeping the model supervised *SoD* after doing no action has a probability p and offers the third higher reward.

Figure 4 depicts the result from the MDP calculation using three distinct repre-sentations. In the top left corner, the value function is presented at each stage k, and each p value is separated. We observe that increasing p drives to increased value function. In the top right corner, the elicited evolutions to fulfill the value function are depicted. For each p the set of evolutions differ (each set correspond here to a different color). In the bottom, for each p, we represent the percentage of time spent in each model. Here, we observe that changing p implies change in the percentage of time spent in each model.

---

[5] Toolbox public available at http://www7.inra.fr/mia/T/MDPtoolbox.

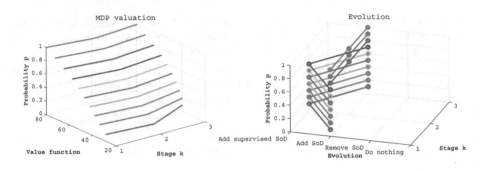

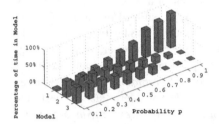

Fig. 4. MDP calculation: P_{ij}^a cf. Table 1; R cf. Table 2; $\gamma = 0.95$ and $p \in [0.1,\ldots,1.0{:}0.1]$.

Aggregating the previous results, the solution that maximizes the value function, is to always keep M1, however, it demands $p = 1$. The interpretation is straightforward and intuitive – if the organization can be fully controlled with no risk of going astray, then it is easy to maximize value. Unfortunately, due to the occurrence of workarounds, it is not expected that any organizational operation will behave 100 % as prescribed [33, 34]. Moreover, when $p \in [0.8,\ldots,1.0[$ then it is possible to avoid φ4 (add extra transaction with supervised *SoD*) which imposes implementation costs. Yet, if p [0.1,…,0.8] then φ4 is required and extra costs are incurred. Therefore, in this case study, the probability (p) to succeed with an evolution (φ) seems to be the relevant variable to maximize the value function.

Furthermore, following the rigor imposed by DSR methodology, these results are analysed using the four principles of *(i)* abstraction, *(ii)* originality, *(iii)* justification and *(iv)* benefit as proposed by [35]:

1. *Abstraction* (the proposed solution must be applicable to a class of problems) – the solution may be used to evaluate other EA models, considering the fact that MDP evaluation depends on the estimation process that is defined for each reality.
2. *Originality* (the proposed solution must substantially contribute to the advancement of the body of knowledge) – by gathering the related literature combined with a stochastic approach, a novel solution is presented, representing a contribution over and above what has been found in the related work Sect.
3. *Justification* (the proposed solution must be justified in a comprehensible manner and must allow validation) – the presented solution depends on *(i)* EA modeling, then *(ii)* converting EA models into a non-deterministic finite automaton

representation, and finally *(iii)* parameter estimation. The calculation results are repeatable using any MDP computational environment.

4. *Benefit* (the proposed solution must deliver benefit, immediately or in the future for the respective stakeholder groups) – the solution explores the benefits of using stochastic approaches supporting EA architect decisions. This goal can be achieved if engineers are empowered with all pertinent information to forecast the impacts of their decisions in the near future of the organization. With this proposal, the architect is able to simulate different configurations (and evaluate them) before its implementation, and subsequently understand the impact of actions in the operation of the organization.

5 Conclusions

This paper proposes an EA-driven organizational evolution process based on MDP calculations. Our goal is to support EA evolution decisions with an informed decision-making process, and thus enable better-informed transformational changes. We argue that the benefit of having a fully informed decision-making solution is the capability to empower the organizational decisions with tools to forecast the impacts in the near/middle/long -terms for the organization. Subsequently, the organization will be able to decide upon which is the best, and the most timely, action to be enacted.

Our solution is illustrated using a stochastic approach that is grounded in Markov Decision Processes theory. Three distinct EA models are considered and four distinguishable evolutions are available afterward. Therefore, this illustration raises the challenge of choosing between twelve different EA evolution options. In this sense, the challenge is to identify the EA evolution option that maximizes value. We remark that a stochastic approach does not address unknown exception situations; however, it covers a significant part of the reality of how actors behave within their social and human interactions. Moreover, this solution is able to show the valuation throughout the intermediate EA evolution stages. Therefore, the organization is able to forecast not only the final valuation to be achieved, but also the value that will be returned throughout time.

The main weakness of the method presented is, of course, that it has not yet been applied to a real case. Clearly, this constitutes the most important direction for future work, where not least the elicitation of probabilities and the full complexity of EA evolution options will be important challenges to overcome. By finding suitable industry partners, we hope to develop an informed decision-making approach that works, side-by-side, with humans taking dynamic decisions. Some potential alternatives and complements are business intelligence, business analytics, process mining, and event calculus. In such real-world environments, the richness of detailed data available might also call for the use of simulation methods that go beyond the analytic solutions demonstrated here.

References

1. Lankhorst, M.M.: Enterprise Architecture at Work – Modelling, Communication and Analysis. The Enterprise Engineering Series, 4th edn. Springer, Berlin (2013)
2. Greefhorst, D., Proper, H.A.: Architecture Principles – The Cornerstones of Enterprise Architecture. Enterprise Engineering Series. Springer, Heidelberg (2011)
3. Gaaloul, K., Guerreiro, S.: A decision-oriented approach supporting enterprise architecture evolution. In: 2015 IEEE 24th International Conference on Enabling Technologies: Infrastructure for Collaborative Enterprises (WETICE), pp. 116–121. IEEE (2015a)
4. Aier, S., Gleichauf, B.: Application of enterprise models for engineering enterprise transformation. Enterp. Model. Inf. Syst. Architect. 5(1), 58–75 (2010)
5. Dietz, J.L.: Enterprise Ontology: Theory and Methodology. Springer, Berlin (2006)
6. Roth, S., Hauder, M., Matthes, F.: A tool for collaborative evolution of enterprise architecture models at runtime. In: 8th International Workshop on Models at Runtime, Miami, USA. IEEE Computer Society (2013)
7. Bernard, S.A.: An Introduction to Enterprise Architecture: 3rd edn. Published by AuthorHouse (2012)
8. TOGAF: The Open Group – TOGAF Version 9. Van Haren Publishing, Zaltbommel (2009)
9. Hevner, A.R., March, S.T., Park, J., Ram, S.: Design science in information systems research. MIS Q. 28(1), 75–105 (2004)
10. Winter, R.: Design science research in Europe. Eur. J. Inf. Syst. 17(5), 470–475 (2008)
11. Johnson, P., Lagerström, R., Närman, P., Simonsson, M.: Enterprise architecture analysis with extended influence diagrams. Inf. Syst. Front. 9(2–3), 163–180 (2007)
12. Sommestad, T., Ekstedt, M., Johnson, P.: A probabilistic relational model for security risk analysis. Comput. Secur. 29(6), 659–679 (2010)
13. Närman, P., Buschle, M., König, J., Johnson, P.: Hybrid probabilistic relational models for system quality analysis. In: 2010 14th IEEE International Enterprise Distributed Object Computing Conference (EDOC), pp. 57–66. IEEE, October 2010
14. Johnson, P., Ullberg, J., Buschle, M., Franke, U., Shahzad, K.: An architecture modeling framework for probabilistic prediction. Inf. Syst. e-Bus. Manag. 12(4), 595–622 (2014)
15. Mikaelian, T., Nightingale, D.J., Rhodes, D.H., Hastings, D.E.: Real options in enterprise architecture: a holistic mapping of mechanisms and types for uncertainty management. IEEE Trans. Eng. Manag. 58(3), 457–470 (2011)
16. Quartel, D., Engelsman, W., Jonkers, H., Van Sinderen, M.: A goal-oriented requirements modelling language for enterprise architecture. In: IEEE International Enterprise Distributed Object Computing Conference, 2009, EDOC 2009, pp. 3–13. IEEE, September 2009
17. Stuart Rance: ITIL Service Transition. The Stationery Office (2011). ISBN 978-0113313068
18. Gaaloul, K., Guerreiro, S.: A risk-based approach supporting enterprise architecture evolution. In: Ralyté, J., España, S., Pastor, Ó. (eds.) PoEM 2015. LNBIP, vol. 235, pp. 43–56. Springer, Heidelberg (2015). doi:10.1007/978-3-319-25897-3_4
19. Bock, A.: The concepts of decision making: an analysis of classical approaches and avenues for the field of enterprise modeling. In: Ralyté, J., España, S., Pastor, Ó. (eds.) PoEM 2015. LNBIP, vol. 235, pp. 306–321. Springer, Heidelberg (2015). doi:10.1007/978-3-319-25897-3_20
20. Franke, U., Johnson, P., König, J.: An architecture framework for enterprise IT service availability analysis. Softw. Syst. Model. 13(4), 1417–1445 (2014)
21. Aier, S., Buckl, S., Franke, U., Gleichauf, B., Johnson, P., Närman, P., Schweda C.M., Ullberg, J.: A survival analysis of application life spans based on enterprise architecture models. In: EMISA, pp. 141–154 (2009)

22. Lankhorst, M.M., et al.: Enterprise architecture modelling—the issue of integration. Adv. Eng. Inform. **18**(4), 205–216 (2004)
23. Ferraiolo, D.F., Sandhu, R., Gavrila, S., Kuhn, D.R., Chandramouli, R.: Proposed NIST standard for role-based access control. ACM Trans. Inf. Syst. Secur. **4**(3), 224–274 (2001)
24. Botha, R.A., Eloff, J.H.P.: Separation of duties for access control enforcement in workflow environments. IBM Syst. J. **40**(3), 666–682 (2001)
25. Russell, S., Norvig, P.: Artificial Intelligence: A Modern Approach. Artificial Intelligence, 3rd edn. Prentice Hall, Upper Saddle River (2010)
26. Puterman, M.L.: Markov Decision Processes: Discrete Stochastic Dynamic Programming. Wiley, New York (1994)
27. Guerreiro, S.: Decision-making in partially observable environments. In: 2014 IEEE 16th Conference on Business Informatics (CBI), vol. 1, pp. 159–166 (2014)
28. Guerreiro, S.: Engineering the decision-making process using multiple Markov theories and DEMO. In: Aveiro, D., Pergl, R., Valenta, M. (eds.) EEWC 2015. LNBIP, vol. 211, pp. 19–33. Springer, Heidelberg (2015). doi:10.1007/978-3-319-19297-0_2
29. Franke, U., Johnson, P., König, J., von Würtemberg, L.M.: Availability of enterprise IT systems: an expert-based Bayesian framework. Softw. Qual. J. **20**(2), 369–394 (2012)
30. Närman, P., Holm, H., Johnson, P., König, J., Chenine, M., Ekstedt, M.: Data accuracy assessment using enterprise architecture. Enterp. Inf. Syst. **5**(1), 37–58 (2011)
31. Ameller, D., Franch, X.: Assisting software architects in architectural decision-making using quark. CLEI Electron. J. **17**(3), 2 (2014)
32. Österlind, M., Johnson, P., Karnati, K., Lagerström, R., Välja, M.: Enterprise architecture evaluation using utility theory. In: 17th IEEE International Enterprise Distributed Object Computing Conference Workshops, Vancouver, BC, pp. 347–351 (2013)
33. Guerreiro, S., Tribolet, J.: Conceptualizing enterprise dynamic systems control for run-time business transactions. In: European Conference on Information Systems (ECIS) 2013, paper 5 (2013)
34. Alter, S.: Theory of workarounds. Commun. Assoc. Inf. Syst. **34**(55), 1041–1066 (2014)
35. Österle, H., et al.: Memorandum on design-oriented information systems research. Eur. J. Inf. Syst. **20**(1), 7–10 (2011)

Multi-Level Event and Anomaly Correlation Based on Enterprise Architecture Information

Jörg Landthaler, Martin Kleehaus, and Florian Matthes(✉)

TU München, Boltzmannstr. 3, 85748 München, Germany
{joerg.landthaler,martin.kleehaus,matthes}@tum.de
http://wwwmatthes.in.tum.de

Abstract. Growing IT landscapes in and among enterprises face the challenge of increasing complexity, which complicates root cause analysis and calls for automated support. This paper presents an approach to correlate events, e.g. anomalies in multi-level monitoring stream data, for instance conversion rates or network load monitoring. Events, e.g. operational activities like application deployments and marketing activities can be taken into account, too. We exploit an Enterprise Architecture documented as a graph to focus on those correlations, where relationships are already known. Therefore, different data source types are identified. We present a minimal prototypical implementation called MLAC that shows first results of the feasibility of the approach, in particular to correlate events and level shift anomalies in an artificial web-shop setup. It includes a dynamic visualization of the correlations in the EA graph.

Keywords: Event correlation · Anomaly detection · Outlier detection · Stream data types · Anomaly types · Enterprise architecture · Multi-level monitoring · Runtime monitoring · Time series data

1 Introduction

The management of large IT landscapes is a big challenge for enterprises. Digitalization is currently recognized as a major trend. Therefore, IT landscapes of enterprises can be assumed to become even larger and more complex, also due to the interconnection of IT landscapes from different enterprises. One key challenge is to identify root causes for problems occurring within these IT landscapes. This is difficult, because often a bunch of monitoring tools is used, which complicates the correlation of events. Moreover, the effects of problems sometimes emerge in multiple key performance indicators (KPIs), e.g. in monitoring data recorded from business processes, applications, hardware and networks. Thus, a monitoring solution covering all sources is desirable. In addition to that, our hypothesis is that the dependency information, such as captured by Enterprise Architecture Management (EAM) tools, could facilitate the identification of root causes.

© Springer International Publishing AG 2016
R. Pergl et al. (Eds.): EOMAS 2016, LNBIP 272, pp. 52–66, 2016.
DOI: 10.1007/978-3-319-49454-8_4

A layered perspective on monitoring solutions is not new, cf. [1]. Similar to that a standard Enterprise Architecture Management (EAM) model distinguishes between business, application and infrastructure layers, where each performance indicator can be assigned to. Moreover, events constitute an efficient way of dealing with relevant information from time series data and has been used by several researchers, cf. Sect. 2. Our idea is to perform anomaly detection on each of the performance indicators and to correlate changes of different performance indicators and also events induced by operational activities on the basis of the information contained in EA models. An Enterprise Architecture (EA) model can be used to document dependencies of performance indicators of different EA layers *a priori* and is often maintained by EA specialists for their own needs. This can be exploited to focus first on correlations, where relationships are already documented. We assume that the correlations detected by this approach speed up the process of root cause analysis, because there is already a documented dependency. Figure 1 illustrates the idea of our approach. Furthermore, approaches exist to discover these dependencies automatically, known as EA discovery, that could be used to automate the process of the graph generation at least to some degree.

A simple use case to illustrate the applicability of our approach could be for example the conversion rate as a KPI in the business layer of an EA that depends on multiple servers. On the servers the corresponding web-shop application or parts of it (e.g. load-balancer, web-servers, databases) are deployed and running. Here, several standard performance indicators of servers could be used to detect erroneous behavior of the server, e.g. ping results, cpu load, network bandwidth and alike.

This work is part of the integrated multi-level monitoring part-project [2,3] of the TUM Living Lab Connected Mobility (LLCM) project. The inter-disciplinary TUM LLCM project [4] envisions an open platform to support and provide new mobility concepts. For this open platform central integrated monitoring services shall be developed including a capability to logically connect monitoring information from different layers of the EA model. However, our general-purpose approach can be applied to a multitude of application scenarios.

The key contributions of this work are a new approach to detect correlations of different types of anomalies and events occurring in an IT landscape based on information gathered from an enterprise architecture and a minimal viable prototype called MLAC to demonstrate the feasibility of the approach. Therefore, we also identify different data source types and discuss potential anomaly detection methods and further suitable events.

The remainder of this paper is organized as follows: Sect. 2 shortly reviews relevant prior and related work. Our general idea of multi-level anomaly correlation (MLAC) is described in Sect. 3. In Sect. 4 we identify different types of data streams and their anomalies and changes. The prototypical implementation is described in Sect. 5. In Sect. 6 we discuss limitations of both: the idea and our prototype. We also present ideas for future work. Finally, Sect. 7 briefly concludes this paper.

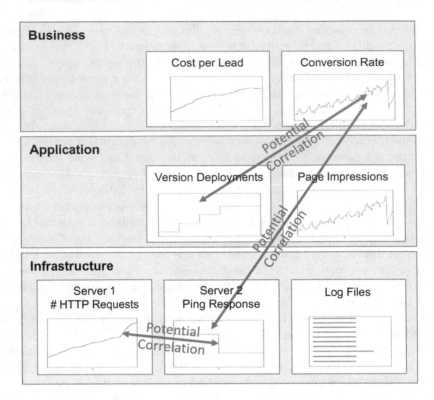

Fig. 1. Illustration of our approach for the correlation of anomalies in KPI streams (monitoring data) and events among different layers of an enterprise architecture model. Correlations can be detected among anomalies and anomalies, anomalies and events and on events and events within one or across multiple layers of the EA.

2   Related Work

Time series data typically occurs in the domain of monitoring. A plethora of work has been done on monitoring KPIs for each of the EA layers, including extensive reviews, e.g. on the topics of business process monitoring [5], network monitoring, e.g. [6] or application monitoring, e.g. [7]. Several monitoring approaches monitor data from two layers, e.g. grid monitoring [8] or eventually even three layers, e.g. cloud monitoring, see e.g. [9].

A handful of approaches attempt to combine event data extracted from monitoring data from several EA layers. For instance Zeginis et al. [10] collect monitoring data from all EA layers, but they do not correlate the data. Vierhauser et al. [11] propose the ReMinds framwork that uses complex event processing to correlate events based on monitoring data, but only uses monitoring data from the infrastructure and application layers. Baresi and Guinea [12] and Mos et al. [13] correlate events from all EA layers. However, none of these approaches exploits the structural information among the entities in the layers.

The domain of detecting outliers and anomalies has a long history. Even the very first definition of an outlier dates back to 1980, and is given by Douglas M. Hawkins [14] "An outlier is an observation that differs so much from other observations as to arouse suspicion that it was generated by a different mechanism." In the following decades, especially in the domain of time series forecasting many methods have been developed, e.g. robust regression [15], ARMA models [16–19], and ARIMA models [20,21], mostly for forecasting purposes. They have been used for anomaly detection later on.

Albeit anomaly and outlier detection can be applied on several data types, we only focus on work capable of using time series data. Analogue to the time series forecasting domain many methods are designed for specific application domains. Aggarwal [22], Chandola et al. [23] and Hodge and Austin [24] provide an extensive overview of outlier detection techniques spanning multiple research areas and application domains. Gupta et al. [25] provide an extensive overview of anomaly detection for temporal data like time series data, data stream, distributed data, spatio-temporal data or network data. Ranshous et al. [26] compiled a considerable survey about anomaly types that occur in dynamic networks and introduced five methods how to detect these anomalies. A further survey conducted by Akoglu et al. [27] comprises not only anomalies types and detection methods in dynamic networks but also provides an extensive overview about static, dynamic, attributed and plain graphs. Furthermore, the authors highlight the effectiveness, scalability, generality, and robustness aspects of the introduced methods and address major techniques that facilitate the root cause analysis of the detected anomalies. We restrict ourselves to a suitable amount of types for the illustration of our approach.

Finding the root causes of anomalies has been extensively studied in various domains. In computer networks, effort has been made on handling both real-time events and link information by means of an extension of the Principal Component Analysis (PCA) algorithm [28], or by the so-called hierarchical domain-oriented reasoning mechanism [29]. Yan et al. [30] present an approach to determine the anomaly localization by passively monitoring the end-to-end performance associated with end-users from inside an Internet Service Provider (ISP) network. The authors of [31] describe a fault localization methodology in an end-to-end service system by using belief networks. The graph models the dependency among network components layered in a multi-level system. Each layer is associated with multiple possible failure modes. After detecting anomalies in the system, belief propagation algorithms are running on the graph and the posterior beliefs are examined to pick out the most likely causes for the anomalies.

Although these aforementioned techniques are good approaches to determine the root cause of anomalies by incorporating multiple data flow layers, they provide only a very inaccurate investigation of the troubleshooting and does not consider the business processes on top of the described network. The developers of the large-scale monitoring systems VScope [32] and Monalytics [33] attempt to efficiently find the root causes of anomalies by considering the relationships between components and sensors. In contrast, our approach attempts to find the root cause of anomalies by comparing simultaneously occurring outliers in time series data and events collected from several enterprise architecture layers.

Many proposals leverage machine learning and data mining techniques for finding root causes in systems. One approach is to learn from historical data and find anomalies in the current data. [34] presents a decision tree learning approach to diagnose failures in large internet sites. The authors of [35] uncover root causes of failures in sensor network applications by performing discriminative frequent pattern mining based on frequent patterns generated by the so-called Apriori algorithm. Both methods employ supervised algorithms, whereas Kim et al. [36] introduce an unsupervised model for finding the cause of anomalies in a service oriented web architecture. The model combines historical and latest service metric data to rank sensors that are potentially contributing to a given anomaly. All listed methods do not attempt to find the root cause of anomalies by detecting correlations between time series data created by means of relevant KPIs based on the particular enterprise layer.

From the wide variety of outlier detection techniques available, we choose the BIRCH algorithm proposed by Zhang et al. [37]. BIRCH is an unsupervised stream data clustering method based on balanced trees. It has notable advantages in comparison to other algorithms: It performs effectively over large data sets, which is often the case in high frequency time series data and it produces good clustering from only one scan of the entire data set.

3   Multi-Level Anomaly and Event Correlation (MLAC)

Our approach attempts to find potential correlations of events in an IT landscape. The main assumption for our approach is that anomalies or events that are causally linked occur together within a certain time frame. Events can be anomalies detected in monitoring time series data or events encoding operational activities, e.g. version deployments or marketing activities. Therefore, each data source is considered as a time series (monitoring data and operational events), see also Sect. 4.

After the first processing step only events (anomalies detected in time series data or operational events) are considered. For each event it is assessed, whether other events occurred within a reasonable time frame. The total number of possible correlations is reduced by taking into account the information extracted from an EA, i.e. possible correlations are considered only if a path between the different data source layers exists in the graph representing the EA.

Within each time step of our algorithm, a limited amount of data is collected for each data source. Subsequently, the time series pre-processing/change detection is performed and the events are assessed for possible correlations according to the EA graph. Moreover, a time window describing the maximal distance in time for the possible correlation of events can be set. This process is repeated for each time step.

It is possible to detect correlations among events only, anomalies detected in time series data and events and also among anomalies stemming from different time series data only, with the latter being of course the most interesting combination. This approach requires the user to maintain a correct and possibly large EA graph on the one hand. On the other hand, it allows a large flexibility with respect to the different data source types.

4 Data Source Types and Anomaly Detection Methods

Our approach takes into account anomalies detected on time series data as well as special events. There are two views on this. Events can be imagined as time series data with only binary or ordinal values, as depicted in Fig. 3. Of course, they can be saved much more efficiently by only saving the time stamp and the value when changes occur. Similarly, anomalies can be imagined as events in time series data. This relationship of the input data is depicted in Fig. 2. Consequently, the input to our algorithm can always be assumed to be a time series and the output of the anomaly detection or event detection methods can always be assumed to be events (except for log data).

Nevertheless, there is a multitude of events in time series data that can be relevant for the detection of possible correlations in the IT landscape. In the literature different types of anomalies in time series data have been identified, e.g. by [21,38,39]:

- **additive outlier (AO)** affects only a single observation and jumps back to the normal behavior after the anomaly occurred. Additive outliers can adopt a seasonal characteristic which appears as a surprisingly large or small value occurring repeatedly at regular intervals.
- **innovative outlier (IO)** presents an unusual innovation in the time series and affects all later observation. In detail the observation can increase, decrease or follow a constant shift. A mixed innovative outlier can be observed when only one characteristic of the time series, e.g. trend or seasonal component, is changed by the innovation.
- **level shifts (LS)** characterize outliers which experience a move in their original level. Like an innovative outlier LS anomalies affect many observations and have a permanent effect.

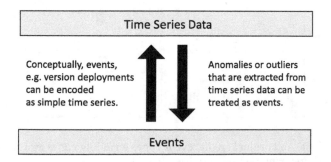

Fig. 2. Illustration of the relation between different possible inputs to our approach.

- **temporary changes (TC)** describe an anomaly which produces an initial effect that dies out gradually with time.
- **reallocation outlier (RO)** introduced by Wu and Hosking [39] affects a series of coherent additive outliers. In addition, reallocation outliers exhibit the particular characteristic that all the affects add up to null.

For our approach, the user needs to manually decide what type of anomalies or events are relevant for each data source. Therefore, we classify a selection of the possible events that can occur in the IT landscape:

- Events that can be encoded in **binary or ordinal valued time series**, e.g. server ping responses, version deployments or marketing activities: Fig. 3.
- Simple events in real-valued time series data (Figs. 4 and 5), e.g. exceeding an **upper bound threshold** or falling below a certain **lower bound threshold**, see Fig. 6 for an illustration.
- Anomalies extracted from linear or cyclical time series models using **anomaly or outlier detection methods**.
- **Complex time series data** can be reduced to trend, cyclical, seasonal and noise components using time series decomposition. The trend and cyclical components can then be fed into anomaly and outlier detection methods for linear or cyclical time series data.
- Events extracted from semi-structured or structured **text documents**, e.g. log files.

Some events in the IT landscape can be encoded simply as binary on/off values, e.g. server ping responses. Marketing activities and relatively sparse events in time can easily be encoded as ordinal time series values. The automated detection of outliers in real-valued time series data is much more challenging. There are several types of anomalies. As already discussed there are single outliers as well as qualitative changes. The latter might be more relevant for concrete use cases. Furthermore, there exists a plethora of different algorithms for anomaly and outlier detection on time series and stream data. For each data source a specific use case requires one or several different types of anomalies to be detected.

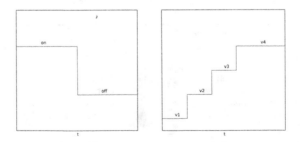

Fig. 3. Binary (left) and ordinal (right) event types encoding e.g. server ping responses, version deployments or marketing activities (e.g. TV spots)

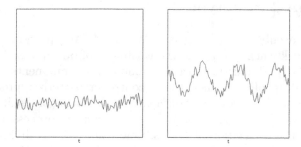

Fig. 4. Trend (left) and seasonal or cyclical (right) time series data modeling for example conversion rates or network load monitoring data.

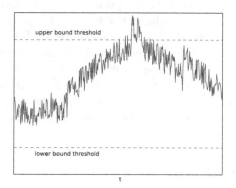

Fig. 5. Upper and lower bound thresholds on time series data that encodes e.g. preventive alerts on network bandwidth load monitoring data.

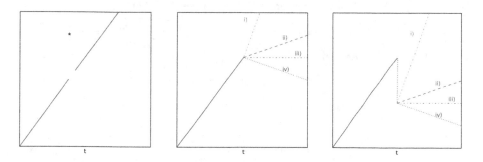

Fig. 6. Illustration of different anomaly types extracted from time series data known in the literature, e.g. additive (left), innovative (middle) and level shift (right). Most relevant for a conversion rate time series are innovative anomalies. However an increasing growth depicted in (i) can be desirable, whereas smaller decreases (ii) or a stopping of growth could be considered normal, and (iii) switching to a decrease in growth could be considered as a relevant anomaly. Additionally, these changes in the trend can be preceded by a significant drop or rise in the values of the time series.

5   The MLAC Prototype

The Multi-level events and anomaly correlation (MLAC) prototype is currently designed as a workbench to evaluate the feasibility of our approach. The overall architecture of MLAC and the data flow among its components is depicted in Fig. 7. In general, it follows a model-view-controller pattern approach, separating data management, processing of data and visualization of results. Within the processing part it can be divided into two sub parts: pre-processing of the time series data and the correlation of events. One result of this division into components is that each component can rather easily be improved or replaced. The individual components of the MLAC prototype are described in the following:

- **Database/Data Warehouse, Data Integrator, Data Generator:** Currently, we generate artificial streaming data in a Data Generator component and store it in a HSQLDB database. For real world applications a time series database or a data warehouse to keep data is essential, e.g. Pentaho that collects data using a Data Integrator component from various sources, e.g. from marketing analysis tools like Google Universal or Piwik.
- **Data Collector:** This component of MLAC is an interface to access relevant time series data from a database or adData warehouse. It queries the data store and selects only time series data within the configured time frame.

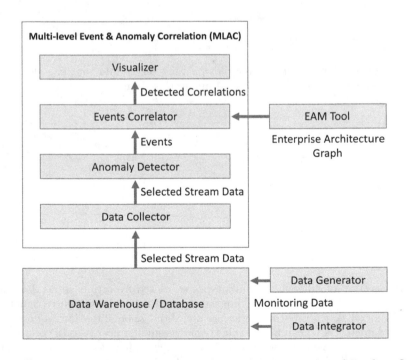

Fig. 7. Illustration of the architecture of the MLAC prototype and its data flows.

- **Anomaly Detector:** The quality of the proposed correlations heavily depends upon the quality of the detected anomalies or changes. Therefore, the Anomaly Detector component provides an interface to invoke a suitable anomaly detection algorithm on the time series data.
- **Anomaly Correlator:** The core component of MLAC is the Anomaly Correlator. It runs in an endless loop, where within each loop the algorithm matches all detected anomalies with respect to the edges in the EA graph and time constraints.
- **EAM Tool:** The EA architecture in an enterprise context is often documented in an EAM tool, e.g. ArchiMate or alike. Currently, the graph is directly modeled in MLAC, but a component that imports the graph information from EAM tools is planned.
- **Visualizer:** The visualizer component depicts the EA as a graph and highlights edges.

In order to perform a first evaluation of the feasibility of our approach, we choose a very simple and artificial setup. The enterprise architecture setup of a simple web-shop example is depicted in Fig. 8(b): Ten servers on the infrastructure level contribute to two different business level KPIs (conversion rates). Five servers contribute linearly to each of the conversion rates. The server availability is simulated and measured as simple binary time series (cf. Fig. 3) representing the server ping responses.

If one server is not running, the conversion rate will drop for one fifth of its normal value. Note that multiple servers can shut down in parallel. The conversion rate hence contains level shifts and we perform an outlier detection using the BIRCH algorithm on the conversion rates. We use the common heuristic to consider the smallest cluster to contain most likely outliers. The idea is that the detection of changes in the server ping responses is sharp. This is done to evaluate if the BIRCH algorithm is a suitable algorithm to detect level shift changes in the conversion rates. Figure 8 illustrates the textual and visual output of our prototype.

Using this simple artificial setup, we can see that the BIRCH algorithm needs to be fine-tuned using the distance threshold parameter that controls the diameter of clusters and indirectly also controls the total possible number of clusters for a particular data set. It is necessary to find a value in a range so that the BIRCH algorithm results neither in a single large cluster nor in as many cluster centers as there are values. Despite these manual needs for fine-tuning, the BIRCH algorithm is capable of detecting the points in time, where level shifts occur. Using the heuristic that the smallest cluster center contains the outliers, it is not possible to detect zero outliers (if there are none in human terms). We use a value that detects more outliers than necessary. This is due to the simple setup. Moreover, using the EA graph we can filter out unnecessary outliers, because there are no other events in the system at the same time.

So far a simple evaluation with a toy setup shows that the approach is feasible in general and that a fine-tuning of the distance threshold parameter influences the quality of the detected anomalies. It is possible to tune it in a way that

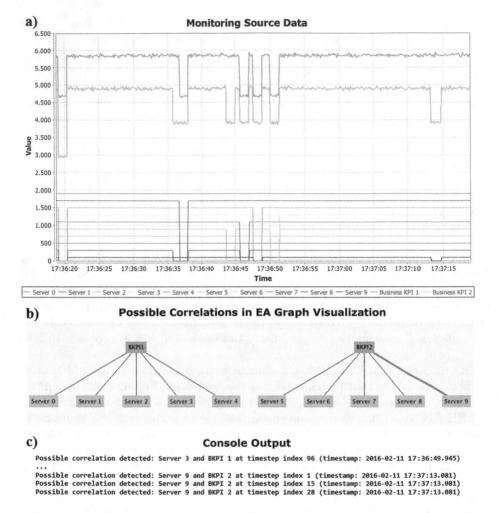

Fig. 8. Screenshots of the prototype's different outputs: (a) Illustration of source data streams (multiple time series depicted in one plot for a clear graphical presentation), (b) Graphical illustration of the detected correlations in the EA model depicted as a graph: Correlations indicated by bold red edges, (c) Textual output of detected correlations. In this example two business KPIs (conversion rates) are plotted in the upper part of (a) and the lower of the two drops around 17:37:14 for about one second. At the same time server 9, the bottom line in plot (a) fails to answer. For this artificial example our approach is capable of detecting the correlation, which is displayed textually in the three bottom lines of (c) and also indicated by the bold red line in (b). Note that [40] is used for (b). (Color figure online)

relatively simple level shifts in a time series with small noise can be detected and that a small over-fitting can be accepted because of the sharp nature of the events of the toy example.

6   Limitations and Future Work

A current limitation of the prototype and subject to future work is that changes
are not correlated among disjoint time steps, i.e. a change that occurs a short
time period before or after a change on a different stream are not considered
to be correlated. This can be resolved by a window of a fixed number of time
steps around the currently considered time step. However, it would increase the
total number of necessary comparisons by the number of considered time steps.
Moreover, a current limitation is that the data streams need a joint time axis.
A support for variable time axis granularity is planned.

Currently the prototype is build purely in Java. It should be extended to be
accessible and configurable via a web-based frontend in the future. Additionally,
the data should be stored in either a time series database or a data warehouse
like Pentaho [41]. A time series database has the advantage of a highly optimized
software for storing and querying time series data. In contrast to that Pentaho
has the advantage of easy integration of existing data sources. Moreover, the
integration of a complex event processing framework, e.g. Drools Fusion [42]
could simplify and empower the configuration of the prototype.

A major limitation of our approach in general is that it depends heavily on a
properly maintained enterprise architecture documentation (the EA graph) and
the quality of the detected anomalies and changes. With respect to the quality of
detected anomalies several improvements can be thought of: Anomalies depend
on the size of the sliding window, i.e. the number of data points considered.
Hence, the anomaly detection methods could be performed on different window
sizes and a subsequent majority voting could improve the anomaly detection.
Also, machine learning methods could be applied on the resulting anomalies to
improve the quality of the anomaly detection. Last but not least, several different
methods like BIRCH and AnyOut could be applied simultaneously on the same
data in order to detect anomalies of higher quality.

As future work we intend to experiment with different anomaly detection
algorithms, especially after the application of time series decomposition algorithms on real world data.

7   Conclusion

The MLAC prototype correlates changes in monitoring data streams from different elements in enterprise architecture. A major benefit is the reduction of
necessary comparisons by comparing only anomalies or changes along the edges
of a graph encoding an enterprise architecture. Anomalies can be detected with
any anomaly or outlier detection algorithm. Therefore, we identified different
types of anomalies from a use case point of view. Moreover, we can extend the
approach to encode changes or activities like software deployments or marketing
activities as monitoring data streams. We achieve promising results with our
first minimal viable prototype. It encodes server availability of multiple servers
that linearly influence fictive business KPIs. We use a BIRCH implementation

to detect anomalies on the business KPI monitoring data streams. However, it is clear that the quality of detected possible correlations heavily depends upon the quality of detected anomalies.

For future work it is essential to evaluate the approach on real world data. Besides this, the prototype can be extended in various ways with the most interesting being the test of different anomaly detection algorithms for different monitoring stream data.

Acknowledgments. This work is part of TUM Living Lab Connected Mobility (TUM LLCM) project and has been funded by the Bayerisches Staatsministerium für Wirtschaft und Medien, Energie und Technologie (StMWi). We also thank our reviewers for their valuable feedback and constructive reviews.

References

1. Hershey, P., Silio, C.B.: Systems of systems approach for monitoring and response across net-centric enterprise systems. In: 2010 4th Annual IEEE Systems Conference, pp. 1–6, April 2010
2. TUM LLCM: Integrated monitoring (2016). http://tum-llcm.de/project/ap3/tp32/. Accessed 3 Feb 2016
3. TUM LLCM: Visual service-management control panel (2016). http://tum-llcm.de/project/ap3/tp33/. Accessed 3 Feb 2016
4. TUM LLCM: Living lab connected mobility (2016). http://www.tum-llcm.de. Accessed 3 Feb 2016
5. Ly, L.T., Maggi, F.M., Montali, M., Rinderle-Ma, S., van der Aalst, W.: Compliance monitoring in business processes: functionalities, application, and tool-support. Inf. Syst. **54**, 209–234 (2015)
6. Tennenhouse, D.L., Smith, J.M., Sincoskie, W.D., Wetherall, D.J., Minden, G.J.: A survey of active network research. IEEE Commun. Mag. **35**(1), 80–86 (1997)
7. Delgado, N., Gates, A.Q., Roach, S.: A taxonomy and catalog of runtime software-fault monitoring tools. IEEE Trans. Softw. Eng. **30**(12), 859–872 (2004)
8. Zanikolas, S., Sakellariou, R.: A taxonomy of grid monitoring systems. Future Gener. Comput. Syst. **21**(1), 163–188 (2005)
9. Aceto, G., Botta, A., De Donato, W., Pescapè, A.: Survey cloud monitoring: a survey. Comput. Netw. **57**(9), 2093–2115 (2013)
10. Zeginis, C., Kritikos, K., Garefalakis, P., Konsolaki, K., Magoutis, K., Plexousakis, D.: Towards cross-layer monitoring of multi-cloud service-based applications. In: Aiello, M., Johnsen, E.B., Dustdar, S., Georgievski, I. (eds.) ESOCC 2016. LNCS, vol. 9846, pp. 188–195. Springer, Heidelberg (2013). doi:10.1007/978-3-642-40651-5_16
11. Vierhauser, M., Rabiser, R., Grnbacher, P., Seyerlehner, K., Wallner, S., Zeisel, H.: ReMinds: a flexible runtime monitoring framework for systems of systems. J. Syst. Softw. (2015)
12. Baresi, L., Guinea, S.: Event-based multi-level service monitoring. In: ICWS, pp. 83–90. IEEE Computer Society (2013)

13. Mos, A., Pedrinaci, C., Rey, G.A., Gomez, J.M., Liu, D., Vaudaux-Ruth, G., Quaireau, S.: Multi-level monitoring and analysis of web-scale service based applications. In: Dan, A., Gittler, F., Toumani, F. (eds.) ICSOC/ServiceWave 2009. LNCS, vol. 6275, pp. 269–282. Springer, Heidelberg (2010). doi:10.1007/978-3-642-16132-2_26
14. Hawkins, D.: Identification of Outliers. Monographs on Statistics and Applied Probability. Springer, Netherlands (1980)
15. Rousseeuw, P.J., Leroy, A.M.: Robust Regression and Outlier Detection. Wiley, New York (1987)
16. Abraham, B., Chuang, A.: Outlier detection and time series modeling. Technometrics **31**(2), 241–248 (1989)
17. Abraham, B., Box, G.E.P.: Bayesian analysis of some outlier problems in time series. Biometrika **66**(2), 229–236 (1979)
18. Galeano, P., Peña, D., Tsay, R.: Outlier detection in multivariate time series by projection pursuit. J. Am. Stat. Assoc. **101**(474), 654–669 (2006)
19. Zeevi, A., Meir, R., Adler, R.: Time series prediction using mixtures of experts. Adv. Neural Inf. Process. **9**, 309–315 (1997)
20. Bianco, A.M., García Ben, M., Martínez, E.J., Yohai, V.J.: Outlier detection in regression models with ARIMA errors using robust estimates. J. Forecast. **20**(8), 565–579 (2001)
21. Tsay, R.S.: Outliers, level shifts, and variance changes in time series. J. Forecast. **7**(1), 1–20 (1988)
22. Aggarwal, C.C.: Outlier Analysis, 1st edn. Springer, New York (2013)
23. Chandola, V., Banerjee, A., Kumar, V.: Anomaly detection: a survey. ACM Comput. Surv. (CSUR) **41**, 1–58 (2009)
24. Hodge, V.J., Austin, J.: A survey of outlier detection methodologies. Artif. Intell. Rev. **22**(2), 85–126 (2004)
25. Gupta, M., Gao, J., Aggarwal, C., Han, J.: Outlier detection for temporal data: a survey. IEEE Trans. Knowl. Data Eng. **26**(9), 2250–2267 (2014)
26. Ranshous, S., Shen, S., Koutra, D., Harenberg, S., Faloutsos, C., Samatova, N.F.: Anomaly detection in dynamic networks: a survey. Wiley Interdiscip. Rev. Comput. Stat. **7**, 1–27 (2015)
27. Akoglu, L., Tong, H., Koutra, D.: Graph based anomaly detection and description: a survey. Data Min. Knowl. Disc. **29**(3), 626–688 (2015)
28. Jiang, R., Fei, H., Huan, J.: Anomaly localization for network data streams with graph joint sparse PCA. IN: Proceedings of 17th ACM SIGKDD International Conference on Knowledge Discovery and Data Mining, pp. 886–894 (2011)
29. Chao, C.S., Yang, D.L., Liu, A.C.: An automated fault diagnosis system using hierarchical reasoning, alarm correlation. In: Proceedings 1999 IEEE Workshop on Internet Applications, vol. 9, no. 2, pp. 183–202 (1999)
30. Yan, H., Flavel, A., Ge, Z., Gerber, A., Massey, D., Papadopoulos, C., Shah, H., Yates, J.: Argus: end-to-end service anomaly detection and localization from an ISP's point of view. In: Proceedings of IEEE INFOCOM, pp. 3038–3042 (2012)
31. Steinder, M., Sethi, A.: End-to-end service failure diagnosis using belief networks. In: IEEE/IFIP Network Operations and Management Symposium, pp. 375–390 (2002)
32. Wang, C., Rayan, I.A., Eisenhauer, G., Schwan, K., Talwar, V., Wolf, M., Huneycutt, C.: VScope: middleware for troubleshooting time-sensitive data center applications. In: Narasimhan, P., Triantafillou, P. (eds.) Middleware 2012. LNCS, vol. 7662, pp. 121–141. Springer, Heidelberg (2012). doi:10.1007/978-3-642-35170-9_7

33. Wang, C., Schwan, K., Talwar, V., Eisenhauer, G., Hu, L., Wolf, M.: A flexible architecture integrating monitoring and analytics for managing large-scale data centers. In: Proceedings of 8th ACM International Conference on Autonomic Computing, pp. 141–150 (2011)
34. Chen, M., Zheng, A., Lloyd, J., Jordan, M., Brewer, E.: Failure diagnosis using decision trees. In: Autonomic Computing, pp. 36–43 (2004)
35. Khan, M.M.H., Le, H.K., Ahmadi, H., Abdelzaher, T.F., Han, J.: Dustminer: troubleshooting interactive complexity bugs in sensor networks. In: Proceedings of 6th ACM Conference on Embedded Network Sensor Systems, pp. 99–112 (2008)
36. Kim, M., Sumbaly, R., Shah, S.: Root cause detection in a service-oriented architecture. In: Proceedings of ACM SIGMET- RICS/International Conference on Measurement and Modeling of Computer Systems, vol. 41, no. 1, pp. 93–104 (2013)
37. Zhang, T., Ramakrishnan, R., Livny, M.: BIRCH: an efficient data clustering databases method for very large databases. In: ACM SIGMOD International Conference on Management of Data, vol. 25, no. 2, pp. 103–114 (1996)
38. Fox, A.J.: Outliers in time series. J. Roy. Stat. Soc. **34**(3), 350–363 (1972)
39. Wu, L.S.-Y., Hosking, J.R.M.: Reallocation outliers in time series. J. Roy. Stat. Soc. **42**(2), 301–313 (1991)
40. Dutot, A., Guinand, F., Olivier, D., Pigné, Y.: GraphStream: a tool for bridging the gap between complex systems and dynamic graphs. In: Emergent Properties in Natural and Artificial Complex Systems, Satellite Conference within the 4th European Conference on Complex Systems (ECCS 2007), Dresden, Germany, October 2007
41. Pentaho Corporation: Pentaho—data integration, business analytics and big data leaders (2016). http://www.pentaho.com/. Accessed 15 Feb 2016
42. Red Hat: Drools - business rules management system (2016). http://www.drools.org/. Accessed 15 Feb 2016

Towards OntoUML for Software Engineering: Introduction to The Transformation of OntoUML into Relational Databases

Zdeněk Rybola$^{(\boxtimes)}$ and Robert Pergl

Faculty of Information Technology,
Czech Technical University in Prague, Prague, Czech Republic
{zdenek.rybola,robert.pergl}@fit.cvut.cz
http://ccmi.fit.cvut.cz

Abstract. OntoUML is an ontologically well-founded conceptual modelling language that distinguishes various types of classifiers and relations providing precise meaning to the modelled entities. Efforts arise to incorporate OntoUML into the Model-Driven Development approach as the conceptual modelling language for the platform independent model of application data. This paper discusses the transformation of an OntoUML platform independent model into an implementation specific model of a relational database schema, while preserving the semantics of the OntoUML universal types.

Keywords: OntoUML · UML · Relational database · Transformation · MDD

1 Introduction

Software engineering is a demanding discipline that deals with complex systems [6]. The goal of software engineering is to ensure high quality software implementation of these complex systems. To achieve this, various software development approaches have been developed.

Model-Driven Development (MDD) is a very popular approach in the recent years. It is a software development approach based on elaborating models and performing their transformations [13]. The product to be developed is described using various types of models specifying the requirements, functions, structure and deployment of the product. These models are used to construct the product using transformations between models and code generation. MDD was originally based on Model-Driven Architecture (MDA) [15] defining these types of models:

- Computation Independent Model (CIM),
- Platform Independent Model (PIM),

This research was partially supported by grant by Student Grant Competition No. SGS16/120/OHK3/1T/18.

R. Pergl et al. (Eds.): EOMAS 2016, LNBIP 272, pp. 67–83, 2016.
DOI: 10.1007/978-3-319-49454-8_5

- Platform Specific Model (PSM),
- Implementation Specific Model (ISM) [1].

The most usual part of the MDD approach used in the practice is the process of *forward engineering*: transformations of more abstract models into more specific ones. The most common use-case of such process is the development of conceptual data models and their transformation into source codes or database scripts.

To achieve a high-quality software system, high-quality expressive models are necessary to define the requirements for the system [6]. To use such models in the Model-Driven Development approach, the model should define all the requirements and all constraints of the system. Moreover, it should hold that more specific models persist the constraints defined in the more abstract models [8].

OntoUML was formulated in 2005 as a graphical modelling language for developing ontologically well-founded conceptual models [8]. As OntoUML is domain-agnostic, it may be used for any domain. In our research, we focus on the domain of software application data and therefore we use OntoUML to create the PIM of the system. Such model can be then transformed into a PSM of the data persistence. However, as OntoUML uses various types of entities and relations to provide additional ontological meaning to the model elements, the transformation needs to deal with these aspects.

As relational databases are still the most common type of data storage, this paper deals with the transformation of an OntoUML PIM of application data into an ISM of a relational database. To achieve that, we divide the transformation into the following steps:

1. Transform an OntoUML PIM into a UML PIM including all the aspects defined by the OntoUML constructs.
2. Transform the UML PIM with the additional constraints into a PSM of a relational database including the required additional constraints.
3. Transform the PSM with the additional constraints into the ISM to define the constructs in the database to hold the data and maintain the constraints.

In this paper, we outline the various possibilities of the transformation of selected OntoUML universal types and we illustrate them using a running example. In Sect. 2, the work related to our approach including the OntoUML notation is discussed. In Sect. 3, the running example of the OntoUML PIM is explained. In Sect. 4, our approach is discussed and illustrated on the running example. Finally, in Sect. 5, conclusions of the paper are provided.

2   Background and Related Work

2.1   Model-Driven Development

The Model-Driven Development approach is based on the Model-Driven Architecture (MDA) defined by OMG [15]. Although established already in 2001, there is still deep interest in this approach as can be seen in recent publications. The book *Model-Driven Software Development: Technology, Engineering, Management* by Stahl et al. [25] provides a great overview of the MDD approach including the terminology, specifications, transformations and case studies. Another book *Model-Driven Software Engineering in Practice* by Brambilla et al. [3] presents the foundations of MDSE approach and also deals with the technical aspects of MDSE including the basics of domain-specific languages, transformations and tools. Also, the survey by da Silva [5] provides a good overview of the MDD approach and terminology related to MDE, MDD and MDA. Another survey was published by Whittle et al. [26] that focused on the support of the MDE approach in tools and provides a taxonomy of tool-related considerations.

2.2   UML and OCL

Unified Modeling Language (UML) [14,17] is a very popular modelling language for creating and maintaining variety of models using diagrams and additional components [5]. UML defines a set of building blocks – various types of elements (i.e. classes, use cases, components, etc.), relations (i.e. association, generalization, dependency, etc.) and diagrams (class diagram, use case diagram, sequence diagram, etc.). It defines also the syntax and semantics of models and a general architecture of the model [1]. In context of the data modelling, UML Class Diagram is the notation mostly used to define conceptual models of application data. The UML Data Model profile as an extension to the UML Class Diagrams may be used to describe the structure of relational databases in UML [24].

Object Constraint Language (OCL) [16] is a specification language that is part of the UML standard. It can be used for the following purposes:

– to access model elements and their values,
– to define constraints and restrictions for model elements and their values,
– and to define query operations [1].

In [19], the authors define basic syntax and semantics of OCL constructs and introduce several tools that support modelling and evaluation of OCL constraints. In [4], the authors define a technique for transformations of OCL constructs into other equivalent forms to support their definition, validation and transformation.

2.3   OntoUML

OntoUML is a conceptual modelling language focused on building ontologically well-founded models. It was formulated in Guizzardi's PhD Thesis [8] as an extension of UML based on UML profiles.

The language is based on *Unified Foundational Ontology* (UFO), which is based on the cognitive science and modal logic and related mathematical foundations such as sets and relations. Thanks to this fact, it provides expressive and precise constructs for modellers to capture the domain of interest. Unlike other extensions of UML, OntoUML does not build on the UML's ontologically vague "class" notion, but builds on the notion of *universals* and *individuals*. It uses the basic notation of UML class diagram like classes, associations and generalization/specialization together with stereotypes and meta-attributes to define the nature of individual elements more specifically. On the other hand, it omits a set of other problematic concepts (for instance aggregation and composition) and replaces them with its own ontologically correct concepts.

UFO and OntoUML address many problems in conceptual modelling, such as part-whole relations [10] or roles and the counting problem [9]. The language has been successfully applied in different domains such as interoperability for medical protocols in electrophysiology [7] and the evaluation of an ITU-T standard for transport networks [2]. Being domain-agnostic, we believe that it may be suitable for conceptual modelling of application data in the context of MDD.

The following description of the OntoUML and UFO aspects is based on [8].

Universals and Individuals. UFO distinguishes two types of things. *Universals* are general classifiers of various objects and they are represented as classes in OntoUML (e.g. Person). There are various types of universals according to their properties and constraints as discussed later. *Individuals*, on the other hand, are the individual objects instantiating the universals (e.g. Mark, Dan, Kate).

The fact that an individual is an instance of a universal means that – in the given context – we perceive the object *to be* the Universal (e.g. Mark is a Person). Important feature of UFO is the fact that an individual may instantiate multiple universals at the same time but all the universals must have a common ancestor providing the identity principle (e.g. Mark is a Person and he is a Student as well).

Identity Principle. Identity principle is a key feature of UFO, which enables individuals to be distinguished from each other. Various universals define different identity principles and thus different ways how to distinguish their individuals (e.g. a Person is something else than a University); different individuals of the same universal have different identities (e.g. Mark is not Kate even when both are Persons).

Each individual always needs to have a single specific identity, otherwise there is a clash of identities (e.g. Mark is a Person and therefore it can never be confused with another concept such as a University). The identity of an individual is determined at the time the individual comes to existence and it is immutable – it can never be changed (e.g. Mark will always be Mark and he will always be a Person).

The types of universals that provide the identity principle for their instances are called *Sortal universals* (e.g. Person, Student). The types of universals not providing the identity principle are called *Non-Sortal universals* (e.g. a Customer may be a Person or a Company). In this paper, we discuss only the transformations of the Sortal types of universals, as they form the basis of models.

Rigidity. UFO and OntoUML are built on the notion of worlds coming from Modal Logic – various configurations of the individuals in various circumstances and contexts of time and space. Rigidity is a meta-property of the universals that defines the fact that the extension of a universal (i.e. the set of all instances of the universal) is world invariant [11]. UFO distinguishes rigid, anti-rigid and semi-rigid universals:

Rigid universals are such types of universals whose extension is rigid – instances of the Rigid universals cannot cease to be their instance without ceasing to exist (e.g. Mark will always be a Person). Certain types of both Sortal and Non-Sortal universals are rigid.

Anti-rigid universals are such types of universals that contain an instance in their extension in one world which is not included in the extension in another world. It means that an individual that is an instance of the Anti-rigid universal in one world may not be an instance of that universal in another world without ceasing to exist (e.g. Mark is a Student now but he will not be a Student 50 years later). Certain types of both Sortal and Non-Sortal universals are anti-rigid.

Semi-rigid universals are such types of universals that can include both rigid and anti-rigid instances in their extension. Only Non-Sortal types of universals are semi-rigid.

Generalization and Specialization. In UML, the generalization relation expresses the fact that a subclass is a special case of its superclass. According to Arlow and Neustadt [1], an object is considered to be an instance of exactly one class (the subclass) and it may inherit additional properties from the superclass. However, according to the *substitution principle* and UML 2.4.1 specification [14], an instance of a subclass may be also considered to be an instance of the superclass. Nevertheless, the relation is rigid and holds in all situations.

Although not very common in UML models, the subclasses may form generalization sets to define a partition of subclasses with common sense. For each generalization set, the *isCovering* and *isDisjoint* meta-properties should be set to restrict the relation of an instance to the individual subclasses. The default setting of these properties differ in the versions of UML: UML 2.4.1 [14] and older define the {*incomplete, disjoint*} as default, while UML 2.5 [17] defines the {*incomplete, overlapping*} as default. Also, an instance of the superclass may be an instance of various subclasses from multiple generalization sets at the same time.

In contrast to UML, in UFO and OntoUML, the generalization relation defines the inheritance of the *identity principle*. According to that, an instance of the subclass is also considered the instance of the superclass automatically through inheriting the identity principle from the superclass. Also, the relation may be non-rigid and therefore a single individual may be an instance of both the superclass and subclass in one world and it may be an instance of only the superclass in another world.

The generalization sets in OntoUML are much more common as they define the relation between various universal types. Unless altered, {*incomplete, non-disjoint*} is considered the default value of the meta-properties.

Kinds and Subkinds. The backbone of an OntoUML model is created by Kinds. *Kind* is a Rigid Sortal type of universals that defines the identity principle for its instances, thus defining the way how we are able to distinguish individual instances of that universal. In OntoUML, the Kind universals are depicted as classes with the ≪ *Kind* ≫ stereotype. Examples of Kind universals are a Person and a University.

Subkind is a Rigid Sortal universal type that does not define its own identity principle but it inherits it from its ancestor and provides it to its instances. Therefore, Subkind universals form generalization sets of other Kind or Subkind universals; they form inheritance hierarchies with the root in a Kind universal. In other words, each instance of a Subkind universal is automatically – through the transitive generalization relation – also an instance of all the ancestral Kind and Subkind universals, receiving the identity principle from the root Kind universal. The inheritance may have any combination of values of the *isDisjoint* and *isCovering* meta-properties. Examples of Subkind universals may be a Man and a Woman as subkinds of a Person.

Roles. *Role* is an Anti-rigid Sortal universal type. It is used to define certain facts and the properties of individuals when they are related to some other individuals – i.e. they play a role in the context defined by their relation to the other individual. As the Role universals are anti-rigid, the individuals can change their instantiation of the Role universal depending on the *world*.

A Role universal does not define its own identity principle but it inherits it through the generalization relation from another universal defining an identity principle. In fact, the universal related through the generalization relation is the one whose instances may play the role in the relation. The generalization relations of Role universals usually do not form generalization sets as a single instance of the parent universal may be an instance of multiple child Role universals at the same time.

Furthermore, the Role universals are relational-dependent. It means that for each Role universal there must be a mandatory relation to another universal (i.e. minimal multiplicity value equal or greater than 1) so that all instances of the Role universal are related to some instances of the other universal.

In OntoUML, a Role universal is depicted by a class with the ≪ *Role* ≫ stereotype and a generalization relation to its ancestor. Example of a Role universal may be a Student, which is a role of a Person when attending a University.

Phases. *Phase* is another Anti-rigid Sortal universal type. It is used to define various states of instances of a universal. These states may vary in properties or meaning, defining various stages in the history of the individual. As the

Phase universals are anti-rigid, the individuals may change the phase they are an instance of.

The Phase universals do not define their own identity principle but they inherit it from an ancestry Sortal universal through a generalization relation. An instance of a Phase universal is automatically – through the generalization relation – an instance of its parent universal, as well, and so it gets its identity principle.

Phase universals always form *complete* and *disjoint* generalization sets and thus defining all possible states in which an instance of the parent universal may be. Such generalization set is usually called a *Phase partition*. This means that each instance of the parent universal is automatically – through the specialization relation – an instance of one of the Phase universals in the generalization set, as well. Moreover, there can be multiple Phase partitions for a single universal and the instance of this universal is always an instance of one Phase universal from each of the Phase partitions.

In OntoUML, a Phase universal is depicted as a class with the ≪ *Phase* ≫ stereotype and a generalization relation to its identity ancestor that forms the Phase partition. Examples of Phase universals may be `Child` and `Adult` phases of a `Person`.

Other Universal Types. UFO and OntoUML define several other universal types such as Relator, Mixin, Quantity et al. However, they are out of scope of this paper.

2.4   Tools

There are some tools supporting certain parts of the transformation process described in Sect. 4. Although none of them supports the full transformation, they can be used for the individual steps or serve as an inspiration for a complex tool to be deeloped.

Enterprise Architect[1] is a complex CASE tool supporting the whole software development process. Beside the modeling in UML and other notations, it offers transformation between models and source code generation. In context of our work, the transformation of a class model into a database model and the generation of SQL DDL scripts are useful. Beside Enterprise Architect, there are many other tools providing similar functions for UML and relational databases (e.g. Visual Paradigm[2]).

There are also several tools supporting definition of OCL constraints and their evaluation on a given model instance, such as DresdenOCL[3], OCLE[4] or USE[5]. DresdenOCL even provides functions to generate Java source code with

---

[1] http://www.sparxsystems.com.au/products/ea/.
[2] https://www.visual-paradigm.com/.
[3] https://github.com/dresden-ocl.
[4] http://lci.cs.ubbcluj.ro/ocle/.
[5] http://sourceforge.net/projects/useocl/.

AspectJ for the OCL constraints or SQL DDL scripts with views for the OCL constraints.

For OntoUML, there is a few of tools as well. OntoUML lightweight editor (OLED)[6] is an environment for modelling with OntoUML which also offers functions for model evaluation or transformations into OWL. However, it does not offer transformations into UML nor relational databases. Mentor Editor[7] is a successor of OLED, providing more convenient environment for modelling and providing transformations of an OntoUML model along with OCL constraints into OWL, RDF and UML. There is also an Enterprise Architect plugin[8] and a palette for UMLet editor[9] available for OntoUML modelling in other tools.

2.5   Previous Work

OntoUML is mostly used for ontological conceptual modelling. Its usage in the software development process is still not wide-spread. Therefore, the transformation of an OntoUML model into a relational database is not yet fully elaborated. However, some of our previous work can be applied to certain parts of this approach.

In [22,23], we focused on the transformation of special multiplicity values in a UML PIM into PSM for relational databases and the possible realizations of such constraints. The approaches described in these contributions may be used for the realization of the constraints derived from the OntoUML constructs used in the PIM as discussed in this paper.

In [18], we focused on the transformation of an ontological conceptual model in OntoUML into a pure object implementation model in UML and also the instantiation of such model to validate it. The approach of the transformation into a pure object UML model is similar to our approach for the transformation into relational databases, however, certain parts of the model must be transformed in a different way because of the specifics of the relational database technology.

3   Running Example

Our approach to OntoUML PIM transformation will be demonstrated on the running example in Fig. 1.

The model defines a domain where various persons can attend various universities. The persons are defined as the ≪ *Kind* ≫ class Person, the universities by the ≪ *Kind* ≫ class University. A person can either be a man or a woman which is defined as ≪ *Subkind* ≫ subclasses of the Person class as it is not supposed that a person can change their gender. The generalization set of Man

---

[6] https://github.com/nemo-ufes/ontouml-lightweight-editor.
[7] http://www.menthor.net/menthor-editor.html.
[8] http://www.menthor.net/ea-plugin.html.
[9] https://zenodo.org/record/51859.

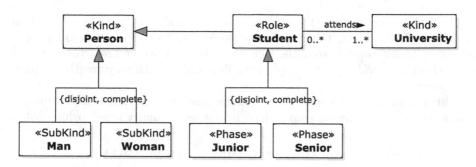

Fig. 1. PIM in OntoUML for the running example

and Woman subclasses of Person is complete and disjoint because every person is either a man or a woman.

When a person attends a university, they are considered to be a student. This fact is modelled by the ≪ Role ≫ class Student defined as a subclass of Person and its relation attends to the University class. As a person is considered a student only when attending at least one university – while they can attend multiple universities at the same time – the multiplicity of the universities in the relation is 1..*.

When a person is a student, we distinguish two states. Junior students are students under 26 years who are supported by the state in context of the social and health insurance[10]. Senior students are older students who do not receive this support. This feature is defined by the phase partition of the Student class composed of the ≪ Phase ≫ classes Junior and Senior.

4   Our Approach

Our approach to transformation of a PIM in OntoUML into its realization in a relational database consists of three steps which are discussed in the following sections:

1. Subsection 4.1 discusses the transformation of an OntoUML PIM into a UML PIM with additional constraints,
2. Subsection 4.2 discusses the transformation of the UML PIM into a PSM for relational database including the additional constraints,
3. Subsection 4.3 discusses the transformation of the PSM and the additional constraints into an ISM of the relational database.

Although the transformation could be done in a single step consisting of generating SQL DDL scripts directly from an OntoUML model, our approach brings several advantages. First, existing know-how for the transformation of

---

[10] This is a fact of Czech legislative, however, it serves the purpose of describing the transformation of the phases.

UML models into relational databases may be used (e.g. [12,23]), as well as existing tools supporting this transformation (e.g. Enterprise Architect). Second, after each transformation step, the model may be analysed and refactored, based on the resulting model and the application domain[11], which may greatly simplify the model[12].

Furthermore, in our approach, we assume just binary relationships as n-ary relationships can be always transformed into a set of binary relationships [20].

4.1 Transformation of OntoUML PIM into UML PIM

This phase of the transformation deals with the transformation of various types of universals in an OntoUML model into a pure UML model while preserving all the semantics defined by the universal types.

The resulting transformed model of the running example is shown in Fig. 2. In the following sections, the transformation of the individual OntoUML universal types is discussed.

Kinds and Subkinds. As Kind and Subkind universals are rigid and their instances persist the type in all possible worlds, their representation in UML may stay the same. Each ≪ Kind ≫ and ≪ Subkind ≫ class is transformed into a standard UML class including all its properties.

Thanks to the rigidity, also the generalization set of ≪ Subkind ≫ classes can be transformed into standard UML generalization set – only the generalization meta-properties must be adapted accordingly. If it is the only generalization set of ≪ Subkind ≫ classes and it is complete, the ≪ Kind ≫ class may be defined abstract and the set may stay incomplete. Otherwise the generalization set must be set complete.

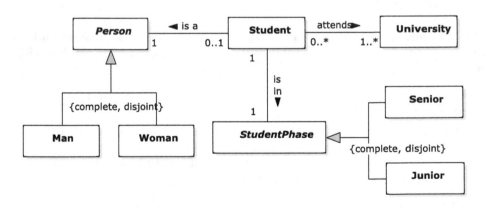

Fig. 2. PIM in UML for the running example

---

[11] For instance, phases without attributes may be refactored into a simple flag or enumeration attribute of the identity bearer.

[12] These finer bits are, however, out of scope e of this paper.

The result of this transformation can be seen in Fig. 2 on classes `Person`, `Man`, `Woman` and `University`.

Roles. The Role universals can be realized as standard classes as well. However, as Role universals are anti-rigid, the relation to their parent is also anti-rigid. Because the generalization in UML is rigid, this relation in the OntoUML model cannot be realized as generalization in the UML model. Instead, an association must be used for this relation. This association has the role of *is a* relationship as it binds the identity for the individual which is the instance of the role. The relation has the following multiplicities:

- The parent class multiplicity is `1..1` as in fact this binds the identity of the role instance.
- The role class multiplicity is `0..1` as the object's role is optional.

This transformation can be seen in Fig. 2 for the class `Student`.

Phases. As Phase universals are anti-rigid, the generalization relation to their identity principle bearer cannot be realized by UML generalization. It might be realized by associations to the individual phase classes instead. Exactly one phase should be bound to the object and the phase instance is unique for each object. We may achieve this using two possible approaches: (i) Making two associations and formulating an additional constraint, e.g. in the OCL language (not discussed in this paper, see [18]); (ii) Introducing a special virtual class as a parent of all the phase classes (`StudentPhase` in Fig. 2). Then, the association between the identity principle bearer's class and the phase superclass is `1..1` to `1..1`. As the phase partition in OntoUML defines all possible phases and it is `complete` and `disjoint`, also the generalization set of the phase superclass must be `complete` and `disjoint`.

Associations. In fact, there is no transformation of associations from the OntoUML PIM into the UML PIM in our case. The representation is the very same. However, OntoUML uses some additional constructs for relations between individuals that are not discussed in this paper.

4.2 Transformation of PIM into PSM

The second step is the transformation of the UML PIM into a PSM of a relational database. During this transformation, classes are transformed into database tables, class' attributes are transformed into table columns and associations are transformed into FOREIGN KEY constraints. Also, PRIMARY KEY constraints are defined for unique identification of individual rows in the tables. The basic rules for this transformation were already discussed in [23]. In this paper, we focus on the constraints derived from the OntoUML universal types.

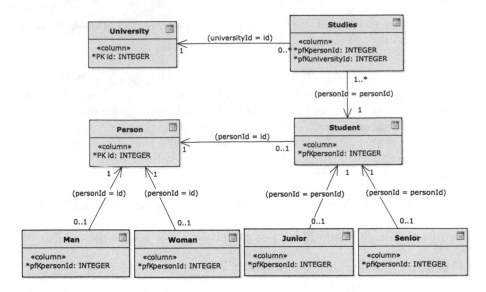

Fig. 3. PSM of relational database schema in UML for the running example

The UML Data Model profile – an extension to the UML class diagrams – is used to describe the structure of relational databases in UML+[24]. Additional constraints required to preserve the semantics derived from the OntoUML model are defined as OCL invariants, as OCL is part of the UML standard and there are tools supporting the transformation of OCL constraints into database constructs such as DresdenOCL.

The final transformed PSM of the relational database is shown in Fig. 3. In the following sections, the transformation of various OntoUML-related aspects is discussed.

Kinds and Subkinds. The transformation of classes representing various Kind universals is straightforward – the class with its attributes is transformed into a table with its columns as discussed in [23]. However, more complicated situation arises for subclasses representing the Subkind universals. There are multiple standard variants of the transformation of subclasses, however, they have certain limitations regarding the OntoUML Subkind universal constraints:

A. Transform the subclasses into additional columns of the parent class' table. As OntoUML is based on the principle that an instance of a universal really has the properties defined by the universal and it does not have empty values – the optionality of having the properties is defined by the anti-rigid universal types – all columns of the class' table should be NOT NULL. However, in this variant, it is more complicated to define such constraints as the NOT NULL constraint applies only for a subset of the columns depending on the fact instance of which subclass the record represents – the other column may be NULL. Furthermore, constraints should be defined for the columns based on the meta-properties of the generalization set. Finer details of this variant are not discussed here.

B. Transform the subclasses into individual tables containing the columns for the superclass's columns. In this variant, the NOT NULL constraints for the columns of the individual classes can be defined easily on the column level, as each table represents only a single entity with all the columns valid for it. However, it is more complicated to ensure the unique values for attributes of the superclass (if needed), as the data are distributed in several distinct tables. Also, this variant cannot be used for an `incomplete` generalization set as it does not allow the storing of an instance of only the superclass. Moreover, this variant is not suitable for `overlapping` generalization sets either, as storing the data of multiple subclasses to their respective tables also duplicate the data of the superclass. Finer details of this variant are not discussed here.

C. Transform both the superclass and the subclasses into individual tables. The tables of the individual subclasses contain a FOREIGN KEY referring to the parent class' table. This direction is determined by the fact that an instance of the subclass is also an instance of the superclass. Therefore a record in the subclass' table requires exactly one record in the superclass' table – thus being related to `1..1` parent records. More details about determination of the FOREIGN KEY direction can be found in [21].

This variant makes it easier to define the NOT NULL constraints for the columns of the subclasses' attributes as all columns in the table belong to the same entity. However, an additional constraint must be defined for the meta-properties of the generalization set of the subclasses according to the following variants:

{`complete`, `disjoint`}—exactly one row from only one of the subclass' tables refers to the row in the superclass' table.
{`complete`, `overlapping`}—at most one row from each of the subclass' tables refers to the row in the superclass' table, but at least one in total.
{`incomplete`, `disjoint`}—at most one row from only one of the subclass' tables refers to the row in the superclass' table.
{`incomplete`, `overlapping`}—at most one row from each of the subclass' tables refers to the row in the superclass' table.

The restriction of *at most one row from a table* can be realized by a UNIQUE KEY constraint on the FK column; the same column may also be part of the PRIMARY KEY constraint. The exclusivity must be checked by a special constraint, then.

In the running example, the subclasses `Man` and `Woman` are transformed into the respective tables (see Fig. 3). As their generalization set is `complete` and `disjoint`, the FK column is part of the PRIMARY KEY constraint to make it unique. Furthermore, the constraint shown in Listing 1 must be defined. The other variants of the generalization meta-properties are not discussed here.

Listing 1. OCL invariant for generalization set of Man and Woman

```
context p:Person inv ManOrWoman:
def: man:Boolean = Man.allInstances()
    ->exists(m |    m.personId = p.id)
def: woman:Boolean = Woman.allInstance()
    ->exists(w | w.personId = p.id)
man.xor(woman)
```

Roles. As Role universals are anti-rigid and the UML generalization is rigid, the Role classes in UML PIM are related to their identity principle bearers by an association with the multiplicities 0..1 to 1..1. Because of this, the FOREIGN KEY constraint is defined in the Role's table and it should be defined UNIQUE as discussed in [21]. No other constraint is needed.

Phases. As the virtual superclass of the Phase classes forms a `complete` and `disjoint` specialization set, it would require the same realization as discussed for the Subkinds. However, it does not hold any meaning in the model and it would only complicate the queries by joining an additional table without any useful data. Therefore, this virtual class is not worth realizing.

Instead, only tables for the individual Phase classes are defined with FOREIGN KEY constraints referring to the table of their identity principle bearer as shown in Fig. 3. Also, the FK columns are defined UNIQUE so there is always only one row in that Phase class' column referring to a single row in the other table.

To enforce the disjointness of the phases, the following constraint must be defined:

Listing 2. OCL invariant for the phase partition of Junior and Senior student

```
context s:Student inv JuniorOrSenior:
def: junior:Boolean = Junior.allInstances()
    ->exists(j | j.personId = s.personId)
def: senior:Boolean = Senior.allInstances()
    ->exists(e | e.personId = s.personId)
junior.xor(senior)
```

4.3   Transformation of PSM into ISM

The last step is the transformation of the PSM of a relational database into an ISM. This model consists of real database scripts for the creation of the database tables, constraints and other constructs.

As we have the PSM of the relational database, the transformation is quite easy. Most of the current CASE tools such as Enterprise Architect can be used to generate the SQL DDL scripts. These scripts usually include the CREATE commands for the tables, their columns, NOT NULL constraints and PRIMARY and FOREIGN KEY constraints.

However, the OCL invariants of the additional constraints require special transformation. Only a few tools currently seem to offer transformation of such constraints (e.g. DresdenOCL).

There are various options for the realization of OCL invariants from the PSM: database views, CHECK constraints and triggers. Each of the options has its own advantages and disadvantages as discussed in [23].

The same approach should be also used for special multiplicity values in the PSM. An example of such special multiplicity value is the relation between the Study and Student tables as the minimal multiplicity of the source table – the table with the FOREIGN KEY constraint – is 1. Such constraint can be expressed as the OCL invariant shown in Listing 3. Applying the approach presented in [23], this invariant might be realized by the view shown in Listing 4.

Listing 3. OCL invariant for the multiplicity of Studies of a Student

```
context  s:Student  inv  StudyExists:
Study.allInstances()->exists(t | t.personId = s.personId)
```

Listing 4. SQL DDL of the view for the multiplicity of Studies of a Student

```
CREATE VIEW ValidStudent AS
  SELECT * FROM Student s WHERE EXISTS
    (SELECT 1 FROM Study t WHERE t.personId = s.personId)
```

The same approach might be used even for the other constraints derived from the OntoUML Universal types, such as the phase partition constraint defined in Listing 2. The view realizing this constraint is shown in Listing 5.

Listing 5. SQL DDL of the view for the phase partition of Junior and Senior student

```
CREATE VIEW ValidStudentInPhase AS
SELECT * FROM Student s WHERE
  (EXISTS (SELECT 1 FROM Junior j
      WHERE j.personId = s.id)
        AND NOT EXISTS (SELECT 1 FROM Senior e
          WHERE e.personId = s.id))
  OR
  (NOT EXISTS (SELECT 1 FROM Junior j
      WHERE j.personId = s.id)
        AND EXISTS (SELECT 1 FROM Senior e
          WHERE e.personId = s.id))
```

As we can see, the views in Listing 4 and in Listing 5 are defined over the same table, each checking a different constraint. To make the database consistent according to all the constraints at the same time, the views need to be merged into a single view, which is a common situation for more complex industrial applications.

5   Discussion and Conclusion

In this paper, we introduced our approach to the transformation of an OntoUML PIM of application data into an ISM of a relational database. This transformation is separated into three sequential steps: a transformation of OntoUML PIM into a UML PIM, a transformation of the UML PIM into a PSM for relational database and a transformation of the PSM into an ISM of a relational database.

During these transformations, various options and additional constraints should be defined and realized to maintain the semantics defined by the OntoUML universal types. These options and constraints and their transformation were outlined in this paper.

Our approach was illustrated on a simple example of an OntoUML model. For industrial applications, the model will be orders of magnitude complicated. However, the constraints derived from the OntoUML universal types outlined here are independent of each other, therefore there should not arise any complications from their mutual bindings.

In this paper, we provided an overview and introduction to the topic and its challenges. More details about the transformation of individual OntoUML universal types (i.e. Rigid Sortals, Anti-rigid Sortals, Non-sortals, Relationship types, etc.) are about to be elaborated in consecutive papers.

References

1. Arlow, J., Neustadt, I.: UML 2.0 and the Unified Process: Practical Object-Oriented Analysis and Design, 2nd edn. Addison-Wesley Professional, Salt Lake City (2005)
2. Barcelos, P.P.F., Guizzardi, G., Garcia, A.S., Monteiro, M.E.: Ontological evaluation of the ITU-T recommendation G. 805, vol. 18. IEEE Press, Cyprus (2011)
3. Brambilla, M., Cabot, J., Wimmer, M.: Model-driven software engineering in practice. Synth. Lect. Softw. Eng. **1**(1), 1–182 (2012)
4. Cabot, J., Teniente, E.: Transformation techniques for OCL constraints. Sci. Comput. Program. **68**(3), 179–195 (2007)
5. Collis, D.J., Montgomery, C.A.: Model-driven engineering: a survey supported by the unified conceptual model. Comput. Lang. Syst. Struct. **43**, 139–155 (2015)
6. Ghezzi, C., Jazayeri, M., Mandrioli, D.: Fundamentals of Software Engineering, 2nd edn. Prentice Hall PTR, Upper Saddle River (2002)
7. Goncalves, B., Guizzardi, G., Pereira Filho, J.G.: Using an ECG reference ontology for semantic interoperability of ECG data. Special Issue on Ontologies for Clinical and Translational Research (2011)
8. Guizzardi, G.: Ontological Foundations for Structural Conceptual Models, vol. 015. University of Twente, Enschede (2005)
9. Guizzardi, G.: Agent roles, qua individuals and *the counting problem*. In: Garcia, A., Choren, R., Lucena, C., Giorgini, P., Holvoet, T., Romanovsky, A. (eds.) SELMAS 2005. LNCS, vol. 3914, pp. 143–160. Springer, Heidelberg (2006). doi:10.1007/11738817_9
10. Guizzardi, G.: The problem of transitivity of part-whole relations in conceptual modeling revisited. In: Eck, P., Gordijn, J., Wieringa, R. (eds.) CAiSE 2009. LNCS, vol. 5565, pp. 94–109. Springer, Heidelberg (2009). doi:10.1007/978-3-642-02144-2_12

11. Guizzardi, G., Wagner, G., Guarino, N., Sinderen, M.: An ontologically well-founded profile for UML conceptual models. In: Persson, A., Stirna, J. (eds.) CAiSE 2004. LNCS, vol. 3084, pp. 112–126. Springer, Heidelberg (2004). doi:10.1007/978-3-540-25975-6_10

12. Kuskorn, W., Lekcharoen, S.: An adaptive translation of class diagram to relational database. In: International Conference on Information and Multimedia Technology, ICIMT 2009, pp. 144–148, December 2009

13. Mellor, S.J., Clark, A.N., Futagami, T.: Model-driven development. IEEE Softw. **20**(5), 14 (2003)

14. OMG. UML 2.4.1, August 2011. http://www.omg.org/spec/UML/2.4.1/. Accessed 08 Feb 2016

15. OMG. MDA guide revision 2.0, June 2014. http://www.omg.org/cgi-bin/doc?ormsc/14-06-01. Accessed 10 Mar 2016

16. OMG. Object constraint language (OCL), version 2.4, February 2014. http://www.omg.org/spec/OCL/2.4/. Accessed 23 Feb 2016

17. OMG. UML 2.5, March 2015. http://www.omg.org/spec/UML/2.5/. Accessed 08 Feb 2016

18. Pergl, R., Sales, T.P., Rybola, Z.: Towards OntoUML for software engineering: from domain ontology to implementation model. In: Cuzzocrea, A., Maabout, S. (eds.) MEDI 2013. LNCS, vol. 8216, pp. 249–263. Springer, Heidelberg (2013). doi:10.1007/978-3-642-41366-7_21

19. Richters, M., Gogolla, M.: OCL: syntax, semantics, and tools. In: Clark, T., Warmer, J. (eds.) Object Modeling with the OCL. LNCS, vol. 2263, pp. 42–68. Springer, Heidelberg (2002). doi:10.1007/3-540-45669-4_4

20. Rob, P., Coronel, C.: Database Systems: Design, Implementation, and Management, 2nd edn. Boyd & Fraser, San Francisco (1995)

21. Rybola, Z., Richta, K.: Transformation of binary relationship with particular multiplicity. In: DATESO 2011, vol. 11, Písek, Czech Republic, pp. 25–38. Department of Computer Science, FEECS VSB - Technical University of Ostrava, April 2011

22. Rybola, Z., Richta, K.: Transformation of specialmultiplicity constraints - comparison of possible realizations. In: Proceedings of the Federated Conference on Computer Science and Information Systems, FedCSIS, Wroclaw, Poland, pp. 1357–1364, September 2012

23. Rybola, Z., Richta, K.: Possible realizations of multiplicity constraints. Comput. Sci. Inf. Syst. **10**(4), 1621–1646 (2013). WOS:000327912000006

24. Sparks, G.: Database Modeling in UML. http://www.eetimes.com/document.asp?doc_id=1255046. Accessed 02 Feb 2016

25. Stahl, T., Völter, M., Bettin, J., Haase, A., Helsen, S.: Model-Driven Software Development: Technology, Engineering, Management. Wiley, Hoboken (2013)

26. Whittle, J., Hutchinson, J., Rouncefield, M., Burden, H., Heldal, R.: Industrial adoption of model-driven engineering: are the tools really the problem? In: Moreira, A., Schätz, B., Gray, J., Vallecillo, A., Clarke, P. (eds.) MODELS 2013. LNCS, vol. 8107, pp. 1–17. Springer, Heidelberg (2013). doi:10.1007/978-3-642-41533-3_1

Towards a Formal Approach to Solution of Ontological Competence Distribution Problem

Alexey Sergeev[1,2(✉)] and Eduard Babkin[1]

[1] Department of Information Systems and Technologies,
Higher School of Economics, National Research University,
Bol. Pecherskaya 25, 603155 Nizhny Novgorod, Russia
aisergeev@yahoo.com, eababkin@hse.ru
[2] Department of Engineering and Management, Instituto Superior Técnico,
Technical University of Lisbon, Lisbon, Portugal

Abstract. Competence is a well-known term in the field of enterprise engineering, however, there is very little practical application of competences found in the enterprise engineering literature. This paper proposes the extension of DEMO notation in order to include competences representation, and an algorithm for competence-based enterprise restructuring. The competence distribution problem is appearing during application of the proposed algorithm. The goal of the paper is to provide mathematical formulation of this problem based on the simple competence model and choose possible methods and algorithms for its solution. Literature review on problem solution methods and algorithms, and future research proposal are concluding the paper.

Keywords: DEMO · Enterprise engineering · Enterprise restructuring · Competence · Workforce planning · Task assignment

1 Introduction

In [1] we agreed to use the following definition of competence:

Competence is a specialized system of individual or collective abilities or skills that are necessary to perform a particular action.

It was also highlighted that the term competence was well known in the area of enterprise engineering. For example, Dietz [2] considers competence as one of the main attributes of an actor, along with authority and responsibility, and defines competence as the ability of a subject to perform particular P-acts as well as the corresponding C-acts. However, in corresponding DEMO methodology there is no any practical usage of specific units of competence (skills, knowledge) while building the ontological model of the enterprise and using it for enterprise engineering/reengineering. No any model, while being part of DEMO, includes competence in detail enough for its practical usage.

It is of particular importance when applied to enterprise governance. Henriques et al. [3] use the same definition of competence. In reference method they propose, step

© Springer International Publishing AG 2016
R. Pergl et al. (Eds.): EOMAS 2016, LNBIP 272, pp. 84–97, 2016.
DOI: 10.1007/978-3-319-49454-8_6

3 is to "identify the competence domains and define a set of competence principles for each actor role". Competence domains can be perceived as attributes that will guide the evaluation process to check if a person has the adequate competence to exercise its job. Competence principle purposes to restrict the detailed design freedom regarding the actors' production acts. This is the step towards considering competences in the ontological model of the enterprise and using competences while enterprise engineering and reengineering. In the next section development of this idea in a way of algorithm proposal is provided.

Hoogervorst in [4] provides the definition of competence as 'a coherent whole of organizational skills, knowledge and technology – anchored in the competencies of employees'. Author states that central to the notion of competence is the integration of various enterprise resources. In view of the above, Hoogervorst defines an enterprise competence as an integrated whole of enterprise skills, knowledge and technology. Understandably, competences must be organized: they are thus an organizational capacity or ability to produce something. And as previously mentioned, integration does not occur spontaneously: intentional activities are required for integration to happen. Author concludes that competence-based view on the enterprise is important and is a base for competence-based governance approach. However, no practical framework for using competences in enterprise engineering and reengineering activities is being proposed.

There are many publications related to competence definition and modelling [5–8]. In [5] authors describe electronic market of competences to solve team building problem. They provide classification of different flavors of competence: knowledge, enabling technologies, fields of experience, personal traits; and use competence trees for competence structure representation. Authors state that competence vocabulary is required to provide common language for competence modelling. While the paper provides some insight into competence modelling, it does not really explore practical usage of competences after they are modelled. The competence tree structure is not practically relevant to our research as will be shown later in this paper, as well as competence taxonomy mentioned before. Another work [6] confirms our finding that no practical application of competences was previously explored in the literature related to business process modelling. In particular, authors state that "despite several approaches to business process modeling, such as BPMN, IDEF3, Event Process Chains and Role Activity Diagrams, focus on different modeling perspectives, such as activity coordination and resource modeling, they all lack the means to describe the competencies required to execute an activity and those provided by the organizational actors. Consequently, the information on the organization's competencies cannot be directly traced to its business processes. This hinders skill management from a process perspective and promotes mismatches within the description of the enterprise architecture". In this research [6], competence modelling framework is being provided. It includes 3 phases: competence definition, competence aggregation, and competence analysis. Using this framework, authors build complicated structure of competences and state that such structure will help to build competence marketplace, and certain steps may be automated (such as proposing a team or assisting the team formation process). However, no practical recommendations for such implementation are being provided, as well as any evidence that such representation of competences is being optimal for conducting this task. Papers [7, 8] propose an algebraic approach for competences modelling and their usage in a Competence Management System (CMS). The approach is based on a case study conducted with Italian aerospace company and describes an approach used in existing CMS, which may make it inapplicable to many other companies from different industries. To add to this, proposed algebraic approach represents competence structure which is overcomplicated for our case. In summary, existing papers on competence modelling lack examples of practical applicability, especially for the area of enterprise engineering, and their findings cannot be directly applied to our research due to different requirements for competence hierarchy and structure. The goal of this research is to provide mathematical formulation of the competence distribution problem based on the simple competence model and choose possible methods and algorithms for its solution. The future research will include further complication of the problem to map reusable ontology to the optimization algorithms, taking into account intrinsic features of ontology such as partial competence matching, hierarchical (de)composition, exclusive or inclusive competences, and derived competences.

The paper is organized as follows. Section 2 describes the algorithm for competence-based enterprise engineering using ontologies. In Sect. 3 we formulate mathematical problem as a part of the proposed algorithm practical application. Section 4 includes literature review on the methods and algorithms used to solve similar problems. Section 5 proposes topics for future research and Sect. 6 concludes the paper.

2 Proposed Algorithm for Competence-Based Enterprise Restructuring Using Ontologies

For design of our algorithm we use basic principles of DEMO methodology and introduce several new concepts. In our research we assume that there are actors in the enterprise which fulfil certain actor roles in order to execute certain (ontological) transactions. Actors possess individual competences and actors are mapped to actor roles contributing their competence to actor role competence on one side. On the other side, there are competence requirements for ontological transactions execution. There may be an inconsistency in requirements and existing competences.

We can draw a map of actors assigned to certain actor roles. Assuming we know individual competences of actors (the problem of retrieving the list of individual competences is beyond the scope of this paper), we can conclude about competences present in actor roles in the current implementation of the enterprise.

We can extend this map by adding competence requirements to the actor roles. Competence requirements are dependent on the ontological transactions being initiated and executed by this actor role (assume that initiation of a transaction also requires certain competences) and on the implementation of the ontological model of the enterprise. DEMO's Actor Transaction Diagram includes both transactions with their competence requirements and actor roles, so we can actually use ATD as the base for such map drawing. This approach for competence representation provides enough detail for us to use competences in frames of outlined problem.

Resulting map will actually be a graph with 3 types of vertices – namely actors, actor roles and transactions. Actors are connected only to actor roles, transactions are also connected only to actor roles. There is no direct connection between vertices of the same type and between actors and transactions. Each vertex has a set of attributes

– atomic competence items. Attributes for actors are atomic individual competences. Attributes for transactions are atomic competence requirements on the ontological level. Attributes for actor roles are atomic competence requirements on the implementation level. We will call such map an Ontological Competence Map (OCM); word "ontological" in this context means that the map was produced based on ATD with only ontological transactions represented.

Example of such OCM for the 2nd phase of Pizzeria case (adopted from [2]) – see Fig. 1 for original ATD, Fig. 2 for OCM.

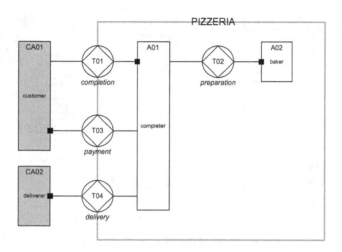

Fig. 1. Original ATD of the Pizzeria, 2nd phase (adopted from [2]).

With this map, the algorithm for competence-based enterprise restructuring is being proposed. Similar to the method described in [9] for considering costs during enterprise restructuring, this algorithm focuses on competence-based models. The algorithm consists of ten steps, which leverage usage of the aforementioned competence map and enables enterprise restructuring using enterprise ontology. It must be noted that for the current stage of the research the approach to competence modelling with extending DEMO models has advantages over other competence modelling methods and frameworks proposed in the literature [5–8], because in the case described no competence hierarchy or relationships between competences are required, so using DEMO provides the most concise method with less modelling efforts.

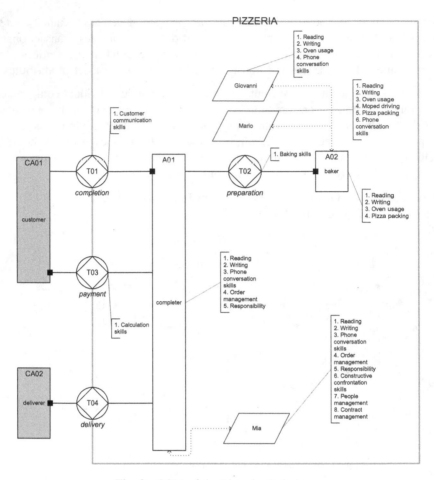

Fig. 2. OCM of the Pizzeria, 2nd phase.

Algorithm description:

Step 1. Create ontological model of the current state of the enterprise using DEMO. Refer to [2] for more details on the DEMO models creation. Outcome of this step is the set of DEMO models of the current state of the enterprise.

Step 2. Based on the Actor Transaction Diagram, create Ontological Competence Map of the current state of the enterprise. This step requires participation of subject matter experts in order to gather competence requirements for each transaction, participation of business managers to gather information about current assignment of employees to actor roles, and information about individual competences of employees (this information can be gathered from Competence Management Systems, if they are implemented within the enterprise). Outcome of this step is the OCM of the current state of the enterprise.

Step 3. Create ontological model of the planned state of the enterprise after restructuring using DEMO. Outcome of this step is the set of DEMO models of the future state of the enterprise.

Step 4. Based on the Actor Transaction Diagram, create Ontological Competence Map of the planned state of the enterprise after restructuring. At this step, OCM will be complete in terms of ontological competence requirements, but may be incomplete for implementation competence requirements and individual employee competences. Outcome of this step is the OCM of the future state of the enterprise.

Step 5. Compare OCMs produced on step 2 and 4 in order to understand:
- which new ontological requirements are added to the model and not yet fulfilled;
- which individual competences are removed from the model because of employees leaving the company or changing their roles;
- what are the changes for implementation competence requirements.
   Outcome of this step is the list of changes between current and future states of the enterprise in terms of competence requirements.

Step 6. Analyze OCM produced on step 4 with the information obtained on step 5 in order to finalize implementation competence requirements. Outcome of this step is the final list of competence requirements in the future state of the enterprise.

Step 7. Reassign employees between actor roles based on their individual competences in order to fulfil implementation competence requirements in the most optimal way, where possible. The main aim of this step is to optimize employee functions based on their individual competences, and to minimize number of new employees to be hired. Produce new OCM. Outcome of this step is the new assignment of incumbent employees among actor roles in the optimal way.

Step 8. Based on the OCM produced on step 7, finalize number of people to be hired and competence requirements for them. Produce final OCM for the planned restructuring. Outcomes of this step are the final OCM of the future state of the enterprise, number of people to be hired and the list of competence requirements for those new hires.

Step 9. Hire new employees based on the requirements produced on step 8 and assign them to the actor roles as per the final OCM. Outcome of this step is hiring completed and all employees assigned to their roles.

Step 10. Produce OCM of the state of the enterprise after restructuring ends to validate that no competence gaps exist. If competence gaps exist, proceed with additional employee hiring or employees' trainings to remove the gaps. Outcome of this step is the confirmation that no competence gaps exist or action plan to reach this state through repetition of steps 9 and 10.

Practical relevance of OCM for current enterprise operation is to help understand the lack of competence in order to do reassignment of employees to actor roles, plan employee trainings or hire new employees (and, possibly, fire some existing employees). OCM also helps to optimize employee assignment to actor roles to minimize number of employees to be hired. In case new employees are needed to be hired, OCM shows all competence requirements for new hires.

Proposed algorithm is relevant for enterprise restructuring, because it ensures that no gaps in competence will exist in new structure, helps to plan budgets for employee hiring and training, and helps to build optimal implementation of the ontological model of the enterprise in terms of enterprise competence.

However, as it was outlined in [1], there are remaining questions which are to be answered:

– How to model competences in a way appropriate for analysis?
– How to automate steps 7 and 8?

3   Problem Statement

The first issue which needs to be solved beforehand is how to formalize employees' competence levels. The decision is to use competence level system similar to one used in European e-Competence Framework – "its purpose is to provide general and comprehensive e-Competences specified at five proficiency levels that can then be adapted and customised into different contexts from ICT business and stakeholder application perspectives"[1]. In this work we apply only 5-level proficiency system and not actual competences, which makes it applicable beyond ICT area. European e-CF is in turn based on The European Qualifications Framework for Lifelong Learning[2]. European e-CF has 5 levels of proficiency in competence (from e-1 through e-5), which correspond to levels 3–8 of the EQF in the following way:

e-1: Able to apply knowledge and skills to solve straight forward problems; responsible for own actions; operating in a stable environment.

e-2: Operates with capability and independence in specified boundaries and may supervise others in this environment; conceptual and abstract model building using creative thinking; uses theoretical knowledge and practical skills to solve complex problems within a predictable and sometimes unpredictable context.

e-3: Respected for innovative methods and use of initiative in specific technical or business areas; providing leadership and taking responsibility for team performances and development in unpredictable environments.

e-4: Extensive scope of responsibilities deploying specialized integration capability in complex environments; full responsibility for strategic development of staff working in unfamiliar and unpredictable situations.

e-5: Overall accountability and responsibility; recognized inside and outside the organization for innovative solutions and for shaping the future using outstanding leading edge thinking and knowledge.

It must be noted that potential problems of partial competence matching, hierarchical (de)composition, exclusive or inclusive competences, and derived competences, addressed by other researchers in [5–8], are not applicable for the problem being solved in this paper. For the case described, it is enough to have flat list of competences in

---

[1] http://www.ecompetences.eu/.

[2] http://relaunch.ecompetences.eu/wp-content/uploads/2013/11/EQF_broch_2008_en.pdf.

order to match existing competences with competence requirements. However, one of the goals for future research will be to map reusable ontology to the optimization algorithms, taking into account intrinsic features of ontology such as partial competence matching, hierarchical (de)composition, exclusive or inclusive competences, and derived competences.

Having such 5-level proficiency system, we can now formulate the problem which needs to be solved on step 7 of proposed algorithm:

Let $r \in R$ be actor roles, $a \in A$ - actors, $c \in C$ - competences.

We define:

$r = \{n, c_1^r, c_2^r, \ldots, c_m^r\}$, where n – number of actors, which should play the actor role r, c_i^r - requirements of role r for the level of competence i, $\forall i \in [1,m] : 0 \leq c_i^r \leq 5$, where value of 0 means no requirement for competence, levels 1 through 5 mean competence levels e-1 through e-5, m – overall number of all competences which are included as a requirement to at least one actor role.

$a = \{c_1^a, c_2^a, \ldots, c_m^a\}$, where c_i^a – level of competence i, possessed by actor a, and $\forall i \in [1,m] : 0 \leq c_i^a \leq 5$

Problem statement:

Let k_i^j be the fraction of work time which actor a_i devotes for playing the actor role r_j, $0 \leq k_i^j \leq 1$. For $\forall i,j$ need to find k_i^j, so the following conditions are satisfied (depending on the exact goal of enterprise restructuring):

1. The problem constraints:

$$\forall l \in [1,m] : c_l^{r_j} \geq c_l^{a_i} \tag{1}$$

with the following restrictions (one or more may be used with different priorities):
(1) $\sum_j k_i^j \to 1$ (each actor spends as close to 100 % of time as possible)

(2) $\sum_i k_i^j \geq n_j$ (requirements of each actor role for number of actors are satisfied)
   - this condition can be specified as $\sum_i k_i^j \to n_j$

(3) $\sum_l (c_l^{a_i} - c_l^{r_j}) \to max$ (maximizing positive difference between competence levels and competence requirements)

2. The problem constraints:

$$\sum_l (\min(0; c_l^{a_i} - c_l^{r_j})) \to max \tag{2}$$

with the following restrictions (one or more may be used with different priorities):
(1) $\sum_j k_i^j \to 1$ (each actor spends as close to 100 % of time as possible)

(2) $\sum_i k_i^j \geq n_j$ (requirements of each actor role for number of actors are satisfied)
   - this condition can be specified as $\sum_i k_i^j \to n_j$

(3)
$$\sum_{l}(c_l^{a_i} - c_l^{r_j}) \rightarrow max \qquad (3)$$

(maximizing positive difference between competence levels and competence requirements)

(4)
$$number((c_l^{a_i} - c_l^{r_j}) < 0) \rightarrow min \qquad (4)$$

(minimizing number of situations when competence requirement exceeds competence level).

Next section provides literature review on similar problems and typical methods and algorithms of their solution.

4 Methods and Algorithms for Problem Solution

Ernst et al. [10] reviewed more than 700 papers in the area of personnel scheduling and rostering. They provide comprehensive classification of personnel scheduling problems. The approach proposed in our paper is new, so no research on exactly the same problem has been done, however, literature review showed that in academia there are similar problem statements, as we formulated in Sect. 3, being discussed. Using classification provided in [10], there are two types of problem statements which are essentially close to problem described in our paper:

- Workforce planning (99 papers reviewed by Ernst et al.)
  Workforce planning is more about strategic decisions than operational ones. It involves the determination of the staff levels required if an organization is to achieve its goals. As an example, a workforce planning problem for airlines is to decide how many pilots will be employed.
- Task assignment (32 papers reviewed by Ernst et al.)
  Task assignment is the process of allocating a set of tasks, with specified start and end times and skill requirements, between a group of workers who have typically already been assigned to a set of working shifts.

We must note that the workforce planning type of problem is quite wide, and includes various problem statements. Not all of them are similar to our problem statement. Task assignment type of problem uses essentially the same problem statement as ours, while certain applications may vary.

Based on review of Ernst et al., we conclude that the most widely used algorithms for workforce planning are constructive heuristic (used in 29 papers), simulation (13 papers), queueing (12 papers) and integer programming (11 papers); the most widely used algorithms for task assignment problem are constructive heuristic (10 papers), integer programming (10 papers), simple local search (7 papers) and linear programming (5 papers).

Brief description of each algorithm:

1. Constructive heuristic

   In practice it is sometimes more important to get a sensible feasible solution quickly than to expend a great deal of computational effort to obtain an optimal or near optimal solution. Simple but fast heuristic algorithms provide a means to this end. This is particularly true in the early stages of developing computational approaches for some problems. Moreover, feasible solutions from simple heuristic algorithms often offer a good starting point for obtaining better solutions. Manual solutions for scheduling and rostering can be categorized simple heuristic algorithms.

2. Simple local search

   Local search is used to improve solution quality by iteratively exploring feasible solutions in the neighborhood of the current solution. Simple local search methods do not use the complicated moving strategies employed in many meta-heuristic approaches such as simulated annealing and tabu search. Hill-climbing and descent are two examples of simple local search.

3. Simulation

   Simulation is a technique for imitating the behavior of a real system by means of an analogous computer model. The cause-and-effect relationships of a system are captured in the simulation model which is then used to predict the behavior of the system. One of the main uses of simulation is to carry out what-if analyses on different system scenarios. In personnel scheduling and rostering, simulation modelling is mainly used for demand modelling.

4. Queueing theory

   Queueing theory is the study of the behavior of the queues arising, in the context of rostering demand, from calls to a call center, customer arrivals at bank counters, patient arrivals at a medical facility, and so on. Queueing theory can be used to analyze service performance using measures such as queue length and waiting time, and to determine possible improvements in performance arising from changes to service times or the number and configuration of available servers. Queueing theory is mainly used for demand modelling in personnel scheduling and rostering systems that have dynamic demand. It can be used as an alternative to simulation in some cases.

5. Linear programming

   Linear programming is a method to achieve the best outcome in a mathematical model whose requirements are represented by linear relationships. Linear programming is a special case of mathematical programming.

6. Integer programming

   An integer programming problem is a mathematical optimization or feasibility program in which some or all of the variables are restricted to be integers. In particular, integer linear programming but not specialized branch-and-bound algorithms used by reviewed papers.

We must note that queueing theory is not applicable to our particular problem since we do not have dynamic demand and time duration. Integer programming is not applicable also since some of the restrictions are non-integer.

It must be noted that constructive heuristics are always problem-specific and cannot be easily applied to another type of problem or problem with different restricting conditions. In [11] the problem described is the scheduling proctors for examinations. The problem is somewhat similar to ours (if we consider proctors to be analogues to actors and examinations to be analogues to actor roles), but with different restricting conditions. Authors state that for their particular problem, usage of problem-specific heuristics helps to significantly improve time for solution finding comparing to other methods (in particular, genetic algorithms are being used). The heuristics proposed in [11] cannot be applied to our problem due to different restrictions and conditions used. In [12] authors confirm our finding that heuristics are problem-specific and cannot be directly applied to another problem without adaptation. The problem discussed in this particular paper is scheduling medical residents to multiperiod assignments. The problem differs from ours, so the "Rounding Heuristics" proposed by authors cannot be applied to our problem. In [13] the same authors continue their research and generalize their Rounding Heuristics, though it is still not applicable to our case. Kroon et al. in [14] are solving Tactical Fixed Interval Scheduling Problem of distribution machines across tasks, the constructive heuristic used, again, cannot be applied to our problem. The same applies to work [15] where proposed heuristic is efficient for particular problem in question only.

Extensive review in [10] is limited to papers published prior to 2004. Reviewing more recent literature on the matter, we see the same trends. In [16] authors are using linear programming to solve task distribution problem among employees. Interestingly, authors are also taking competences into account, while their understanding of competence differs from widely used in literature – they consider competence to be the amount of work employee can do in a certain amount of time. In [17] linear programming is being used in order to solve qualified workforce distribution problem. Authors do not consider competences directly, but rating workers as either qualified, non-qualified or temporary. The problem statement differs from ours. Papers [18, 19] propose to use metaheuristic and constructive heuristic approaches such as particle swarm optimization combined with either genetic algorithm or evolution strategy. Authors of [20] are using simulation methods for solving job shop scheduling problem. In [21] authors use a combination of specialized heuristics and linear programming. In [22] authors use guided local search approach, which is heuristically enhanced version of simple local search. Rocha et al. [23] are using integer linear programming to solve cyclic staff scheduling problem. Finally, in [24] the combination of constructive heuristic and linear programming is used to solve workforce planning problem.

By summarizing all of the above, literature review shows that constructive heuristic, simple local search, simulation, and linear programming (or the combination of these) are the most popular algorithms used to solve problems similar to ours.

5 Future Research

The next step of the research will be applying outlined methods (constructive heuristic, simple local search, simulation, and linear programming, or the combination of these) to the problem in question. We also plan to test those methods against enumeration for problems of different sizes in order to understand if those methods are needed at all given growing computing capabilities of modern PCs.

To have test scenario close to real life we will be using case study of a department of a real company as an example. Case describes European customer support department of multinational company. Customer support is outsourced to 3rd-party vendor providing technical and warranty support services to company's customers in the region.

Vendor support center includes:

- Technical support agents – responsible for first-line technical support for customers
- Technical support experts - responsible for second-line technical support for customers
- Technical support team leaders – responsible for technical teams management
- Warranty support agents - responsible for first-line warranty support for customers
- Warranty support team leaders - responsible for warranty teams management
- Reporting specialist – responsible for all reporting activities both internally within vendor support center and externally to company customer support department
- Support center manager – responsible for support center operation from vendor side.

Customer support department includes company employees:

- Regional customer support manager – responsible for all customer support activities in the region
- Escalations handling manager – responsible for handling all non-technical and non-IT escalations from vendor support center (including warranty exceptions approval, dealing with angry customers, etc.) and for all exceptional situations in the region (e.g. lawsuits, customer escalations directly to company executive office, etc.)
- Product support engineers – responsible for handling all technical escalations from vendor support center, technical trainings to technical agents and involved into new products support planning; playing the role of interface between vendor support center and product developers within the company.

The main problem for vendor support center is to maintain the competence set required to provide service to the corporation department given high attrition rate among support agents. Losing of managing or reporting roles is especially painful. Department of corporation is partly sharing this pain since it has targets for technical and warranty support which must be met. To add to this, department is responsible for technical product trainings to vendor support center agents, and also for keeping high level of expertise of product support engineers. The most interesting problem which we will be considering is crisis plan for different cases when many agents are leaving the support center at the time of new product launches and high workload period.

Another goal for future research is to map reusable ontology to the optimization algorithms, taking into account intrinsic features of ontology such as partial competence matching, hierarchical (de)composition, exclusive or inclusive competences, and derived competences.

6 Conclusion

While concept of competence is being used elsewhere in many different fields of research including enterprise engineering, there is no research has been done on the practical application of competences during enterprise restructuring and reengineering. Continuing research topic started in [1], we propose the algorithm for competence-based enterprise restructuring using ontologies. In order to implement this algorithm, we proposed extension to DEMO notation by explicitly adding competence to the ATD diagram – we call it Ontological Competence Map. Step 7 of the algorithm requires solving problem of actors' distribution among actor roles taking competences and competence requirements into account.

Formulation of this problem appeared to be close to two types of employee scheduling problems studied in the academia – namely "workforce planning" and "staff assignment". The former type of problem is more about strategic decisions than operational ones. It involves determination of the staff levels required if an organization is to achieve its goals. The latter one is about the process of allocating a set of tasks, with specified start and end times and skill requirements, between a group of workers who have typically already been assigned to a set of working shifts. Review also revealed that no exact problem statement was discussed in the literature, this is why no ready method or algorithm to solve such a problem exists. Summarizing the review of methods and algorithms typically used to solve either workforce planning or staff assignment types of problems we conclude that the most widely used methods are constructive heuristic, simple local search, simulation, and linear programming (or the combination of these). We will use these algorithms as a basis for future research. We must also note that constructive heuristic type of methods is very diverse and typically very problem-specific, so algorithms of this type cannot be directly applied to problem with even slightly different conditions without adaptation.

Acknowledgments. The reported study was funded by RFBR under research Project No. 16-06-00184 A.

References

1. Sergeev, A., Babkin, E.: Towards competence-based enterprise restructuring using ontologies. In: Aveiro, D., Pergl, R., Valenta, M. (eds.) EEWC 2015. LNBIP, vol. 211, pp. 34–46. Springer, Heidelberg (2015). doi:10.1007/978-3-319-19297-0_3
2. Dietz, J.L.G.: Enterprise Ontology: Theory and Methodology. Springer, Heidelberg (2006). ISBN 10 3-540-29169-5
3. Henriques M., Tribolet J., Hoogervorst J.: Enterprise governance and DEMO - guiding enterprise design and operation by addressing DEMO's competence, authority and responsibility notions. In: Barbosa, L.S., Correia, M.P. (eds.) INForum 2010 - II Simposio de Informatica, pp. 473–476, 9–10 Setembro 2010
4. Hoogervorst, J.A.P.: Enterprise Governance and Enterprise Engineering. The Enterprise Engineering Series, 1st edn. Springer, Berlin (2009)
5. Lang, A., Pigneur, Y.: Digital trade of human competencies. In: Proceedings of 32nd Annual Hawaii International Conference on Systems Sciences, HICSS-32, 9 p. IEEE (1999)

6. Caetano, A., Pombinho, J., Tribolet, J.: Representing organizational competencies. In: Proceedings of 2007 ACM Symposium on Applied Computing, pp. 1257–1262 (2007)
7. Fortunato, L., Lettera, S., Totaro, S., Lazoi, M., Bisconti, C., Corallo, A., Pantalone, G.: Optimizing a competence management system: an algebraic approach. In: Proceeding of 15th World Multi-conference on Systemics, Cybernetics and Informatics, vol. 2, pp. 302–308 (2011)
8. Fortunato, L., Lettera, S., Totaro, S., Lazoi, M., Bisconti, C., Corallo, A., Pantalone, G.: Development of a competence management system: an algebraic approach. In: Wissensmanagement, pp. 123–131 (2011)
9. Babkin, E., Sergeev, A.: Towards developing a model-based decision support method for enterprise restructuring. In: Proper, H.A., Aveiro, D., Gaaloul, K. (eds.) EEWC 2013. LNBIP, vol. 146, pp. 17–27. Springer, Heidelberg (2013). doi:10.1007/978-3-642-38117-1_2
10. Ernst, A.T., Jiang, H., Krishnamoorthy, M., Owens, B., Sier, D.: An annotated bibliography of personnel scheduling and rostering. Ann. Oper. Res. 127, 21–144 (2004)
11. Awad, R., Chinneck, J.: Proctor assignment at Carleton University. Interfaces 28(2), 58–71 (1998)
12. Franz, L., Miller, J.: Scheduling medical residents to rotations – solving the large-scale multiperiod staff assignment problem. Oper. Res. 41(2), 269–279 (1993)
13. Miller, J., Franz, L.: A binary-rounding heuristic for multi-period variable-task-duration assignment problems. Comput. Oper. Res. 23(8), 819–828 (1996)
14. Kroon, L., Salomon, M., Van Wassenhove, L.: Exact and approximation algorithms for the tactical fixed interval scheduling problem. Oper. Res. 45(4), 624–638 (1997)
15. Schaerf, A., Meisels, A.: Solving employee timetabling problems by generalized local search. In: Lamma, E., Mello, P. (eds.) AI*IA 1999. LNCS (LNAI), vol. 1792, pp. 380–389. Springer, Heidelberg (2000). doi:10.1007/3-540-46238-4_33
16. Rizaev, Z.I., Sirazetdinov, R.T.: Algorithms for assessment of accomplishment project and task distribution based on mathematical modelling of competence of employees. Nelineinyi mir (Nonlinear World) 10(5), 9 (2012). (in Russian)
17. Fragnière, E., Gondzio, J., Yang, X.: Operations risk management by optimally planning the qualified workforce capacity. Eur. J. Oper. Res. 202, 518–527 (2010)
18. Liu, L.-l., Shu, Z.-s., Sun, X.-h., Yu, T.: Optimum distribution of resources based on particle swarm optimization and complex network theory. In: Li, K., Fei, M., Jia, L., Irwin, G.W. (eds.) ICSEE/LSMS -2010. LNCS, vol. 6329, pp. 101–109. Springer, Heidelberg (2010). doi:10.1007/978-3-642-15597-0_12
19. Nissen, V., Günther, M.: Staff scheduling with particle swarm optimisation and evolution strategies. In: Cotta, C., Cowling, P. (eds.) EvoCOP 2009. LNCS, vol. 5482, pp. 228–239. Springer, Heidelberg (2009). doi:10.1007/978-3-642-01009-5_20
20. Pérez-Rodríguez, R., Jöns, S., Hernández-Aguirre, A., Alberto-Ochoa, C.: Simulation optimization for a flexible jobshop scheduling problem using an estimation of distribution algorithm. Int. J. Adv. Manuf. Technol. 73, 3–21 (2014)
21. Al-Yakoob, S.M., Sherali, H.D.: Mixed-integer programming models for an employee scheduling problem with multiple shifts and work locations. Ann. Oper. Res. 155, 119–142 (2007)
22. Alsheddy, A., Tsang, E.P.K.: Empowerment scheduling for a field workforce. J. Sched. 14, 639–654 (2011)
23. Rocha, M., Oliveira, J.F., Carravilla, M.A.: Cyclic staff scheduling: optimization models for some real-life problems. J. Sched. 16, 231–242 (2013)
24. Bard, J.F., Morton, D.P., Wang, Y.M.: Workforce planning at USPS mail processing and distribution centers using stochastic optimization. Ann. Oper. Res. 155, 51–78 (2007)

The Algorithmizable Modeling
of the Object-Oriented Data Model
in Craft.CASE

Ondřej Šubrt[1(✉)] and Vojtěch Merunka[1,2]

[1] Faculty of Nuclear Sciences and Physical Engineering,
Department of Software Engineering,
Czech Technical University in Prague, Prague, Czech Republic
`subrton2@fjfi.cvut.cz, vmerunka@gmail.com`
[2] Faculty of Economics and Management, Department of Information Engineering,
Czech University of Life Sciences Prague, Prague, Czech Republic

Abstract. The object-oriented approach usually does not follow any formal design process and is mostly ad hoc in real software development. This makes it more of an art than a science. The quality of the resultant design therefore depends to a large extent on the skills of the individual designer and cannot be evaluated easily. In this paper we present an approach to normalization of the object-oriented conceptual model based on UML class diagrams. The normalization of the object-oriented data model is performed in algorithmic way based on model transformation rules. The algorithm is able to transform the object-oriented data model from one into the other normal form following the transformation rules. The algorithm application rids the design process from the above-mentioned problems and yields a better object model by bringing formalism and taking a scientific approach. Recently, development of the CASE tool based on this approach has been started.

Keywords: Data normalization · Object-Oriented Data Model (ODM) · First object-oriented normal form (1ONF) · Second object-oriented normal form (2ONF) · Third object-oriented normal form (3ONF) · Craft.CASE

1 Introduction

The object-oriented programming (OOP) has its origins in the researching of operating systems, graphic user interfaces, and particularly in programming languages, that took place in the 1970s [1]. It differs from other software engineering approaches by incorporating non-traditional ways of thinking into the field of informatics. We look at systems by abstracting the real world in the same way as in ontological, philosophical streams. The basic element is an object that describes data structures and their behavior. OOP has been and still is explained in many books [2–5]. The [2], written by OOP pioneers, belongs to the best.

© Springer International Publishing AG 2016
R. Pergl et al. (Eds.): EOMAS 2016, LNBIP 272, pp. 98–110, 2016.
DOI: 10.1007/978-3-319-49454-8_7

In real software development, the object-oriented approach usually does not follow any formal design. In this paper, we propose the transformation of object-oriented design to correct one following the transformations rules. Moreover, to make the process of transformation automatic and self-sustaining, we introduce the algorithms handling these transformations. The goal of the paper is to obtain a cohesive framework providing the resultant design with high quality. The final framework could be used in software development for design improvements.

This paper is organized as follows. Section 2 presents three normalization rules for model transformation from one into the other normal form. In Sect. 3, the introduction to Craft.CASE scripting is stated and the description of algorithm for algorithmizable modeling is given. In the last section, the algorithmizable modeling is investigated and evaluated on one more complicated example.

2 Three Object Normal Forms and Transformation Rules

In the data world, there is a common process called data normalization by which the data are organized in such a way as to reduce and even eliminate data redundancy, effectively increasing the cohesiveness of data entities. Data normalization only deals data and not behavior. We need to consider both when normalizing the object schema. Class normalization is a process of reorganizing the structure of object schema in such a way as to increase the cohesion of classes while minimizing the coupling between them.

In this section, three object normal forms are introduced [1,6]. Moreover, the transformation rules from one into the other normal form are discussed in a detailed way [7–11].

2.1 First Normal Form Rule

Definition 1. *A class is in the first object normal form (1ONF) when its objects do not contain group of repetitive attributes. Repetitive attributes must be extracted into objects of a new class. The group of repetitive attributes is then replaced by the link at the collection of the new objects. An object schema is in 1ONF when all of its classes are in 1ONF.*

More formally; Let us have an object a in the object system Ω as $a \in \Omega$, where for $k > 1$ (length of collections of similar attributes) and $n > 1$ (number of repetition of these collections) is $data(a) = [\ldots, x_1^1, \ldots, x_k^1, \ldots, x_1^n, \ldots, x_k^n, \ldots]$ having $\forall i \in (1, \ldots, k) : class(x_i^1) = class(x_i^2) = \ldots = class(x_i^n)$.

Then it is required to modify object a and create new objects $b_j \in \Omega$ for $j \in (1, \ldots, n)$ as $data(a) = [\ldots, \{b_j\}, \ldots]$ and $data(b_j) = [x_1^j, \ldots, x_k^j]$.

In Fig. 1, there is the example of data structure in non-normalized form and in the Fig. 2, there is the same example in 1ONF.

2.2 Second Normal Form Rule

Definition 2. *A class is in the second object normal form (2ONF) when it is in 1ONF and when its objects do not contain attribute or group of attributes,*

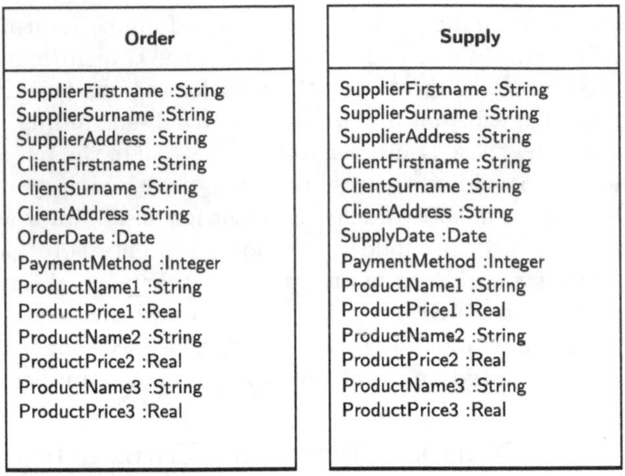

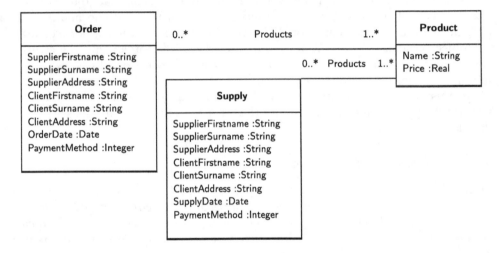

Fig. 1. Model in 0ONF

Fig. 2. Model in 1ONF

which are shared with another object. Shared attributes must be extracted into new objects of a new class, and in all objects, where they appeared, must be replaced by the link to the object of the new class. An object schema is in 2ONF when all of its classes are in 2ONF.

More formally; Let us have two objects $a, b \in \Omega$ for $k > 1$ (length of a collection of shared attributes) as $data(a) = [\ldots, x_1, \ldots, x_k, \ldots]$ and $data(b) \doteq [\ldots, y_1, \ldots, y_k, \ldots]$ having $\forall i \in (1, \ldots, k) : x_i = y_i$.

Then it is required to modify objects a and b and create new object $c \in \Omega$ as $data(a) = [\ldots, c, \ldots]$ and $data(b) = [\ldots, c, \ldots]$ and $data(c) = [x_1, \ldots, x_k] = [y_1, \ldots, y_k]$.

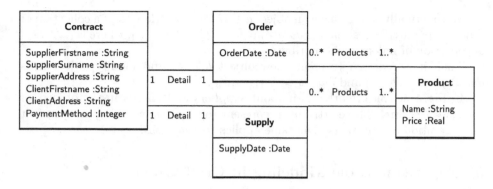

Fig. 3. Model in 2ONF

In Fig. 3, it concerns the attributes *SupplierFirstname*, *SupplierSurname* and *SupplierAddress* for *Supplier* and *ClientFirstname*, *ClientSurname* and *ClientAddress* for *Client* and method of payment in our example. Because these attributes are common for both concrete order and supply, it was necessary to create the new object class *Contract*.

2.3   Third Normal Form Rule

Definition 3. *A class is in the third object normal form (3ONF) when it is in 2ONF and when its objects do not contain attribute or group of attributes, which have the independent interpretation in the modeled system. These attributes must be extracted into objects of a new class and in objects, where they appeared, must be replaced by the link to this new object. An object schema is in 3ONF when all of its classes are in 3ONF.*

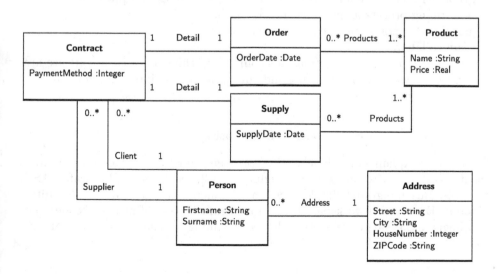

Fig. 4. Model in 3ONF

More formally; Let us have an object $a \in \Omega$ for $k > 1$ (length of a collection of independent attributes) having $data(a) = [\ldots, x_1, \ldots, x_k, \ldots]$, where $[x_1, \ldots, x_k]$ is collection of independent attributes.

Then it is required to create new object $b \in \Omega$ and modify object a as $data(a) = [\ldots, b, \ldots]$ and $data(b) = [x_1, \ldots, x_k]$.

In Fig. 4, it concerns the data about *suppliers* and *clients* in the objects of the class *Contract*. These attributes represent some *persons* having independent interpretation on contracts. The same applies to *addresses*.

3   Algorithmizable Modeling in Craft.CASE

Craft.CASE is a business process analysis (BPA) tool based on a C.C method [12]. The core of this method explains how to progress in a BPA project without forgetting anything. The C.C method consists of small steps, sequences of which are tested and validated as soon - and as often - as possible. Following this method allows processes to remain consistent even if the problem is complex. Craft.CASE leads its users step-by-step according to the C.C method. This means that the notation of the tool is rigid enough to discover, understand, and analyse processes in a consistent way.

Last but not least, another very important feature is the ability to simulate the process. Whether man use it for model validation, verification, or just to present and visualize process progress, depends on his current needs. The list of the most common features is given below:

– guidelines set according to the C.C. method
– process analysis categorization into interview, business and conceptual phases
– ability to set the user-defined properties to individual objects
– graphically visualize any object according to its values and properties
– performing process animations and simulations
– generating reports and specifying their content
– team collaboration
– advanced functions or functions not common in the field of BPA software are defined by users who can define and run their own scripts using our built-in programming language

3.1   Introduction to Craft.CASE Scripting

This section explains some details of C.C programming language and the environment used for programming in the language [6,13], see Table 1. The Craft.CASE tool contains integrated development environment with a source code editor (Module Browser), a workspace (place for instant testing of pieces of code) and a debugger. C.C language is a simple programming language that user can use for:

- querying the process model developed in the Craft.CASE tool
- automatic transformation and modification of the process model in Craft.CASE
- specification of user-defined reports and exports
- extension to the Craft.CASE tool functionality (normalization of models, design patterns application, refactoring, ...)

Table 1. Important objects for normalization of models

conceptual::class	Represents a specific class
conceptual::composition	Represents a specific attribute of some class
conceptual::method	Represents a specific method of some class
conceptual::association	Represents a relation between two classes

We have prepared a simple ODM representing relationship between a car and the owner of this car. In Fig. 5, the ODM of our example is given. We use it for demonstrating of scripting in Craft.CASE.

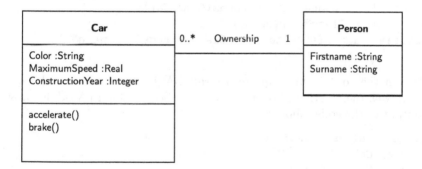

Fig. 5. The ODM representing relationship between a car and the owner of this car

In the following example, the code is printing the list of all attributes, methods and associations to other classes for class *Car* in Craft.CASE.

```
# it gets all classes from project
Classes := project:elements(conceptual::class).
# initialization of ClassCar variable
ClassCar := nil.
# searching for class Car
from 1 to size(Classes) do { :I |
    if ClassCar = nil then
    {
```

```
        if Classes[I]["name"] = "Car" then
        {
            ClassCar := Classes[I].
        }.
    }.
}.
# it gets all attributes and relations to other classes
ClassLinks := element:links(ClassCar).
from 1 to size(ClassLinks) do { :I |
    if element:type(ClassLinks[I]) = "Composition" then
    {
        stream:print-nl("Attribute:" + ClassLinks[I]["name"]).
    }.
    if element:type(ClassLinks[I]) = "Association" then
    {
        stream:print-nl("Relation to class" +
        element:target(ClassLinks[I])["name"] + ":" +
        ClassLinks[I]["name"]).
    }.
}.
# it gets all methods
ClassMethods := conceptual:methods(ClassCar).
from 1 to size(ClassMethods) do { :I |
    stream:print-nl("Method:" + ClassMethods[I]["name"]).
}.
```

We run the code in Workspace of Craft.CASE. To organize code in well-arranged way, the creation of own packages is also possible in Module Browser. The output of the code follows:

```
Relation to class Person: Owner
Attribute: Color
Attribute: MaximumSpeed
Attribute: ConstructionYear
Method: accelerate
Method: brake
```

3.2   Normalization Algorithms for ODM

In this section, we introduce algorithms enabling transformation from one into the other normal form. We call this process as the normalization of ODM. Firstly, the algorithm for transformation from 0ONF to 1ONF is given, see Algorithm 1. To remind, a class is in 1ONF when specific behavior required by an attribute that is actually a collection of similar attributes is encapsulated within its own class. An object schema is in 1ONF when all of its classes are in 1ONF.

Then, the algorithm for transformation from 1ONF to 2ONF is given, see Algorithm 2. To remind, a class is in second object normal form (2ONF) when it

---

Algorithm 1. Transformation from 0ONF into 1ONF algorithm

$Classes \leftarrow$ get all classes in current project
for all $Class \in Classes$ **do**
    $DuplicatedAttributes \leftarrow$ get all duplicated attributes of class $Class$
    for all $DuplicatedAttribute \in DuplicatedAttributes$ **do**
        remove attribute $DuplicatedAttribute$ from class $Class$
    end for
    for all $DuplicatedAttribute \in DuplicatedAttributes$ **do**
        $NewClassName \leftarrow$ get name of new class from name of $DuplicatedAttribute$
        $NewAttributeName \leftarrow$ get name of new attribute from name of $DuplicatedAttribute$
        if class with name $NewClassName$ already exists **then**
            $NewClass \leftarrow$ get class with name $NewClassName$
        else
            $NewClass \leftarrow$ create class with name $NewClassName$
        end if
        if attribute with name $NewAttributeName$ in class $NewClass$ does not exist yet **then**
            create a new attribute with name $NewClassName$ in class $NewClass$
        end if
        if association between $Class$ and $NewClass$ does not exist yet **then**
            create a new association between $Class$ and $NewClass$
        end if
    end for
end for

---

is in 1ONF and when "share" behavior that is needed by more than one instance of the class is encapsulated within its own class(es). An object schema is in 2ONF when all of its classes are in 2ONF.

All attributes are identified only by their names and data types. It means the mentioned algorithms are dependent on well-named attributes and their uniqueness in order to transform model correctly. Of course, the violation of this restriction might cause unsuccessful and incorrect transformations.

Finally, the algorithm for transformation from 2ONF to 3ONF should be also given. To remind, a class is in third object normal form (3ONF) when it is in 2ONF and when it encapsulates only one set of cohesive behaviors. An object schema is in 3ONF when all of its classes are in 3ONF. Unfortunately, the algorithm would be more complex than the previous ones and its implementation is going beyond the scope of this article.

To identify attribute or group of attributes having the independent interpretation in the modeled system is not a straightforward process. It must be considered what each physical attribute represents. It is not a simple task to identify these representations without any information handling them from other models (participants, function and scenarios, participant relations, business interactions, business diagrams, etc.) incorporated in a whole process of analysis.

Algorithm 2. Transformation from 1ONF into 2ONF algorithm

$Classes \leftarrow$ get all classes in current project
$AgreementNumber \leftarrow 0$
$ClassXGlobal \leftarrow nil$
$ClassYGlobal \leftarrow nil$
$TransformationTo2ONFDone \leftarrow false$
while $\neg TransformationTo2ONFDone$ **do**
    for all $ClassX, ClassY \in Classes$ **do**
        if $ClassX \neq ClassY$ **then**
            $CurrentAgreementNumber \leftarrow 0$
            $AttributesX \leftarrow$ get all attributes of class $ClassX$
            $AttributesY \leftarrow$ get all attributes of class $ClassY$
            for all $AttributeX \in AttributesX, AttributeY \in AttributesY$ **do**
                if $AttributeX$ and $AttributeY$ represent same attribute **then**
                    $CurrentAgreementNumber \leftarrow CurrentAgreementNumber + 1$
                end if
            end for
            if $AgreementNumber < CurrentAgreementNumber$ **then**   ▷ searching for
                two classes with the highest agreement
                $AgreementNumber \leftarrow CurrentAgreementNumber$
                $ClassXGlobal \leftarrow ClassX$
                $ClassYGlobal \leftarrow ClassY$
            end if
        else
            $Attributes \leftarrow$ get all attributes of class $ClassX$ with the same $Prefix$
            if $Attributes \neq \emptyset$ **then**
                remove attributes $Attributes$ from class $ClassX$
                $NewClass \leftarrow$ create class with name $Prefix$
                create all attributes $Attributes$ in class $NewClass$
                create a new association between $ClassX$ and $NewClass$
            end if
        end if
    end for
    if $AgreementNumber > 0$ **then**
        $AttributesX \leftarrow$ get all attributes of class $ClassXGlobal$
        $AttributesY \leftarrow$ get all attributes of class $ClassYGlobal$
        $NewClassName \leftarrow$ get name of new class from name of $ClassXGlobal$ and
            $ClassYGlobal$
        $NewClass \leftarrow$ create class with name $NewClassName$
        for all $AttributeX \in AttributesX, AttributeY \in AttributesY$ **do**
            if $AttributeX$ and $AttributeY$ represent the same attribute **then**
                remove attribute $AttributeX$ from class $ClassXGlobal$
                remove attribute $AttributeY$ from class $ClassYGlobal$
                create a new attribute represent the same attribute in class $NewClass$
            end if
        end for
        create a new association between $ClassXGlobal$ and $NewClass$
        create a new association between $ClassYGlobal$ and $NewClass$
        $AgreementNumber \leftarrow 0$
        $ClassXGlobal \leftarrow nil$
        $ClassYGlobal \leftarrow nil$
    else
        $TransformationTo2ONFDone \leftarrow true$
    end if
end while

For the identification of attributes representation, it could be also used clustering, pattern recognition, reinforcement learning, neural networks, etc. In sum, any technique based on the machine learning. We can see repeating groups of data from a data entity.

4 Test Case

In this section, we test, investigate and evaluate proposed algorithms on the example. The example is quite well-known. We can find it also in several other publications [1,14].

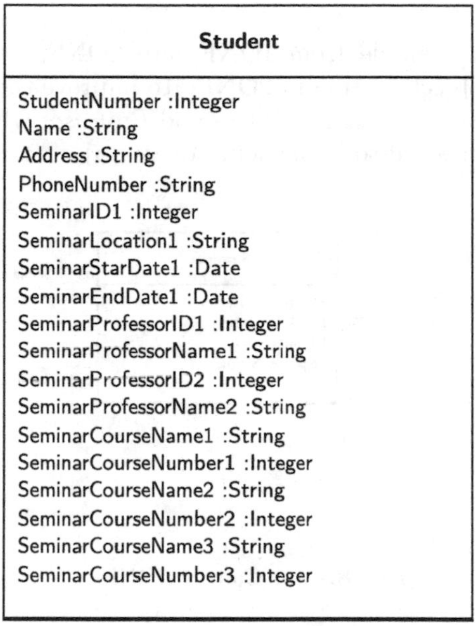

Student
StudentNumber :Integer
Name :String
Address :String
PhoneNumber :String
SeminarID1 :Integer
SeminarLocation1 :String
SeminarStarDate1 :Date
SeminarEndDate1 :Date
SeminarProfessorID1 :Integer
SeminarProfessorName1 :String
SeminarProfessorID2 :Integer
SeminarProfessorName2 :String
SeminarCourseName1 :String
SeminarCourseNumber1 :Integer
SeminarCourseName2 :String
SeminarCourseNumber2 :Integer
SeminarCourseName3 :String
SeminarCourseNumber3 :Integer

Fig. 6. Test Case in 0ONF

Consider the class *Student* in Fig. 6. This design is clearly not very cohesive. This single class is implementing functionality that is appropriate to several concepts. To transform this example from 0ONF into 1ONF, we use Algorithm 1.

With 1ONF we remove repeating groups of data from a data entity and create a new class *Seminar*. All these repeating attributes have been moved to this class. In Fig. 7, we can see the resultant design in 1ONF.

Consider *Seminar* in Fig. 7. It implements the behavior of maintaining both information about the course that is being taught in the seminar and about the professor teaching that course. Although this approach would work, it unfortunately does not work very well. When the name of a course changes we would have to change the course name for every seminar of that course.

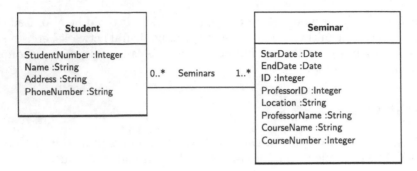

Fig. 7. Test Case in 1ONF

To transform our example from 1ONF into 2ONF, we use Algorithm 2. Figure 8 depicts the object schema in 2ONF. To improve the design of *Seminar* we have introduced two new classes, *Course* and *Professor* which encapsulate the appropriate behavior needed to implement course objects and professor objects.

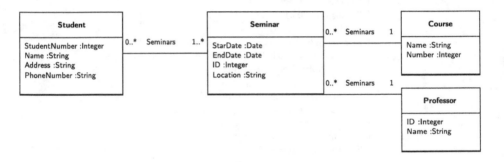

Fig. 8. Test Case in 2ONF

Unfortunately, we do not have any algorithm for transformation from 2ONF into 3ONF, since it is going beyond the scope of this article. The exact reasons have already been mentioned in previous section.

To have the whole transformation process complete, we introduce also the model design in 3ONF, however, the final transformation from 2ONF into 3ONF is done manually.

In Fig. 8, the *Student* class encapsulates the behavior for both students and addresses. The first step would be to refactor *Student* into two classes, *Student* and *Address*. This would make our design more cohesive and more flexible because there is a very good chance that students are not the only things that have addresses. This realization leads to the class diagram presented in Fig. 9.

We are still not done, because the *Seminar* class of Fig. 8 implements "date range" behavior. It has a start date and an end date. Because this sort of behavior

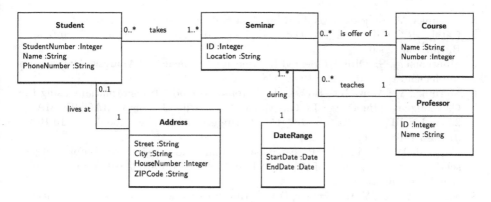

Fig. 9. Test Case in 3ONF

forms a cohesive whole, and because it is more than likely needed in other places, it makes sense to introduce the class *DateRange* of Fig. 9.

5 Conclusion

In this paper we have shown that the principle of normalization can be applied to object-oriented design. This framework thus provides us with a formal mechanism of methodically analyzing an object-oriented design and improving its overall quality by applying these normalizations in a systematic and scientific manner.

Moreover, all normalization processes have been automated using our transformation algorithms. All classes containing well-named, unique attributes are transformable, firstly, from 0ONF into 1ONF, secondly, from 1ONF into 2ONF. The requirement on well-named and unique attributes in classes is the constraint of our research and it is absolutely essential, since we have used them for identification of particular transformation rules.

Our future research can focus on several directions. One direction could be describing the rules of our object-oriented normal forms as a sequence of refactoring steps. The algorithm for transformation from 2ONF into 3ONF is also still waiting for a deeper investigation. Moreover, there is also possibility to make our algorithms less dependent on well-named attributes and their uniqueness in our model.

References

1. Merunka, V., Tůma, J.: Normalization rules of the object-oriented data model. In: Innovations and Advances in Computer, Information, Systems Sciences, and Engineering, pp. 1077–1089. Springer, New York (2013)
2. Goldberg, A., Rubin, K.S.: Succeeding with Objects: Decision Frameworks for Project Management. Addison-Weysley, Boston (1995)

3. Merunka, V.: Objektové modelování. Alfa Nakladatelství, s.r.o. (2008)
4. Catell, R.G.: The Object Data Standard: ODMG 3.0. Morgan Kaufmann, Burlington (2000)
5. Montgomery, S.: Object-Oriented Information Engineering: Analysis, Design, and Implementation. Academic Press, Cambridge (2012)
6. Merunka, V., Nouza, O., Brožek, J.: Automated model transformations using the C.C language. In: Dietz, J.L.G., Albani, A., Barjis, J. (eds.) CIAO!/EOMAS - 2008. LNBIP, vol. 10, pp. 137–151. Springer, Heidelberg (2008). doi:10.1007/978-3-540-68644-6_10
7. Yonghui, W., Aoying, Z.: Research on normalization design for complex object schemes. In: Proceedings of ICII 2001 Info-Tech and Info-Net, vol. 5, pp. 101–106. IEEE, Beijing (2001)
8. Mok, W.Y., Ng, Y.-K., Embley, D.W.: An improved nested normal form for use in object-oriented software systems. In: Proceedings of the 2nd International Computer Science Conference Data and Knowledge Engineering: Theory and Applications, pp. 446–452, Hong Kong (1992)
9. Tari, Z., Stokes, J., Spaccapietra, S.: ACM transactions on database systems. In: Object Normal Forms and Dependency Constraints for Object-Oriented Schemata, vol. 22, pp. 513–569. ACM, New York (1997)
10. Lee, B.S.: ACM SIGMOD record. In: Normalization in OODB Design, vol. 24, pp. 23–27. ACM, New York (1995)
11. Mala, G.S.A., Uma, G.V.: Automatic construction of object oriented design models [UML Diagrams] from natural language requirements specification. In: Yang, Q., Webb, G. (eds.) PRICAI 2006. LNCS (LNAI), vol. 4099, pp. 1155–1159. Springer, Heidelberg (2006). doi:10.1007/978-3-540-36668-3_152
12. Craft.CASE Ltd.: Official web sites of Craft.CASE tool (2016). http://www.craftcase.com/. Accessed 1 Mar 2016
13. e-FRACTAL: Craft.CASE scripting manual, November 2015. http://www.e-fractal.cz/
14. Ambler, S.W.: Introduction to class normalization (2016). http://www.agiledata.org/essays/classNormalization.html. Accessed 1 Mar 2016
15. Lodhi, F., Mehdi, H.: Normalization of object-oriented design. In: 7th International Multi Topic Conference, INMIC 2003, pp. 446–450. IEEE (2003)

Human-Centric Approaches

Exploring Human Resource Management in Crowdsourcing Platforms

Cristina Cabanillas[✉]

Vienna University of Economics and Business, Vienna, Austria
cristina.cabanillas@wu.ac.at

Abstract. The correct execution of process activities is usually responsibility of the employees (i.e., human resources) of an organisation. In the last years, notable support has been developed to make resource management in business processes more efficient and customisable. Recently, a new way of working has emerged and caught significant attention in the market: crowdsourcing. Crowdsourcing consists of outsourcing activities in the form of an open call to an undefined network of people, i.e., the crowd. While in traditional resource management in business processes resources are known and task assignment is usually controlled, the workers in crowdsourcing platforms are unknown and are allowed to select the tasks they want to perform. These and other differences between resource management in business processes and in crowdsourcing platforms have not been explicitly investigated so far. Taking as reference the existing mature work on resource management in business processes, this paper presents the results of a study on the existing support for resource management in crowdsourcing platforms.

Keywords: Business Process Management · Crowdsourcing · Empirical study · Resource management

1 Introduction

Work is materialised in activities that must be completed, usually under temporal constraints. Nowadays, there are several ways to distribute the execution of activities. Business processes or workflows constitute a controlled definition (and execution) of the activities carried out in an organisation and are characterised as follows: (i) the workers are generally employees of the organisation and hence, easily accessible; (ii) the workers are typically offered or allocated the activities they can work on depending on their expertise; and (iii) each activity has one person responsible who can act individually or in collaboration with other workers for the completion of the job, being the outcome of an activity the result of a single execution (a.k.a. activity instance). On the other hand, in the last 10 years a new way of working known as *crowdsourcing* has become

This work is funded by the Austrian Research Promotion Agency (FFG) under grant 845638 (SHAPE).

R. Pergl et al. (Eds.): EOMAS 2016, LNBIP 272, pp. 113–128, 2016.
DOI: 10.1007/978-3-319-49454-8_8

popular. Crowdsourcing consists of a web-based completion of publicly available activities ranging from simple tasks (e.g., picture tagging) to complex activities (e.g., software development). A crowdsourcing platform acts as an intermediary between a client (a company or an individual that needs an activity to be done) and the crowd (any person registered at the platform) in charge of executing the activities [1]. All the crowdsourcing platforms have in common that: (i) the workers are loosely coupled with the client as they do not have a contract with them but are paid for each activity "correctly" completed; (ii) usually, the workers can access any activity published on the platform and work on its execution; and (iii) due to the varied nature of activities and the high risk of cheating and misbehaviour, several instances of an activity are usually concurrently executed by different workers, and one or more results are taken into consideration for the final outcome of the job.

Despite their differences, similar steps must be carried out for work distribution in both the Business Process Management (BPM) and the crowdsourcing domains, such as the allocation of activities to suitable resources. In BPM, human resource[1] management has been widely investigated in the last years [2–4]. However, in the domain of crowdsourcing, the research efforts have been put on how to incentive workers [5] and how to assure quality of the results of the executions [6]. To the best of our knowledge, resource management in crowdsourcing platforms has not yet been investigated in a systematic way, so there might be room for improvement.

To address this gap, we have conducted a survey on the support for resource management in crowdsourcing platforms framed by the resource management concepts from BPM as well as quality assurance features described in the crowdsourcing literature and found in an exploration of crowdsourcing systems. This work contributes to understanding the current support and to discovering potential directions for future work in the crowdsourcing domain.

The paper is structured as follows. Section 2 introduces the vocabulary required to understand the study. Section 3 presents the hypotheses and the survey design. Section 4 analyses the results of the survey and outlines the limitations of the work. Finally, Sect. 5 draws conclusions and points out future work.

2   Background

In the following, we introduce the main concepts related to resource management in BPM and in crowdsourcing.

2.1   Resource Management in Business Processes

In BPM, resource management explores how resources are involved in the activities of the processes executed in an organisation. Three steps can be distinguished in resource management in BPM [7]. Figure 1 illustrates them.

---

[1] From now on *resource* for the sake of brevity.

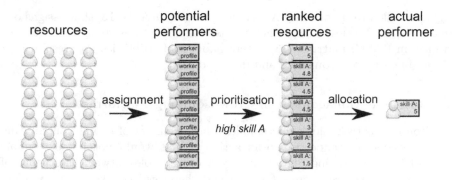

Fig. 1. Resource management in business processes

Resource assignment defines the set of conditions that resources must meet to be allowed to take part in an activity. These conditions are defined at design time and are evaluated at run time when a process instance is executing, resulting in the set of *potential performers* of an activity instance. The languages for resource assignment rely on the concept of organisational model as a description of the part of the organisation involved in a business process. Common terms in organisational models are: person, role, position, organisational unit and the notion of capability or skill [8]. There are textual [4] as well as graphical [9] and hybrid [3,10] resource assignment languages, which differ in their expressiveness to define the selection conditions (e.g., based on organisational roles or on skills). A subset of the workflow resource patterns called creation patterns is typically used as an evaluation framework of the expressiveness [2]. The most expressive languages support all of them [3,4].

Resource allocation is the process of selecting one specific resource from the set of potential performers as the *actual performer* of an activity instance. BPM systems usually perform resource allocation by offering an activity to one single resource or to several resources, or by allocating the activity directly to a specific resource. These and other techniques are collected in the subset of workflow resource patterns called push patterns [2]. Smarter ways of choosing the most appropriate resource for an activity instance to optimise, a.o., time or cost, are increasingly being investigated in the context of BPM [11].

Resource prioritisation is the definition of preferences to sort out the set of potential performers prior to resource allocation [12]. Properties that can be used for defining the preferences are, e.g., personal and organisational data, such as the value of predefined skills, the length of the worklist of resources at a specific point in time, or historic information that points out the ability of a resource for performing certain work. The outcome of the prioritisation is thus a ranking of potential performers that serves as input for the resource allocation technique.

These three steps apply not only to select the resource responsible for the execution of an activity but also for other responsibilities that may be associated with it. Responsibility is generally modelled in process-oriented organisations by using a so-called Responsibility Assignment Matrix (RAM) [13] that assigns one or more responsibilities to a specific organisational role for a process activity. For instance, in RASCI matrices [13] the available responsibilities are: responsible, accountable, support, consulted and informed.

2.2 Resource Management in Crowdsourcing Platforms

Crowdsourcing is technology that enables a large number of people contributing their knowledge and expertise to an activity[2] that would not be so valuable alone [14]. Crowdsourcing platforms play a crucial role between two types of registered users: the requesters (clients) and the crowd (workers). A complete crowdsourcing workflow is made up of four steps:

1. A requester submits an activity description to the platform defining, a.o., the due completion date and the associated remuneration. Ideally, on the platform the requester can specify if the task is available to the whole crowd or only to workers with specific characteristics as well as preferences for the performer of the activity.
2. All workers who are able to see the activity description can generally claim for its execution, except for activities restricted to a limited number of workers.
3. The workers that requested the activity may be ranked by the platform according to the criteria previously specified by the requester, and shown to the requester.
4. The requester can decide which worker(s) should perform the activity.
5. The selected worker(s) will then start their work and submit the results to the platform.
6. When the activity deadline is reached or all the requested activity instances are completed, the platform collects all the results from the workers and sends them to the requester, who proceeds to pay the workers for their job.

As can be observed, the resource management steps described for traditional BPM are also represented in the crowdsourcing domain, specifically: resource assignment maps to step 1, resource prioritisation maps to step 3 and resource allocation maps to step 4.

Unlike in traditional BPM, one of the biggest problems in crowdsourcing environments nowadays is the challenging mission of quality assurance. Wikis were the first crowdsourced applications run by non-profit organisations [14,15] with the rise of the Web 2.0. Afterwards, with the emergence of commercial crowdsourcing platforms, like Amazon Mechanical Turk (AMT)[3], remuneration was a driving factor for people to join a crowdsourcing platform. Money-driven engagement implies that some workers try and cheat the system to maximize their earnings without delivering any useful contribution. Hence, every contribution of every worker may be incorrect and has to be checked against fraud

---

[2] The term *task* is more common in the crowdsourcing domain but we will use *activity* for the sake of consistency.
[3] https://www.mturk.com/mturk/welcome.

and validity [15,16]. Quality assurance can take place at several stages of the aforementioned workflow, e.g., by means of tests after a new worker is registered to the platform or before the results of an activity are sent to the requester for the subsequent invoicing, and it constitutes a critical matter to be considered in the management of resources in the crowdsourcing domain [6].

Two main classes of crowdsourcing platforms can be distinguished. *Marketplaces* are crowdsourcing platforms in a narrow sense, i.e., a platform where individuals and companies can post their activities and get them done by crowdworkers [17]. Steps 1 to 6 are performed as described above. Advanced mechanisms for quality assurance are not expected. Examples of marketplaces are oDesk, AMT and Microworkers. *Brokers* act as intermediaries and helpers between the requesters and the crowd, so that the requesters do not need to frame the task and post it to a marketplace. In addition, the broker typically offers complementary services such as quality control [17]. Examples of brokers are CrowdFlowers, CrowdControl and Microtask.

3   Research Design

Our aim is to explore resource management in marketplace and broker crowdsourcing platforms in terms of the support for resource assignment, resource prioritisation, resource allocation and quality assurance, as these are the characteristics that stand out regarding work distribution and completion.

We use an online questionnaire as research method because: (i) it supports geographical independence, i.e., any crowdsourcing company is accessible regardless of its location; (ii) it keeps confidentiality while providing insights, i.e., we can get precise information not publicly available while respecting privacy; and (iii) it keeps the balance between effort, results and drawbacks (low response rate and different perceptions [18]).

A typical workflow of a questionnaire is composed of six steps [19]. The first one is the selection of the sample (cf. Sect. 3.1). Afterwards, the research model with hypotheses must be defined (cf. Sect. 3.2). To make the research model measurable, an operationalidation step is crucial, whose resulting items must be arranged in a questionnaire (cf. Sect. 3.3). With the feedback collected from a pretest round, the questionnaire can be optimised and the data collection can be started (cf. Sect. 3.4). Afterwards, the analysis of the data and the evaluation uses the research model and tries to falsify the hypotheses (cf. Sect. 4).

3.1   Selection of the Sample

Our research on marketplaces and brokers resulted in a list of 55 companies, whose identities are kept confidential in this paper. For each of them, a contact person was identified through the websites of the companies, under the requirement of having a technical understanding and knowledge about their product. After the evaluation of the population the sample size was determined. We used the formula of Krejcie and Morgan [20] (cf. Eq. 1) with the parameters shown in

Table 1. Equation parameters for estimating the sample size

Parameter	Value	Description
N	55.00	Discovered platforms
X	1.96	Confidence level of 95 %
P	0.5	Population proportion: 0.5 to get maximum sample size
d	0.05	Accuracy of 5 % (margin of error)

Table 1. This results in a number of 48 platforms that should respond in order to reach the given confidence and accuracy.

$$s = \frac{X^2 N P(1 - P)}{d^2(N - 1) + X^2 P(1 - P)} \tag{1}$$

3.2 Hypotheses

From now on we will differentiate between (i) *criteria*, which describe the conditions that can be defined for resource assignment and prioritisation, such as based on roles or skills (cf. Sect. 2.1); and (ii) *features*, which comprise the functionality that is provided, i.e., support for assignment, prioritisation, allocation and quality assurance functionalities. We want to discover the features implemented in the platforms and, for those platforms supporting assignment and prioritisation, the criteria used in them.

Our hypotheses are outlined in Table 2 and the derived research model is depicted in Fig. 2. The model is composed of seven constructs (boxes) connected through arrows that illustrate how the constructs are influenced by the hypotheses: (+) indicates a positive influence and (i) indicates a negative influence. The construct Task Type (TT) has been introduced for statistical purposes and thus has no influence on any other construct of a hypothesis.

Table 2. Hypotheses

ID	Description
H1	A broker platform will support more features than a marketplace platform
H2	A marketplace platform will support more criteria for resource assignment and prioritisation than a broker platform
H3	The supported criteria/features are rated as helpful
H4	The higher the helpfulness of a supported criteria/feature, the higher the frequent usage
H5	The unsupported criteria/features are rated as potentially unhelpful
H6	The higher the necessity of supporting a criteria/feature in the future, the higher the perceived helpfulness

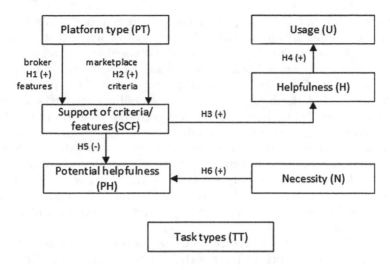

Fig. 2. Research model

In Sect. 2.2 we distinguished two types of crowdsourcing platforms: marketplaces and brokers. Brokers, by definition, provide additional features for requesters such as quality assurance. This leads to hypothesis H1. On the other hand, marketplaces are more specialised and hence, might have greater support of criteria for assignment and prioritisation. This leads to hypothesis H2. If a platform supports a criterion or feature it might be assumed that the criterion or feature is perceived as helpful for requesters. This leads to hypothesis H3. Furthermore, if a criterion or feature is perceived as helpful there should be evidence of it in the form of a more frequent usage than other less helpful criteria or features. This leads to hypothesis H4. On the contrary, if a platform does not support a criterion or feature it might be assumed that the criterion or feature is perceived as potentially unhelpful for requesters. This leads to hypothesis H5. Finally, another construct which might influence the potential helpfulness of criteria and features is the necessity of supporting it in the future due to a high business competition. This leads to hypothesis H6.

3.3 Questionnaire

In order to measure the seven factors involved in the research model (cf. Fig. 2) we introduce measurement items in the form of questions in the questionnaire:

- Platform type (PT) is measured by a nominal scale with three items, only one of which can be selected by the user: (1) a definition of marketplace platform, (2) a definition of broker platform and (3) a free text field for platforms which would not classify themselves this way.
- Support of criteria/features (SCF) is measured by a multiple item choice table which contains various criteria or features. Due to space limitations, we refer to [21] for a complete description of the features and criteria used.

– Helpfulness (H) and usage (U) are measured by a 5-point Likert scale as it is a rating scale which measures the strength of agreement on a set of clearly defined statements [22]. The items are phrased so that a participant is requested to express his or her level of agreement from Strongly Disagree (1) to Strongly Agree (5). These questions are only asked if the participant has stated that their platform supports the corresponding criterion or feature. These two factors (H+U) are grouped by the corresponding criterion or feature and asked in a single multiple choice table.

– Potential helpfulness (PH) and necessity (N) are also measured by a 5-point Likert scale ranging from Strongly Disagree (1) to Strongly Agree (5). In this case, the questions are only shown to participants who indicated that the feature or criterion is not supported by the platform. These two factors (PH+N) are grouped by the corresponding criterion or feature and asked in a single multiple choice table.

– Task types (TT) is a multiple choice scale where a participant can to make one or several choices on which task types their platform supports. The available task types, such as development, picture tagging, translation services and logo design, have been collected from the platform websites and generalised to reduce the number of types [21].

Table 3. Structure of the questionnaire

Section name	Questioned factors	Goals
1. Introduction	–	Introduction to the survey, purpose and usage of collected data
2. Worker selection and ranking	SCF, H, U, PH, N	Criteria supported for resource assignment and prioritisation
3. Support for the requester	SCF, H, U, PH, N	Features that help the requester decide upon resource allocation
4. Quality assurance	SCF, H, U, PH, N	Features to ensure quality of results
5. Advanced task assignment	SCF, H, U, PH, N	Support for functionality like, e.g., team composition
6. About the platform	PT, TT	Type of platform and tasks
7. About you	–	Basic corporate information

To improve the clarity of the questionnaire the items were structured and aggregated into topical groups, as depicted in Table 3. Several tools were evaluated for the generation of the questionnaire and Qualtrics[4] was selected to serve as online survey platform for this study, as it is open-source and it supports conditional table rows for multiple choice questions.

3.4   Data Collection

According to Beywl and Schepp-Winter, a pretest should be done by four to six participants [23]. We sent the questionnaire to four colleagues familiar with

---

[4] http://qualtrics.com.

the topic, obtaining a positive final statement from all them accompanied with suggestions for minor language improvements, such as word order and typos. All the improvements were considered and integrated into the final version of the questionnaire, available in [21].

The questionnaire was sent to 55 companies that we had identified as marketplaces or brokers. We contacted associates of the management hierarchies (Chief/Head of Product, Product Manager, Chief Technology/Technical Officer (CTO), Chief Operating Officer (COO) or Chief Executive Officer (CEO)) but stated in the invitation e-mail that it could be forwarded to a capable person. On average, every 4 days for a 2-month period a reminder was sent to the companies that had not responded to the questionnaire so far. In the end, we received 14 valid questionnaires. This means a response rate of 25 %, which is a quite good number for internet surveys w.r.t. the average rates of 20 % to 30 % [18]. Nevertheless, we did not achieve the required 48 responses to draw statistically reliable and accurate conclusions, for which we would have required a response rate higher than 89 %. Due to the low response rate we achieved an accuracy of approximately 22 % instead of desired 5 %. However, the data analysis and evaluation already showed interesting results, which are summarised next.

4   Analysis

In the following we describe the result of the survey as well as the limitations and potential improvements discovered.

4.1   Result of the Survey

The evaluation of the results has been done with Microsoft Excel 2013 and with R [24]. The values are rounded to two decimals for better readability, except in cases where all values are too small to display anything (e.g., p-values). We use the significance level $\alpha = 0.05$ for all statistical tests, which indicates a 5 % risk of concluding that a difference exists when there is no actual difference. Due to space limitations, the analysis of the data is summarised and grouped by hypothesis. For a detailed description of the evaluation, we refer to [21].

The first evaluation performed relates to hypothesis H1. Table 4 illustrates the number of platforms that support each feature (grouped according to the structure of the questionnaire: Sects. 3–5 - cf. Table 3) in both absolute and relative numbers. To evaluate whether H1 can be validated or not, we have to compare the means of supported features for both marketplaces and brokers. Broker platforms have on average 1.17 more features than marketplace platforms. We performed a statistical T-test to determine if the deviation is significant. The resulting p-value of 0.2496 indicates that the difference is not significant ($\alpha \leq p$). Hence, we propose to reject hypothesis H1 and thus, we conclude that no significant difference in feature support exists between marketplaces and brokers.

The evaluation of hypothesis H2 brought up the findings outlined in Table 5. On average, 8.25 platforms support criteria for resource assignment and only

Table 4. Evaluation of the features supported by the platforms

Feature	Marketplace		Broker		Total	
	abs	%	abs	%	abs.	%
Filter workers	5	62.50	4	66.67	9	64.29
Manual offer to workers	4	50.00	5	83.33	9	64.29
Team composition	4	50.00	4	66.67	8	57.14
Preferences	3	37.50	4	66.67	7	50.00
Redundant execution	7	87.50	4	66.67	11	78.57
Skill tests	6	75.00	5	83.33	11	78.57
Feedback on performance	5	62.50	5	83.33	10	71.43
Training tasks	3	37.50	3	50.00	6	42.86
Delegation	1	12.50	1	16.67	2	14.29
Accountable worker(s)	4	50.00	3	50.00	7	50.00
Supportive worker(s)	5	62.50	3	50.00	8	57.14
Consulted worker(s)	2	25.00	3	50.00	5	35.71
Informed worker(s)	3	37.50	2	33.33	5	35.71
Mean	6.50		7.67		7.54	
p-value	0.2496		-		-	

Table 5. Evaluation of the criteria supported by the platforms

Criterion	Marketplace				Broker			
	Assignment		Prioritisation		Assignment		Prioritisation	
	abs	%	abs	%	abs	%	abs	%
Skills	6	75.00	5	62.50	5	83.33	2	33.33
Geographical position	6	75.00	3	37.50	4	66.67	2	33.33
Familiarity with tasks	7	87.50	5	62.50	4	66.67	3	50.00
Familiarity with requester	5	62.50	3	37.50	2	33.33	2	33.33
Expected salary	3	37.50	3	37.50	3	50.00	2	33.33
Success rate	5	62.50	5	62.50	3	50.00	2	33.33
Quality ranking	4	50.00	3	37.50	3	50.00	2	33.33
Completion pace	5	62.50	5	62.50	1	16.67	1	16.67
Mean	5.13		4.00		4.17		2.67	
p-value	0.2801		0.2410		-		-	

6 platforms support criteria for resource prioritisation. In summary, the criterion *familiarity with tasks* is the most supported one for marketplaces concerning assignment and for brokers concerning prioritisation. On the other hand, the criterion *skills* is the most supported one for broker platforms for resource

assignment. For marketplaces covering resource prioritisation, there are 4 top supported criteria: *skills*, *familiarity with tasks*, *success rate* and *completion pace*. The statistical analysis shows that marketplaces support more criteria in the two categories (assignment = +1.13, prioritisation = +1.50) but none of the probability values indicates a significant difference as no value was below 0.24. Since the difference between marketplaces and brokers for resource assignment is very small, a statistical T-test was performed on the data to calculate the significance of the differences. No category got a significant result. Therefore, we suggest that H2 is invalid, and thus, there is no significant difference between marketplaces and brokers regarding the criteria supported.

Hypothesis H3 states that the supported criteria are rated as helpful which means that the values have to be greater than 3. This hypothesis has been evaluated two times: for the supported criteria (Sect. 2 of the questionnaire) and for the supported features (Sects. 3–5 of the questionnaire). Table 6 shows the mean values and the p-values of the factor H of all criteria for assignment and prioritisation. As no value is below 3, the respondents have not declined the helpfulness of the criteria. To validate this part of the hypothesis statistically a one-sided T-test was performed and the p-values were evaluated. 10 out of 16 possible criteria show a significant higher value than 3. Hence, we suggest that H3 is valid. As for the supported features, the situation is similar (cf. Table 7). No participant rated a supported feature as unhelpful. The only outlier is the feature *delegation*, which was rated as neutral. 8 of 13 features had also a significant positive rating. Hence, we can confirm hypothesis H3 as valid for features. Therefore, as both parts could validate H3 we suggest that H3 is valid.

Hypothesis H4 states that the higher the helpfulness of a supported criteria/feature, the higher the frequent usage. This hypothesis has also been evaluated twice. Table 6 shows an overview of the evaluation for the supported criteria, specifically, the Pearson correlation coefficient between the two factors H and U; and the p-value, which indicates whether the correlation is significant or not.

Table 6. Evaluation of factor H and of the correlations of factors H and U for supported criteria (* = significant value for $\alpha = 0.05$)

Criterion	Assignment				Prioritisation			
	H		$H \rightarrow U$		H		$H \rightarrow U$	
	mean	p-value	cor	p-value	mean	p-value	cor	p-value
Skills	4.27	0.0002*	0.7717	0.0054*	4.00	0.0309*	0.9186	0.0035*
Geographical position	3.40	0.1717	0.8458	0.0020*	4.00	0.0171	−0.3953	0.5101
Familiarity with tasks	4.18	0.0002*	0.6119	0.0454*	4.00	0.0249*	0.9589	0.0002*
Familiarity with requester	3.71	0.1100	0.9626	0.0005*	3.40	0.2935	1.0000	0.0000*
Expected salary	3.67	0.0510	1.0000	0.0000*	3.60	0.0352	0.6124	0.2722
Success rate	4.00	0.0006*	1.0000	0.0000*	3.86	0.0226*	0.9262	0.0027*
Quality ranking	4.29	0.0021*	1.0000	0.0000*	4.60	0.0014*	1.0000	0.0000*
Completion pace	3.33	0.1816	0.9342	0.0064*	3.17	0.3054	0.8677	0.0251*

Table 7. Evaluation of factor H and of the correlations of factors H and U for supported features (* = significant value for $\alpha = 0.05$)

Feature	H		$H \rightarrow U$	
	mean	p-value	cor	p-value
Filter workers	3.78	0.664	0.9761	0.0000*
Manual offer to workers	3.78	0.0040*	0.8740	0.0021*
Team composition	3.63	0.1084	0.5130	0.1936
Preferences	3.57	0.0515	1.000	0.000*
Redundant execution	4.09	0.0030*	0.8503	0.0009*
Skill tests	3.64	0.0130*	0.8752	0.0004*
Feedback on performance	4.40	0.0003*	1.0000	0.0000*
Training tasks	4.50	0.0035*	0.8093	0.0511
Delegation	3.00	NA	NA	NA
Accountable worker(s)	4.14	0.0023*	0.7670	0.0442*
Supportive worker(s)	3.88	0.0105*	0.9078	0.0018*
Consulted worker(s)	3.80	0.0497*	0.8018	0.1027
Informed worker(s)	3.80	0.0889	1.0000	0.0000*

In short, all criteria for resource assignment has significant influence on the usage and only 2 criteria for resource prioritisation has no significant influence. The 2 non-validated criteria for ranking are *geographical position* and *expected salary*, whereas *geographical position* has a negative insignificant influence on the usage. Therefore, we suggest to confirm hypothesis H4 as valid for the criteria. Regarding the features, as shown in Table 7, 11 of 13 features have a strong positive influence on the usage and for 9 of them the influence is significant. Only 2 features (*team composition* and *delegation*) have no positive influence on the usage. Hence, we suggest that hypothesis H4 is also valid for features. Therefore, we could confirm the validity of hypothesis H4 for both criteria and features.

Hypothesis H5 states that the unsupported criteria/features are rated as potentially unhelpful, and has also been evaluated two times. As we are asking about factor potentially helpful (PH) we have to look for values below 3. The means and the p-values per criterion are listed in Table 8, where the means are showing a neutral picture: all values are more or less equal to 3, so are the overall mean and median. Only one criterion has a rating significantly different from neutral (*quality rating*) but this criterion is considered as potentially helpful and not unhelpful. Therefore, we can reject hypothesis H5 for criteria support. Regarding the supported features, the mean ratings of all features have been calculated and a statistical one-sided T-test has been performed. As shown in Table 9, only 4 of 13 features got significant p-values, where only the feature *manual offer to workers* is supporting the hypothesis, due the fact that the other three significant features have a positive rating. As most platforms rated most unsupported features as potentially helpful rather than unhelpful, we suggest to reject the hypothesis H5 for features. Therefore, we could not confirm hypothesis H5 in any category, so we reject it.

Finally, hypothesis H6 states that the higher the necessity of supporting a criteria/feature in future, the higher the perceived helpfulness, and this hypothesis has also been evaluated two times. In the evaluation we check the correlation between the factors PH and N. Regarding the supported criteria, as shown in Table 8, half of the criteria have a significant correlation between necessity and potential helpfulness (*geographical position, familiarity with requester, success rate* and *completion pace*) and 2 more criteria have a strong influence but are not significant (*skills* and *quality rating*). The Pearson correlation coefficient for familiarity with tasks cannot be calculated due to a standard deviation of 0 (all respondents answered *neutral*) for the factor N. Therefore, hypothesis H6 cannot be generally validated or invalidated, it holds true for 4 criteria. As for the features supported, Table 9 shows that the evaluation has 4 significant values and hence, the hypothesis is valid for the following 4 features: *team composition, preferences, redundant execution* and *feedback on performance*. The feature *manual offers to workers*, which has been rated significantly negatively before, has a Pearson correlation coefficient of 0, which means that there is no relationship between the two factors. As only 4 of 13 features have a significant correlation we suggest that the hypothesis H6 is invalid. Therefore, since no category could verify that hypothesis H6 is fully valid, we reject the hypothesis.

Altogether, the results of our evaluations conclude that only hypothesis H3 and H4 are valid for the sample data. However, the invalidation of hypothesis H5 brings some light towards future extensions of the platforms to support the missing features and criteria. Moreover, the rejection of hypothesis H6 may be caused by the low response rate.

Table 8. Evaluation of factor PH and of the correlations of factors PH and N for supported criteria (* = significant value for $\alpha = 0.05$)

Criterion	PH		PH → N	
	mean	p-value	cor	p-value
Skills	3.67	0.0918	0.7559	0.4544
Geographical position	3.00	0.5000	0.9733	0.0267*
Familiarity with tasks	3.33	0.2113	NA	NA
Familiarity with requester	2.71	0.2285	0.9226	0.0031
Expected salary	2.71	0.2285	0.2475	0.5926
Success rate	3.20	0.3744	0.9609	0.0092*
Quality ranking	3.71	0.0041*	0.5916	0.1618
Completion pace	2.88	0.3813	0.8440	0.0084*

Table 9. Evaluation of factor PH and of the correlations of factors PH and N for supported features (* = significant value for $\alpha = 0.05$)

Feature	PH		$PH \rightarrow N$	
	mean	p-value	cor	p-value
Filter workers	4.00	0.0171*	0.8607	0.0611
Manual offer to workers	2.00	0.0171*	0.0000	1.0000
Team composition	3.00	0.5000	0.9576	0.0027*
Preferences	3.14	0.3679	0.9354	0.0020*
Redundant execution	3.33	0.2113	1.0000	0.0000*
Skill tests	3.67	0.0918	NA	NA
Feedback on performance	3.50	0.0908	1.0000	0.0000*
Training tasks	3.50	0.0518	0.3536	0.3903
Delegation	3.42	0.1049	0.0837	0.7958
Accountable worker(s)	3.57	0.0150*	-0.1667	0.7210
Supportive worker(s)	3.17	0.1816	0.5813	0.2262
Consulted worker(s)	3.44	0.0176*	0.6532	0.0565
Informed worker(s)	3.44	0.0845	0.4488	0.2256

4.2 Limitations

This survey presents some limitations. For instance, one respondent had a problem with the question "Which statement describes your platform best?" and selected the option *marketplace*. However, from the description subsequently provided in the text field we could derive that the platform is actually a broker. Consequently, we assumed that the respondent selected *broker*. Therefore, this question should be a point for improvement as it should be easily understood by everyone. Furthermore, the low response rate suggests that the survey approach may not have been the best choice. Several companies did not respond at all, other companies gave harsh declinations. However, this fact may be due to a refusal of the companies to share information deemed confidential because of the increasing competition in this sector. In addition, the research performed was limited to one categorisation of crowdsourcing platforms (conceptual model) including only two types of platforms (marketplaces and brokers). However, there exist other types of platforms and many other distinction models, such as crowdsourcing objectives [25] or the four archetypes [26].

5   Conclusions and Future Work

This paper provides an overview of existing support for resource management in crowdsourcing platforms. The evaluation concludes that current crowdsourcing platforms focus their efforts on supporting features and criteria for resource assignment and prioritisation that have proved to be frequently used and hence, are deemed helpful; while it suggests that some unsupported features and criteria could be considered relevant in the future.

From the limitations of the survey we can conclude that, as a first attempt to extend this study, the questionnaire must be revised aiming at increasing the response rate. The rejected hypotheses can serve as a starting point for further investigations. In case of no success, a different research method should be explored. In addition, further potential extensions include taking into account a broader classification of the platforms.

Acknowledgements. We would like to thank David Kren and Prof. Jan Mendling for their cooperation in the realisation of this work.

References

1. Schall, D., Satzger, B., Psaier, H.: Crowdsourcing tasks to social networks in BPEL4People. WWW **17**(1), 1–32 (2014)
2. Russell, N., Aalst, W.M.P., Hofstede, A.H.M., Edmond, D.: Workflow resource patterns: identification, representation and tool support. In: Pastor, O., Falcão e Cunha, J. (eds.) CAiSE 2005. LNCS, vol. 3520, pp. 216–232. Springer, Heidelberg (2005). doi:10.1007/11431855_16
3. Stroppi, L.J.R., Chiotti, O., Villarreal, P.D. : A BPMN 2.0 extension to define the resource perspective of business process models. In: CIbS2011 (2011)
4. Cabanillas, C., Resinas, M., del Río-Ortega, A., Ruiz-Cortés, A.: Specification and automated design-time analysis of the business process human resource perspective. Inf. Syst. **52**, 55–82 (2015)
5. Singla, A., Krause, A.: Truthful incentives in crowdsourcing tasks using regret minimization mechanisms. In: WWW, pp. 1167–1178 (2013)
6. Allahbakhsh, M., Benatallah, B., Ignjatovic, A., Motahari-Nezhad, H.R., Bertino, E., Dustdar, S.: Quality control in crowdsourcing systems: issues and directions. IEEE Internet Comput. **17**(2), 76–81 (2013)
7. Cabanillas, C.: Enhancing the management of resource-aware business processes. AI Commun. **29**(1), 237–238 (2015)
8. Nicolae, O., Wagner, G.: Modeling and simulating organisations. In: Barjis, J., Eldabi, T., Gupta, A. (eds.) EOMAS 2011. LNBIP, vol. 88, pp. 45–62. Springer, Heidelberg (2011). doi:10.1007/978-3-642-24175-8_4
9. Cabanillas, C., Knuplesch, D., Resinas, M., Reichert, M., Mendling, J., Ruiz-Cortés, A.: RALph: a graphical notation for resource assignments in business processes. In: Zdravkovic, J., Kirikova, M., Johannesson, P. (eds.) CAiSE 2015. LNCS, vol. 9097, pp. 53–68. Springer, Heidelberg (2015). doi:10.1007/978-3-319-19069-3_4
10. van der Aalst, W.M.P., ter Hofstede, A.H.M.: YAWL: yet another workflow language. Inf. Syst. **30**(4), 245–275 (2005)
11. Havur, G., Cabanillas, C., Mendling, J., Polleres, A.: Automated resource allocation in business processes with answer set programming. In: Reichert, M., Reijers, H.A. (eds.) BPM 2015. LNBIP, vol. 256, pp. 191–203. Springer, Heidelberg (2016). doi:10.1007/978-3-319-42887-1_16

12. Cabanillas, C., García, J.M., Resinas, M., Ruiz, D., Mendling, J., Ruiz-Cortés, A.: Priority-based human resource allocation in business processes. In: Basu, S., Pautasso, C., Zhang, L., Fu, X. (eds.) ICSOC 2013. LNCS, vol. 8274, pp. 374–388. Springer, Heidelberg (2013). doi:10.1007/978-3-642-45005-1_26
13. Website, "Understanding Responsibility Assignment Matrix (RACI Matrix)." http://project-management.com/understanding-responsibility-assignment-matrix-raci-matrix/. Accessed Mar 2016
14. Greengard, S.: Following the crowd. Commun. ACM **54**(2), 20–22 (2011)
15. Hirth, M., Hossfeld, T., Tran-Gia, P.: Analyzing costs and accuracy of validation mechanisms for crowdsourcing platforms. Math. Comput. Model. **57**, 2918–2932 (2013)
16. Satzger, B., Psaier, H., Schall, D., Dustdar, S.: Auction-based crowdsourcing supporting skill management. Inf. Syst. **38**(4), 547–560 (2013)
17. Schall, D.: Crowdsourcing task marketplaces. In: Service-Oriented Crowdsourcing. SpringerBriefs in Computer Science, pp. 7–30. Springer, New York (2012). Chap. 2
18. Siau, K., Rossi, M.: Evaluation techniques for systems analysis and design modelling methods - a review and comparative analysis. Inf. Syst. **21**(3), 249–268 (2011)
19. Mayer, H.O.: Interview und schriftliche Befragung: Entwicklung, Durchführung und Auswertung. Mnchen: Oldenbourg Verlag, 4th edn. (2008)
20. Krejcie, R.V., Morgan, D.W.: Determining sample size for research activities. Educ. Psychol. Measur. **30**, 607–610 (1970)
21. Kren, D.: A quantitative study of the support for resource management in crowdsourcing platforms, Master's thesis, Vienna University of Economics and Business (2014)
22. Gena, C.: Methods and techniques for the evaluation of user-adaptive systems. Knowl. Eng. Rev. **20**, 1–37 (2005)
23. Beywl, W., Schepp-Winter, E.: Zielgeführte Evaluation von Programmen: ein Leitfaden. Bundesministerium fr Familie, Senioren, Frauen und Jugend (2000)
24. R Development Core Team, R: A Language and Environment for Statistical Computing. R Foundation for Statistical Computing, Vienna, Austria (2008)
25. Vukovic, M.: Crowdsourcing for enterprises. In: SERVICES, pp. 686–692 (2009)
26. Geiger, D., Rosemann, M., Fielt, E., Schader, M.: Crowdsourcing information systems - definition, typology, and design. In: ICIS (2012)

Assessment of Brand Competences in a Family Business: A Methodological Proposal

Eduard Babkin and Pavel Malyzhenkov$^{(\boxtimes)}$

Department of Information Systems and Technologies,
National Research University – Higher School of Economics,
Bol. Pecherskaya 25, 603155 Nizhny Novgorod, Russia
{eababkin, pmalyzhenkov}@hse.ru

Abstract. Competences represent an important part of business administration and enterprise engineering researches as they constitute a solid source of long-term competitive advantage. Still, little practical applications are known in this area, especially in the field of family business, the object of the present work. This paper proposes to use DEMO notation means (in particular, Competence Ontological Map) for the individuation of both transactions which mainly contribute to the formation of the family brand and those which may easily be outsourced with no negative effects on the enterprise performance.

Keywords: Competences · Ontological map · Family business · Brand · DEMO

1 Introduction

The resource-based view of competitive advantage [15, 21, 24] applies analysis to an enterprise or its units and isolates specific resources that are complex, intangible and dynamic. Family business advantages are often described as specific to a given family and business. In the context of the resource-based view, the set of resources that holds potential for performance advantage is identified as incompatible with a particular firm in a particular environment. Additionally, many of the advantages family firms are said to possess are found in their family and organizational processes [9], which makes family competences a broad field for application of the Enterprise Engineering apparatus. Besides, some research examples [13, 16] in the resource-based view literature demonstrate linkages between firm processes and firm performance.

This work explores the research currently conducted in the area of competences and applies the notion of competence to the field of Enterprise Engineering with a focus on practical usage of competence management for a specific kind of business – family enterprises. Until now the concept of competence was widely used in the area of Enterprise Engineering. So, in [7] competence was introduced as one of the main characteristics of an actor, together with responsibility and authority, and was defined as the ability of a subject to perform certain production acts (P-acts), as well as coordination acts (C-acts). By performing production acts the subjects contribute to bringing about the goods and/or services that are delivered to the environment of the enterprise. The realization of a production act is inherently either material or

© Springer International Publishing AG 2016
R. Pergl et al. (Eds.): EOMAS 2016, LNBIP 272, pp. 129–138, 2016.
DOI: 10.1007/978-3-319-49454-8_9

immaterial. By performing coordination acts subjects enter into and comply with commitments towards each other regarding the performance of production acts [7]. It also assumes particular importance in enterprise governance [11]. Despite different contributions related to the practical usage of competence and competence management in enterprise engineering and reengineering [19] this field still deserves further in-depth exploration. The main contribution of the present work is an attempt to apply ontological-based techniques to a specific field of family business.

Literature references contain a variety of family business definitions and descriptions of their success factors [10, 14, 20], just to cite some of them. For the purposes of our research we introduce the following definition: "familiness" of a firm is a unique combination of tangible and intangible characteristics that are distinctive for a firm as a result of family involvement in business processes.

Still, even such closeness to the family business leaves some space for outsourcing operations. Outsourcing brings different advantages linked to efficiency improvement and specialization development; nevertheless it also creates uncertainty for existing employees and contractors who provide services to the client organization. Such uncertainty can cause this staff to look for employment elsewhere and leave either before or during the introduction of outsourcing, causing a need to either make up for the lost resource or reduce the amount of work performed by the organization. In addition, some of the client staff is temporarily engaged for knowledge transfer to the service provider during the implementation. If the staff is not properly motivated or if the service provider does not do a good job with knowledge transfer, this can result in decreased efficiency in service rendering and possibly introduce operational risk.

All these risks can be eliminated by using formal reference models of work with competences and, in particular, DEMO, as a tool which provides possibilities for a formal approach to competences engineering. The paper is organized as follows: Sect. 2 analyzes the family enterprise phenomenon in the modern business context and the particularities of the role of competences therein; Sect. 3 describes methodological proposals formed on the basis of DEMO; Sect. 4 formulates questions for future research; and Sect. 5 concludes the paper.

2 Family Business: Main Characteristics and Competitive Advantage

According to the results of different works [1–3, 6, 9, 17, 18], family firms have a unique working environment that fosters a family-oriented workplace and inspires greater employee care and loyalty. Besides, they have been said to pay higher wages to employees and to assure the ability to bring out the best in their workers. They are characterized by more flexible work practices for their employees, have lower recruitment costs, lower human resource costs, and are said to be more effective than other companies in labor intensive businesses. Family members have also been described as more productive than nonfamily employees because they have a "family language" that allows them to communicate more efficiently and exchange more information with greater privacy. Family relationships generate unusual motivation, cement loyalties, increase trust and, hence, family firms reportedly have lower transaction costs, a more trustworthy reputation, efficient informal decision-making channels, less organizational structure, and lower monitoring and control costs. Finally, decision making tends to be centralized among top family members, which decreases costs and enhances the flexibility of the firm.

So, the resource-based view is the proven discipline of business administration and management which provides the field of family business with a disciplinary approach to family firm performance and advantage. It also creates an opportunity for Enterprise Engineering researchers to further investigate the unique essence of the family structure of business organization as a distinct form of enterprise.

Competitive advantages of family firms cannot be discussed without reference to a firm's specific resources, skills and competencies. These attributes cannot be assumed to be independent in the particular market and competitive context within which a firm's strategies are implemented. A firm can only be said to have a competitive advantage when implementing a value-creating strategy not simultaneously being implemented by current or potential competitors. This strategy becomes a sustainable competitive advantage when other firms are unable to duplicate the benefits of the strategy [4]. The family business field of studies is multidisciplinary, but most of the literature on the subject has come from fields of organizational science not normally associated with explaining and predicting firm performance. The language is borrowed from traditional industrial economics to describe agency theory (family ownership and management) and transaction cost advantages (higher trust, better communication flow, lower monitoring and control costs, consolidated decision making). But the said advantages for family firms have not been supported by research and analysis accepted by those same fields of study.

Transaction cost economics emerged to provide a "better understanding of the origins and functions of various firms and market structures". In family firms, "the economics of trust, as well as other phenomena can be examined to advantage in transaction cost economizing terms" [22]. The resource-based view moves performance discussions beyond cost reduction to other considerations of organizational advantage, looking for antecedents to these economic outcomes.

These resources also include a broad range of organizational, social, and individual phenomena within firms that are often overlooked by concepts such as "core competence" or "capabilities." The collection of resources is idiosyncratic because there are no two different firms that have the same set of experiences, have acquired the same assets and skills, built the same organizational cultures, or the same collection of resources in the same competitive arena at the same point in time [5].

The same reasoning can be fully applied to competences, too. Being a resource, competencies: (a) must be valuable, in the sense that they exploit opportunities and/or neutralize threats in a firm's environment, (b) must be rare among a firm's current and potential competition, (c) must be imperfectly imitable, and (d) there should not be strategically equivalent substitutes for this resource that are valuable, but neither rare, nor imperfectly imitable [4]. Firm resources can be imperfectly imitable for one or a combination of three reasons: (a) the ability of a firm to obtain a resource is dependent on unique historical conditions, (b) the link between the resources possessed by a firm and a firm's sustained competitive advantage is causally ambiguous, or (c) the resource generating a firm's advantage is socially complex. So, in contrast to the generic approach, specific family firm resources are identified and matched to the firm's capabilities.

At this point we describe family business resources as the "familiness" of a given firm. More specifically, familiness is defined as a unique bundle of resources a particular firm has because of the systemic interaction between the family, its individual members, and the business. Such definition of familiness provides a unified system perspective on family firm performance capabilities and competitive advantage. All research studies using the familiness resource model intrinsically have objective functions that relate to system performance rather than the performance of the individual parts of the system. Therefore, it is proper to conclude that performance research should focus on identifying a firm's familiness and assessing the impact thereof on its strategic capabilities, rather than assessing how family businesses (whatever the definition might be) may or may not have a competitive advantage.

Path-dependent phenomena associated with a firm's unique historical conditions create imperfectly imitable resources, such as the family's value-based organizational culture, a particular geographic location or historical asset, or a firm's reputation.

Causal ambiguity exists when the link between the resources controlled by a firm and a firm's sustained competitive advantage is not completely clear. Family companies may have numerous intuitive-based resources not accounted for in the everyday assessment of their competitive advantage (which may be the reason why family business success seems so unexplainable in the first place).

Grant's model [8] indicates that identifying resources and investing in replenishing, augmenting and upgrading them is a critical part of a firm's long-run enterprise engineering processes. It relates to the component of a firm's familiness that provides them with a familial advantage: allows them to deliver offerings that others can't match and customers prefer as their "distinctive familiness."

What is now required is empirical support for these assertions and further research into the links between performance and the idiosyncratic resources that family firms possess. Only then will the research be actionable and ultimately helpful to practitioners as they strive to assist family companies. The practical outcomes, even before the family determines whether the strategic intervention has had the desired effect, are: (1) it has brought linear focus to a circular emotional debate; (2) it has taught the family to think of their family involvement as a strategic issue; (3) it has trained the family to look for specific performance changes as a result of the intervention; (4) it has designed a business solution with accountability for follow-up; and (5) it has caused the family management team to experience the success of pragmatically discussing a difficult issue.

3   Methodological Proposal for Familiness Assessment

Competence modeling represents a fertile subject for enterprise engineering, and the leading researches in this field [7, 11, 12] have delivered exhaustive definitions opening broad possibilities for application.

We are working on a proposal for the individuation of ontological transactions which could be outsourced. As a methodological base we use the Ontology

Competence Map described in [19] with some modifications affecting the outsourcing decision-making in a family enterprise. In particular, as mentioned in [19], the practical relevance of OCM for an enterprise's current operation is to help understand the lack of competence in order to do reassignment of actor roles to employees, plan employee trainings or hire new employees (and, possibly, fire some existing employees). Yet, where it is impossible to adopt these solutions, another way of OCM application is presented by outsourcing, which in some cases represents a valid strategy for maintaining competitiveness by the means of competences management.

Thus, the following modifications to the described scheme are proposed:

1. At Step 2 "Based on the Actor Transaction Diagram, create Ontological Competence Map of the current state of the enterprise" [19] it is necessary to involve business experts or customers themselves in order to identify what transactions determine the formation of the family brand. Actually, in the scheme adopted in this contribution the family which sells pizza may succeed in both baking and delivering pizza, as well as in organizing the entire cycle of the post-production phase. In this case it gets its brand competencies. So, the keys to its competitive advantage may be the composition of ingredients and the staff's excellence in serving customers;
2. At Step 8 "Based on the OCM finalize number of people to be hired and competence requirements for them. Produce final OCM for the planned restructuring" [19] it is necessary to finalize the set and contents of competences required by them and proceed with searching for a suitable contractor.
3. Step 9 "Hire new employees based on the requirements produced on Step 8 and assign them to the actor roles as per the final OCM" [19] requires termination of transactions based on outsourcing and establishment of contractual terms.
4. At Step 10 "Produce OCM of the state of the enterprise after restructuring ends to validate that no competence gaps exist" [19] it is essential to produce OCM of the state of the enterprise after restructuring completion to validate that no competence gaps exist. If competence gaps exist, proceed with employee hiring or searching for another outsourcing partner.

The proposed framework is relevant for enterprise restructuring, because it ensures that no gaps in competence will exist in the new structure, helps to plan budgets for employee hiring and training, and enables to optimally implement the ontological model of the enterprise in terms of enterprise familiness (as defined above).

Yet, the transactions, analyzed as a whole, leave very little space for analysis of a family brand as an idiosyncratic phenomenon which distinguishes one enterprise from another. For the purpose of our analysis we suppose that familiness, using the DEMO language, is expressed in the coordination acts which constitute the basic transaction pattern (Fig. 1, [7]), namely "request", "promise", "state" or "accept".

So, the familiness which is reflected in customer satisfaction is created by the coordination acts of any transaction. For better understanding of which act contributes largely to the level of satisfaction we can also make use of their opinions collected by the means of questionnaires or surveys which can be offered to customers in the pizzeria and which they can fill in while waiting for their order. From the modelling point of view, such process will not influence the ontological model being an

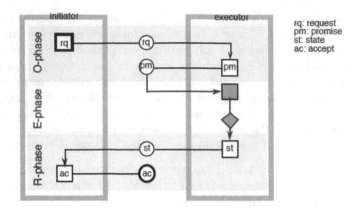

Fig. 1. Basic pattern of the transaction adopted from [7]

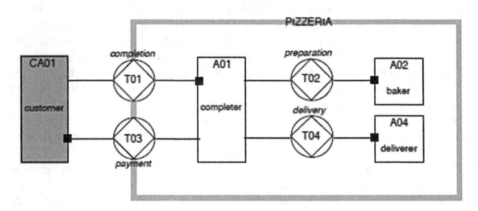

Fig. 2. Detailed ATD of the pizzeria (third phase) adopted from [7]

infological operation, and the opinions of the customers will be further translated into numerical characteristics of every coordination act.

Let us assume that a pizzeria at phase 3 [7] is a family enterprise and the brand Mama Mia is known and appreciated by customers for both baking and delivery (customer serving) processes.

The family advantage is created on the border transactions during the immediate contact with the customer. Actually, such a situation is typical for a modern business characterized by the prevalent presence of immaterial factor. But what exactly distinguishes a family business from all others is that it is propagated onto the subsequent transactions inside the enterprise between all the members of the family, creating the familiness phenomenon that is later manifested in the improved quality of service or product and becomes a competitive advantage of the family brand.

Such "internal propagation" and especially the possibility to express it in quantitative terms may constitute the formal foundation for accepting or rejecting the decision about outsourcing of a certain process/transaction. This propagation will be realized according to a certain formal mechanism. The result may be expressed in quantitative or qualitative terms and, being compared to a preliminarily fixed level of acceptance it may form a decision about the internal maintaining or external transfer of a business function.

An example of implementation of such approach is provided below. Let us suppose that the customers can evaluate the level of their satisfaction according to the following qualitative parameters: "awful", "bad", "satisfactory", "good", and "perfect". Each parameter is converted into the following numerical values: "awful" – 0, "bad" – 0.25, "satisfactory" – 0.5, "good" – 0.75, "perfect" – 1. So, in case of the first transaction T01 "Completion" it can be presented as follows (Fig. 3). It should be mentioned, that in case of border transaction only the C-acts "promise" and "state" can be evaluated, because the acts "request" and "accept" are performed purely by the customer.

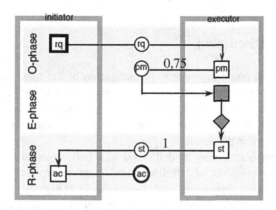

Fig. 3. T01 "Completion" with customer evaluation of C-acts

The same occurs at the phase of T03 realization (we suppose that the completer performs completion and payment in the same manner). After that we sum up these two coefficients obtaining 1.75 and add the coefficient obtained from the customer evaluations of the pizza quality. Let's assume that the customers expressed their satisfaction with pizza as 0.5. The sum of these two values amounts to 2.25. Let us call it the overall value of customer satisfaction related to the baking process.

Still, the situation may change in case of the delivery process. The executor may delay the delivery, be impolite, and so on. So, the total evaluation of the delivery process makes 0.25, giving the overall evaluation of customer satisfaction with the delivery process as 2.

This provides us with the basis for outsourcing acceptance or rejection. In case these values exceed a certain average level of service implementation it is convenient to maintain these functions inside, otherwise they are worth externalizing.

The final evaluation version is presented in Fig. 4.

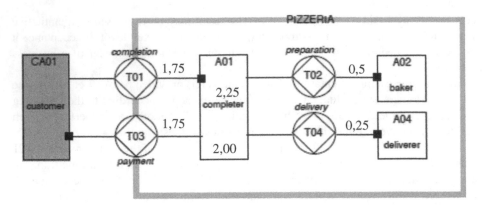

Fig. 4. Final distribution of evaluations

4 Results and Discussion

So, the future research could involve the formalization of the rules according to which the impact of the coordination acts on the border transaction diffuses inside the enterprise and influences other transactions. Based on such impact and, hence, on its contribution to the final brand value we can come to a conclusion whether it is necessary to outsource some processes.

The future research may also be dedicated to a better formalization of the mechanism of internal propagation of familiness inside an enterprise. It could use more sophisticated quantitative techniques and utilize the Ontological Competence Map in order to evaluate the quality of implementation of certain transactions.

One of the article's challenges is to deliver a more precise definition capable of describing the enterprise models.

5 Conclusions

In this paper we have introduced the approach to family enterprise modelling by the means of the DEMO methodology which can be later used in further research. The notion of familiness and the ways of its realization in the field of enterprise engineering has been studied. The proposed approach has been built upon DEMO's Actor Transaction Diagram and the basic pattern of a transaction with a particular emphasis on coordination acts at both ontological and implementation level.

A number of questions have been raised for further research in this field. These questions include the formalization of the process of familiness propagation onto all transactions inside an enterprise and the use of more formal apparatuses like neural networks or Markov nets for the determination of its quantitative impact. In addition, the definitions and the theoretical basis for better modelling of family enterprises could be extended further.

References

1. Aronoff, C.E., Ward, J.L.: Family-owned businesses: a thing of the past or a model of the future? Fam. Bus. Rev. **8**(2), 121–130 (1995)
2. Aronoff, C.E., Astrachan, J.H., Ward, J.L.: Family Business Sourcebook II. Business Owner Resources, Marietta (1996)
3. Astrachan, J.H., Kolenko, T.A.: A neglected factor explaining family business success: human resource practices. Fam. Bus. Rev. **7**(3), 251–262 (1994)
4. Barney, J.B.: Firm resources and sustained competitive advantage. J. Manag. **17**(1), 99–120 (1991)
5. Collis, D.J., Montgomery, C.A.: Competing on resources: strategy in the 1990s. Harvard Bus. Rev. **73**(4), 118–128 (1995)
6. Daily, C.M., Dollinger, M.J.: An empirical examination of ownership structure in family and professionally managed firms. Fam. Bus. Rev. **5**(2), 117–136 (1992)
7. Dietz, J.L.G.: Enterprise Ontology: Theory and Methodology. Springer, Heidelberg (2006)
8. Grant, R.M.: The resource-based theory of competitive advantage: implications for strategy formulation. Calif. Manag. Rev. **33**(3), 114–135 (1991)
9. Habbershon, T.G., Williams, M.L.: A Resource-Based Framework for Assessing the Strategic Advantages of Family Firms, Family Business Review, vol. XII, no. 1, March (1999)
10. Handler, W.C.: Methodological issues and considerations in studying family business. Fam. Bus. Rev. **5**(3), 257–276 (1992)
11. Henriques, M., Tribolet, J., Hoogervorst, J.: Enterprise governance and DEMO – guiding enterprise design and operation by addressing DEMO's competence, authority and responsibility notions. In: Barbosa, L.S., Correia, M.P. (eds) INForum 2010 - II Simposio de Informatica, pp. 473–476, 9–10 Setembro (2010)
12. Hoogervorst, J.A.P.: Enterprise Governance and Enterprise Engineering. The Enterprise Engineering Series, 1st edn. Springer, Heidelberg (2009)
13. Ketchen Jr., D., Thomas, J.B., McDaniel Jr., R.: Process, content, and context: synergistic effects on organizational performance. J. Manag. **22**(2), 231–257 (1996)
14. Litz, R.A.: The family business: toward definitional clarity. Fam. Bus. Rev. **8**(2), 71–81 (1995)
15. Mahoney, J.T., Pandian, J.R.: The resource-based view within the conversation of strategic management. Strateg. Manag. J. **13**(5), 363–380 (1992)
16. McGrath, R.G., MacMillan, I.C., Venkataraman, S.: Defining and developing a competence: a strategic process paradigm. Strateg. Manag. J. **16**(4), 251–275 (1995)
17. Poza, E.J., Alfred, T., Maheshwari, A.: Stakeholder perceptions of culture and management practices in family and family firms - a preliminary report. Fam. Bus. Rev. **10**(2), 135–155 (1997)
18. Tagiuri, R., Davis, J.A.: Bivalent attributes of the family firm. Fam. Bus. Rev. **9**(2), 199–208 (1996)
19. Sergeev, A., Babkin, E.: Towards competence-based enterprise restructuring using ontologies. In: Aveiro, D., Pergl, R., Valenta, M. (eds.) EEWC 2015. LNBIP, vol. 211, pp. 34–46. Springer, Heidelberg (2015). doi:10.1007/978-3-319-19297-0_3
20. Sharma, P., Chrisman, J.J., Chua, J.H.: Strategic management of the family business: past research and future challenges. Fam. Bus. Rev. **10**(1), 1–33 (1997)
21. Wernerfelt, B.: A resource-based view of the firm. Strateg. Manag. J. **5**(2), 171–180 (1984)
22. Williamson, O.E.: Markets and Hierarchies: Analysis and Antitrust Implications. Free Press, New York (1975)

23. Winter, M., Fitzgerald, M.A., Heck, R.K.Z., Haynes, G.W., Danes, Sh.M.: Revisiting the study of family businesses: methodological challenges, dilemmas, and alternative approaches, family business review, vol. XI, no. 3, September (1998)
24. Wortman Jr., M.S.: Theoretical foundations for family-owned business: a conceptual and research-based paradigm. Fam. Bus. Rev. 7(1), 3–27 (1994)

Ontology-Based Translation of the Fusion Free Word Order Languages - Neoslavonic Example

Martin Molhanec[1(✉)], Vojtěch Merunka[2,3], and Emil Heršak[4,5]

[1] Faculty of Electrical Engineering,
Czech Technical University in Prague, Prague, Czech Republic
molhanec@fel.cvut.cz
[2] Faculty of Economics and Management,
Czech University of Life Sciences in Prague, Prague, Czech Republic
vmerunka@gmail.com
[3] Faculty of Nuclear Sciences and Physical Engineering,
Czech Technical University in Prague, Prague, Czech Republic
[4] Zagreb School of Economics and Management, Zagreb, Croatia
ehersak@gmail.com
[5] Faculty of Philosophy, University of Zagreb, Zagreb, Croatia

Abstract. This paper describes the idea of the ontology-based translation of the fusion free word order languages on the practical example of an artificial Neoslavonic zonal constructed language. This article proposes a new approach of the syntactical analysis of free-word-order languages and most accurate machine translation between fusion free-word-order languages.

Keywords: Neoslavonic, zonal constructed language · Analysis of free-word-order languages · Translation between free-word-order languages

1 Introduction

In the history of civilization, many local, i.e., vernacular languages were used in daily life, but there were often attempts to combine these languages or else to standardize them for international communication purposes. Yet there were also tendencies to expand particular languages. In antiquity the Greek Koinē (Κοινή) from the Hellenistic period was used in numerous regions. Later Latin followed this model in certain parts of the Roman Empire and afterwards became a general language in the mediaeval western Christianity. Today English has attained world dominance. However, it seems that in all three of these mentioned cases ideological factors, connected with national-political dominance, were used.

The aim of this work is to propose the use of so called zonal constructed language designed for communication between Slavic peoples. Zonal constructed languages are artificial languages made to facilitate communication between speakers of a certain group of closely related natural languages. Another aim of this work is to define an approach of the conceptual ontology based model of language used for the mutual translation between languages.

© Springer International Publishing AG 2016
R. Pergl et al. (Eds.): EOMAS 2016, LNBIP 272, pp. 139–153, 2016.
DOI: 10.1007/978-3-319-49454-8_10

Current use of ICT for global communication creates an increased need for communication between users of different national languages. Information theory also forms a proper basis for language modelling and the creation of well-designed zonal constructed languages, as well. Instruments of ICT are a driving force for connecting people.

Since all Slavic languages derive from a common Proto-Slavic linguistic form, knowledge of one Slavic language will often allow one to have at least a rough understanding of a text written in another Slavic language - yet not sufficiently enough to achieve a strong comprehension (Derksen 2008). This fact has inspired linguists and others over the centuries to attempt to create a universal zonal Slavic language that would be more understandable to all Slavs (Steenbergen 2011). Old Church Slavonic can be considered the first such attempt. It was initiated in the 9th century by two Byzantine missionaries, Constantine the Philosopher (Cyril) and his brother Methodius, Greeks born in Thessalonica (Tachiaos 2001). Later there would be other international projects, until this present day. What they have in common is that they are all based on the assumption that the Slavic languages are similar enough to make them such an auxiliary zonal language possible at all. All their authors were motivated by the belief that Slavic languages are like dialects of only one Slavic language, rather than separate languages (Steenbergen 2011). There were also some similar projects from the Germanic area (Volapük, for example, later Euronord Folkspraak, etc.) and for the Romanic language zone (Interlingua, for example). Some scientists also argue that the Sanskrit language had been designed on the zonal principles.

Zonal constructed languages are based on a concept that is different from that which has led to the creation of prevalently artificial languages, such as Esperanto. Native speakers from the linguistic areas (i.e., zones) in question often are quite able to passively understand zonal constructed languages, even to a very high level, without the need of prior learning. This means that zonal constructed languages seem to resemble the existing spoken languages. Thus, people very often feel that the zonal artificial language is an unknown dialect of particular real language.

2 How Do Zonal Constructed Languages Differ from Universal Language Structures?

Of course, it would be ideal if a universal language would have a general logical structure – a clear, understandable, but morphologically rich set of rules with minimum exceptions and idioms. In our opinion, Esperanto – even though it has been so far the most successful constructed universal language, has failed, because it includes an awkward system of unnatural pronouns and adverbs, mutually differing in only one vowel or consonant without any analogy to some natural language. Of course, regardless of this problem, the goal of Esperanto was to eliminate the aggressive imposition on other peoples of imperial national languages, and to produce a neutral means of communication, not linked to such dominance.

Some people today will say that English just became popular due to its effect on people. However, author Robert Phillipson (Phillipson 1992), who worked for many years in the British Council, explained in various details that English linguistic imperialism was a policy adopted for political, economic and other goals by Great

Britain and the USA. Strangely enough, some people today think that English is simple and hence a lingua Franca, but as the American founder of linguistic anthropology, Edward Sapir, wrote – English is a "hornet's nest" of problems. Although it does not have many cases (except for the "Saxon genetic"), it is highly complex in its phraseology and vocabulary, let alone in its problems with spelling. On top of this, an extremely high level of homophone tendencies produces problems, both in learning English and, especially, in using it in computer translations.

Yet going back to the topic of universal languages, one key question would be to ask how any widespread universal language can be produced, with only one form, such as Esperanto. Can we tie together all the linguistic details of Indo-European, Sino-Tibetan, Austronesian, Bantu languages, etc. There are, of course, many linguistic researchers today who will claim that there are joint structures for all the languages of the world. And, of course, the name "cat" has quite a general distribution: "gatto" in Italian ("gato" in Spanish), "kot" (=кот) in Russian, "kta" (طق) in Arabic, "kedi" in Turkish, and other alternatives, as in Chinese, "mao" (close to meow) and something similar even in Ancient Egyptian.

3   Neoslavonic Language

Neoslavonic has been created as an auxiliary language that appears to be almost the same as a real spoken language. As such, it is ideal for being used for the following purposes:

1. To share grammar codes and a common vocabulary with modern spoken Slavic languages, in order to build a general language structure which Slavic speakers could understand without any – or with very minimal – prior learning.
2. To be an easily-learned language for those who want to use it actively. People who at first did not speak any Slavic language could use this language as the door to the "big Slavic world". We believe that knowledge of Neoslavonic enables both Slavic and non-Slavic people a greater passive (e.g., receptive) understanding and a better learning of the living Slavic languages.
3. To be a basic conversation platform for Slavic speakers and at first non-Slavic speakers, who would not have to learn a specific real Slavic language.
4. Neoslavonic continues the tradition of Old Church Slavonic. It is designed as a modernized and simplified – but still sufficiently compatible – version of Old Church Slavonic.

Neoslavonic is an artificially constructed language and is much more regular than contemporary spoken Slavic languages, it has not been reduced to an unnatural level as was Esperanto or even Slovio (a Slavic clone of Esperanto). Neoslavonic contains only natural grammatical forms which must be the same or very similar to those in contemporary Slavic languages. As in the case of natural Slavic languages, since Neoslavonic does not reduce its grammar and phonetics to an Esperanto-like style, Slavic speakers using Neoslavonic can make, without problems, the same errors in conjugation patterns (different vowels or accent, for example) as people of various Slavic nations make today, often, when they speak with each other in non-native Slavic languages (for example, when a Czech speaks Russian, or a Pole speaks Croatian, etc.).

In this perspective, we cannot ignore a comment on the Russian language. Russian is the largest spoken Slavic language. The amount of its users (as a first and second language) exceeds the total number of speakers of any other Slavic language. Russian also has an important international status. If the Russian language was sufficiently simple and sufficiently understandable to other Slavs without learning, our project might be unnecessary. However, this is not so. From the linguistic perspective, Russian is specific and distanced from the imaginary linguistic balanced centre of Slavic languages.

Yet the key problem, real or imagined, as in the case of all other languages, and mainly today for English, is that Russian is a national and state language. Of course, this is good for the language itself, but national-state languages, although they may be imagined as neutral on a purely linguistic level, in the real world may bring about political and other problems. Today this is the case with English, because news and other key information, due to English dominance (imperial dominance, as Phillipson wrote) derives for the most part from the US and Great Britain, and regardless of claims of objectivity, it is also directed to the national goals and ethnics of the US and Great Britain, which do not have to be the same as in other countries.

In short, Russian is a nation-state language (as is English) and regardless of the real value of Russian (due to its excellent literature, scientific literature, etc.), such languages are always problematic. And of course, we should add that for Russian speakers as well, Neoslavonic would increase very simply their contacts with other Slavic speakers, and one could imagine also a more realistic and positive impression of Russian culture and ties, on the part of other Slavic populations.

4 Sources of Neoslavonic

There are three main sources of Neoslavonic:

4.1 The Old Church Slavonic Corpus

This is a grammar and a vocabulary of about 6,000 words from the OCS corpus, dating from the period between the 8th and 12th century (Vondrák and Bartoň 2005). The main construction principle from this source is the regularization and the transformation of the original language.

4.2 Interslavic Lexicon and the Interslavic Project

The Interslavic Lexicon is a project managed by Steeven Razdikowski in San Diego, USA. This lexicon of modern words (which are not included in the medieval corpus of the OCS) has about 27,000 words (Interslavic Project 2016).

Modern Slavic conlang projects have joined today into one collaborative community called Interslavic. Interslavic is a common denominator for this collaborative community, which uses the Voting Machine, the statistical algorithm used for finding balanced Interslavic words from the modern Slavic languages. Each of these languages has its own importance and a comprehensibility of the other languages expressed by a different mathematical coefficient (Steenbergen 2016a, 2016b).

4.3   False Friends

This is only one correcting tool for resolving problems in situations where the same word has different meanings in different modern Slavic languages. It is a table-based document of shared word forms which have different meanings between languages, and these similar or identical words with different meanings are known as "false friends". If the voting machine finds a word that is in the "false friends table", this word must be eliminated and the voting machine should be restarted using some synonym. The author of this free document is Daniel Bunčić who made this document under GNU Free Documentation License (GNU and Wikimedia 2016).

We may add, especially for non-Slavic readers, that the Slavic languages are not the only group with "false friend" words. Just compare, in any dictionary, the meanings of the English word *Gift* and the German word *Gift*.

5   Language Example

This Neoslavonic text (here it is shortened at about 1/3 of the original text) has been made for our Interslavic project in the hotel OASIS on the Dead Sea coast for hotel guests coming from the Slavic countries. This real and successful project was organized with the kind assistance of our Israeli colleagues, Ms Viktorija Ajziković from the hotel management and Mr Andrej Teterevov from Ben Gurion University in Be'er Sheva, Israel.

English Text

> *Dear Guests! Check in time after 15:00. Check out time of 11:00.*
> *Breakfast: 07:00–10:30 Dinner: 18:00–20:30.*
> *The lobby bar is open daily from 11:00 until 22:30. Lobby bar offers light snack*
>   *meals all day with live entertainment in the evening. Free entrance in the*
>   *external swimming pool hours are 08:00–18:00.*
> *In addition, our hotel has a private beach. The beach hours are 07:30–18:00. Hotel*
>   *transport to the beach goes each 15 min from the central entrance.*
> *Sincerely, the hotel management.*

Neoslavonic Text - Latin Alphabet

> Dragi gosti! Do hotela se možete priglasiti ot 15:00.
> Iz hotela jest trěba se otglasiti do 11:00.
> Jutrenica: 07:00–10:30 Večerja: 18:00–20:30.
> Lobby-Bar jest otvoreny vsekaky den ot 11:00 do 22:30. Lobby-Bar Vam vsej den
>   predlagaje male jadenja.
> Večerom Vas priglašajemo na veseljenje s živoju muzikoju.
> Bezplatny vstup na otkryty hotelovy bazen jest ot 8:00 do 18:00.
> Hotel takože imaje svoju privatnu plažu. Hotelova plaž jest otvorena ot 7:30 do
>   18:00.

Na plaž ide hotelovy transport vsekakih 15 minut ot centralnogo vhoda.

S uvaženjem, personal hotela.

Neoslavonic Text - Cyrillic Alphabet

Драги гости! До хотела се можете пригласити от 15:00. Из хотела іест трѣба се отгласити до 11:00.

Ютреница: 07:00–10:30 Вечеріа: 18:00–20:30.

Лобы-Бар іест отворены всекакы ден от 11:00 до 22:30.

Лобы-Бар Вам всей ден предлагаіе мале іаденьа.

Вечером Вас приглашаіемо на весельеньс с живою музикою.

Безплатны вступ на открыты хотеловы базен іест от 8:00 до 18:00.

Хотел такоже имаіе свою приватну плажу.

Хотелова плаж іест отворена от 7:30 до 18:00. На плаж иде хотеловы транспорт всекаких 15 минут от централного входа.

С уваженьем, персонал хотела.

A few years ago, prof. Emil Heršak from the University of Zagreb in Croatia (Department of Anthropology, Faculty of Humanities and Social Sciences), together with his students started to analyse the linguistic aspects of Neoslavonic and the advantage that this language would have in Croatia (also in the tourist industry, and as a "parser" through the Internet). Also, in direct co-operation with the Zagreb School of Economics and Management (a university-level private college), a first course of Neoslavonic started in February 2016.

6   Issue of the Machine Processing

In the Neoslavonic language (as well as in all Slavic languages), the word order in a sentence is rather flexible. In English, the position of words in sentences is necessary to inform whether it is a noun, adjective, verb, subject, object or something else. Neoslavonic words have their own endings (declension and conjugation), in which the complete information about their grammatical category is stored, so there is no need for any word to respect a specific position in the sentence. This system of endings is specific to the family of fusional (or inflecting) languages.

Fusional (or also "flective") languages do not need to use the position of words for expressing grammatical categories. Apart from most Slavic languages, other examples of fusional Indo-European languages include Sanskrit (and many of the modern Indo-Aryan languages), Greek (both classical and modern), Latin, Lithuanian, Latvian and Albanian. Italian, German and especially Icelandic are also often placed in this Indo-European list. Another notable group of fusional languages is the Semitic language group (Hebrew, Arabic, Aramaic, etc.). Some degree of fusion is likewise found in many other languages throughout the world.

We can say that Neoslavonic does not need to use the fixed position of words in sentences in order to express information about whether a word is subject, object, verb or something else. It is obvious that fusional languages operate with words containing unambiguous grammatical information without the need to use fixed positions. Free word order can then be used to express the finer details of communication in these languages.

Of course, this does not mean that Neoslavonic words can be mixed in any haphazard way. For example, if adjectives belong to a specific noun, they must be positioned either in front of or behind that corresponding noun, and other elements of the sentence cannot intervene between them. Metaphorically, a Neoslavonic sentence is like a branched tree, whose branches represent particular sentence components. Mutual branches may have a flexible order, but elements within each branch must not be mixed with elements of another branch. From the theoretical perspective, the Neoslavonic sentence is a multidimensional oriented graph rather than a linear sequence of words. (See examples in Figs. 1 and 2.)

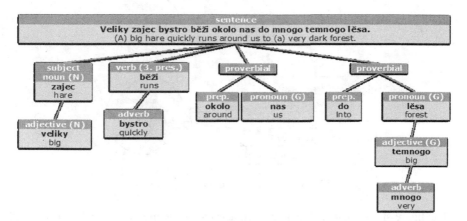

Fig. 1. The sentence linearized by the S-V-O order.

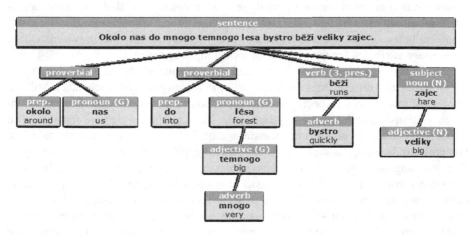

Fig. 2. The same sentence linearized by a different word order.

7 Ontology Based Language Model

Our approach to language modelling is based on the use of the ontological model of the world. The usual linguistic approach is based on Chomsky's conception of language as a tree structure. This is a concept that very well suits the English language and to it similar languages. However, this model is totally unsuitable for inflectional languages like Slavic languages, Latin, and Greek, among others. Our basic principle is the assertion that language is linearly oriented description of the real world. The real world in all its complexity can be described only by ontological model. Our idea is briefly shown in Fig. 3.

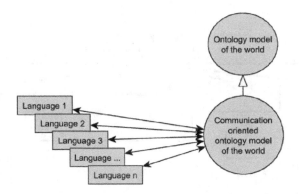

Fig. 3. A general model of language.

The figure shows that each language (linear model) is in two-way relationship with a communication-oriented ontology of the real world. Ontological model is in its essence a general directed graph. The communication-oriented ontology of the real world is a subtype of the general ontology of the real world. The difference between communication-oriented ontology and general ontology is that communication-oriented ontology is enriched with attributes related to communication, therefore, relevant attributes of the speech or written act. Further, it may be impoverished of unnecessary attributes for the purpose of modelling language.

What our model plays a role in the mutual translation of the two languages? The Fig. 4 shows the relationships between multiple languages with each other and our ontological model, with respect to translation. A source language is the language from which we translate and a target language is the language into which we translate. The classic approach is to perform the transformation Tst, or reverse transformation Tts. The problem, however, is that there is no generally 100 % of the semantic overlap of these two languages. Another complication may be that if one language is inflectional and not a second language. This approach can often be improved through the intermediate language translation. We then perform forward transformation Tsi + Tit and reverse transformation Tti + Tis. But even this method will not solve our problem.

Our approach is to perform a transformation between the two languages through the ontological model. Thus, we need to provide, a transformation Ts + Tt or a reverse transformation Tt + Ts. The advantage lies in the fact that the ontological model,

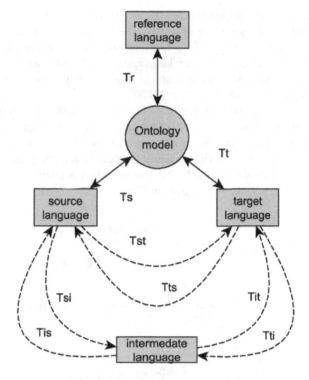

Fig. 4. Translation system model.

100 % semantically covers both languages (source and destination). This follows from its definition (a definition of our ontological model). Furthermore, given that the ontological model is a general graph, we need only perform its linearization and de-linearization. This is easier than transforming one tree to another tree. Because the ontological model is a generic graph that cannot be read as a speech act, we also propose to define a so-called Reference language, between whom and ontological model is an unambiguous transformation Tr. In our case specifically, it is an artificially constructed language (conlang) called Neoslavonic. This language is based on a modern version of the Old Church Slavonic language.

8   Language Model of Translation

We believe that Neoslavonic language is a very useful intermediary tool for the translation between various Slavic languages. Therefore, it is necessary to create a correct model of the language as a parser, i.e., for translation purposes. In our case, this means to create three formal models: a model of the source language, a reference model, and a model of the target language.

The reference model is de facto an ontological model of the real world around us, as seen in general. In the Slavic world, the Neoslavonic language can be used as a common standard of this reference model for translation of all Slavic languages.

Unlike more conventional approaches in linguistics, we do not use the standard language model of a linear sequence of words. The author of the standard model is the very famous contemporary linguist Noah Chomsky (Chomsky 2002), but his scheme is not suitable for Slavic free-word-order languages. That's why we propose to use a different language model based on a conceptual model of linguistic ontology expressed by a directed graph (Davis and Weyuker 1983).

Our new language model expresses the content of a sentence independently of a word order, because it is based on a form of a multidimensional graph. Of course, there does exist a way in which to linearize this graph into a sequence of words. We describe it later in the text. First, we describe a language-independent language model. Meta-model of our model is shown in Fig. 5. Our language-independent language model for a certain class of sentences is then shown in Fig. 6.

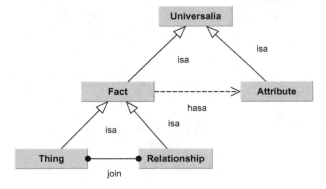

Fig. 5. Metamodel of language-independent language model.

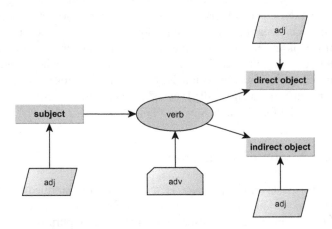

Fig. 6. Language-independent language model for certain class of sentences.

All elements of our model are derived from the root element of our meta-model, i.e., Universalia, which represents whatever. There are two major from it derived classes: (1) class Fact, which represents the facts in the world around us, such as

persons, things, seeing, running, etc., and (2) class Attribute that represents the properties of these facts. Next, there are two subclasses of the class Fact. It is (1) class
Thing, which represents a real or abstract object from the real world as for example:
cars, persons, ideas, and so on, and (2) class Relationship, which represents the relationships between Things. A multiplication between the Thing and Relationship is
many to many. This metamodel is very simple but sufficient for our aim.

A language-independent language model for the class of sentences of type SV2O
(Subject-Verb-Two Objects) is shown in Fig. 6. A Subject and both Objects are of type
Thing and Verb is of type Relationship. An Adj is an Attribute of Thing, thus Subject
or Object. An Adv is an Attribute of Relationship, thus Verb. A model of a particular
sentence is shown in Fig. 7, the sentence is annotated in English, individual elements
of the model are expressed in its basic form, nouns and adjectives are in the nomi-
native, the verb is in the infinitive. This form, however, is not essential in terms of the
model, a model could be annotated in another language as well. The model itself is still
the language-independent. The model expresses a sentence, but only in conceptual
level, not as a sequence of words in any particular language.

The basic norm of language interpretation and translation is very simple. It is based
on graph transformations. In the source model expressed as a graph, we are looking for
a subgraph that corresponds to the transformation rule. If we find such a subgraph in
the source model, we replace it with another subgraph by this rule. Step-by-step, we
apply sequentially all the transformation rules to the source model. The whole process
will end if there is no rule to apply. Finally, we obtain a new graph that represents our
target model. The graph transformations are more general than transformations of linear
sequences to other linear sequences. We can demonstrate our method on an example of
a simple sentence.

A conceptual model of such sentence is shown in Fig. 7. This model corresponds to
linear models[1] of the same sentence, in different languages, see Figs. 8, 9 and 10. To

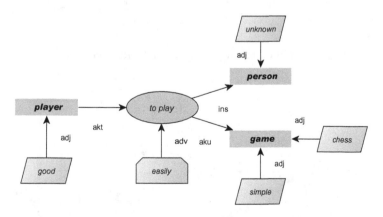

Fig. 7. Language-independent language model of a given sentence.

---

[1] The order of the words after linearization is shown by double body arrows.

create these linear representations (or translations), we use a graph based algorithm, mentioned above. A more detailed description of this algorithm is a subject of the following Author's article.

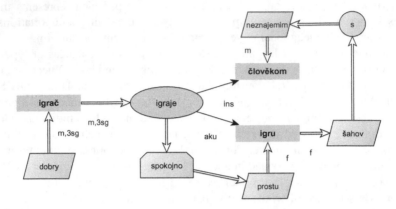

Fig. 8. Model of the given sentence in the Neoslavonic language.

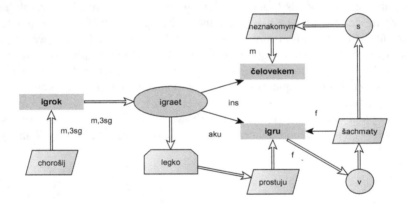

Fig. 9. Model of the given sentence in the Russian language.

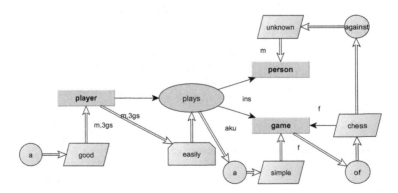

Fig. 10. Model of the given sentence in the English language

9 Survey

Our international survey on the passive intelligibility of the Neoslavonic zonal constructed language was running in all Slavic countries from November 2015 to January 2016. This survey is still available at the website in the Slavic Union. The results were taken in RSForms! for Joomla CMS and processed in Matlab R2015b for MacOS (IZVESTI.info 2011).

The survey consists of 5 pages and takes only a few of minutes to respond. Information about the survey is spread through advertising in social networks Facebook and VKontakte. The target group of the whole Slavic population was aged from 16 to 80 years who identified themselves with knowledge of any Slavic language.

Our statistical hypothesis was whether the Slavic population passively understand the language at a level corresponding to a slightly advanced speaker, which means concretely to be able to understand written text and to recognize at least 5 of 7 missing words. It was inspired by the MICReLa research group, based at the University of Groningen, University of Erlangen, Syddansk University in Odense, University of Copenhagen, University of Ljubljana, and Constantine the Philosopher University in Nitra who developed a similar online game to investigate the matter of passive intelligibility of various national languages of the Member States of the European Union compared to the desirability of English.

We received 1,650 valid responses in total. Answering men outnumbered answering women in the ratio of about 5:1, but the gender differences were only minimal, because their results differ far below the value of only statistical error. Our respondents from different Slavic nations answered in different willingness and frequency (for example, there were more respondents from the small Slovenian nation than from the Russian nation), this is why we did recalculate (by weighted averages) our results according to the size of the population in particular Slavic nations, in order to get correct representation of the whole Slavic population. We also obtained 51 responses from people who have no native Slavic language, but they understand some Slavic language from their surroundings (e.g., learning in school or from friends ...).

Our hypothesis was confirmed with a sufficient degree of probability 0.81. The mean values of all respondents are in the interval from 79 % to 93 %. (These results are in rescaled values, where 100 % equals to 7 correct words from 7 words in total, 86 % equals to 6 correct words from 7 words in total, 71 % equals to 5 correct words from 7 words in total, 57 % equals to 4 correct words from 7 words in total, and so on.) Only 19 % respondents (313 of 1,650) answered worse result than expected hypothesis of 5 correct words from a total of 7 unknown words. Also, our hypothesis met the people who answered no Slavic language as their mother tongue but only a learned language.

The total mean value was 84 %, which almost equals to 6 correct words from 7 words in total. Partial results from this survey are also very interesting:

1. There is no dependency on age. The results differences are under to the statistical error which is about 4 %.
2. There is a group of Slavic nations having the best results: Ruthenians, Czechs, Slovaks, Poles and Belarusians (from 87 % to 93 %), and the group of all South-Slavic nations having the worst results: (from 79 % to 81 %).

3. In contrast to the previous result, the group of all South Slavic nations expressed better aesthetic evaluation (value around 60 %) of Neoslavonic than the other Slavic nations (value around 55 %).
4. All Slavic nations expressed little bit worst values of self-assessment than the real intelligibility. (For example, the total mean value of real intelligibility is 84 %, but the total mean value of self-assessment is only 70 % in comparable rescaled values.)
5. There is a dependency on education. Slavic people having completed university education have 88 % of mean intelligibility, but Slavic people without any university experience have only mean 73 % of the mean (secondary education only) and 72 % of the mean (primary education only).
6. Self-assessment showed that members of smaller nations better understand the similar languages of their neighbours than members of the bigger nations. The biggest contrast shows the situation among Belarusians, Ukrainians, and Russians. Ukrainians understand Russian at the level of 80 % and Belarusians understand Russian at the level of 71 %, but Russians understand Ukrainian at the level of only 46 % and Belarusian at the level of only 39 %. A similar difference is also visible between smaller Slovenian and bigger Croatian nations. Of course, this result is influenced by the fact that older people learned Russian as their obligatory language in the former USSR and satelites, which creates an impression that Russian is automatically understood by all Slavs. This phenomenon will be more elaborated in the future.

In conclusion, we can say that a passive understanding of Neoslavonic without any prior learning meets the conditions that roughly correspond to the local language-skill requirements for immigrants to obtain citizenship in most European countries.

Also, we dare say that if there were Neoslavonic inscriptions on products and public transport (e.g., bus and railway stations, airports...). Then it would be better for many people than current inscriptions in English.

10 Conclusion

The Slavic people of different nations often still feel their mutual cohesiveness and affinity. This is often well manifested when during miscellaneous occasions they tend to speak together not in English, but in some randomly assembled common inter-Slavic language, which is sufficient in many situations. The Neoslavonic language is therefore a professional response to this phenomenon. Neoslavonic would also be an easier and more accurate tool of machine translation between languages.

In general, our idea presented here is the interpretation of a human-language sentence in a form of a multi-dimensional graph rather than a linear sequence of words. This covers also a large group of visual languages such as icons, traffic signs, and sign languages.

Of course, each spoken language is a linear sequence, but it is not the basic formal structure, but only a necessary way of sound-based information transmission. The reference model of many languages can be multi-dimensional. We believe that this approach can be used not only for machine processing of natural free-word-order languages, but also, for example, of another multi-dimensional language, such as sign languages for deaf people, information about road signs, or information stored in various cockpit panels.

Acknowledgment. The authors would like to acknowledge the use of the yED Graph Transformation Tool (yED 2016) and Matlab 2015b, the support of the research grant SGS14/209/OHK4/3T/14, and the support of Slovanská unie z. s. (Slavic Union 2016), which is a voluntary, independent, and non-political association operating as a legal entity #48133396 the Czech and E.U. law. After all, we would like to thank for the thorough and dedicated work of all our colleagues in the project Interslavic, especially the coordinator Mr Jan van Steenbergen.

References

Chomsky, N.: Syntactic Structures. Walter de Gruyter (2002)

Davis, M., Weyuker, E.J.: Computability, Complexity and Languages (Fundamentals of Theoretical Computer Science), 425 pp. Academic Press Inc., New York (1983). ISBN: 0-12-206380-5

Derksen, R.: Etymological Dictionary of the Slavic Inherited Lexicon, Boston (2008)

GNU Free Documentation License sponsored by the Free Software Foundation (2016). http://www.gnu.org

Interslavic Project: The Interslavic-English lexicon, Verb Conjugator, Noun Declinator, Transliterator, and Dynamic Dictionary (2016). http://dict.interslavic.com

IZVESTI.info: On-line interslavic news (2011). http://izvesti.info

Merunka, V.: Neoslavonic Zonal Constructed Language, 2nd edn., Nová Forma 2014 (2014). ISBN: 978-80-7453-291-7 (available in Google Books)

MICReLa Research Group: Mutual intelligibility of closely related languages, the language game. http://www.let.rug.nl/gooskens/project/

Phillipson, R.: Linguistic Imperialism. Oxford University Press, Oxford (1992). ISBN 0-19-437146-8

Slavic Union: Slovanská unie z. s (2016). http://slovane.org

van Steenbergen, J.: The voting machine (2016a). http://steen.free.fr/interslavic/voting_machine.html

van Steenbergen, J.: Dynamic dictionary (2016b). http://steen.free.fr/interslavic/dynamic_dictionary.html

van Steenbergen, J.: Towards a Unified Slavic Language: Past, Present and Future of the Interslavic Language(s). In: The Fourth Language Creation Conference. The Language Creation Society (2011)

Tachiaos, A.E.: Cyril and Methodius of Thessalonica: The Acculturation of the Slavs. St. Vladimir's Seminary, New York (2001)

Vondrák, V., Bartoň, J.: Vocabulary of the classical Old Church Slavonic. Koniash Latin Press, Prague (2005). ISBN 80-85917-60-2

yEd: Graph Editor (2016). http://www.yworks.com/en/products/yfiles/yed

Wikimedia: False friends of the Slavist (2016). http://en.wikibooks.org/wiki/False_Friends_of_the_Slavist

Designing Business Continuity Processes Using DEMO
An Insurance Company Case Study

José Brás[1]([✉]) and Sérgio Guerreiro[1,2]

[1] Lusófona University, Campo Grande 376, 1749-024 Lisbon, Portugal
a21400334@alunos.ulusofona.pt, sergio.guerreiro@ulusofona.pt
[2] Formetis, Hemelrijk 12c, 5281 PS Boxtel, Netherlands
sergio.guerreiro@formetis.nl

Abstract. Business Continuity Plan (BCP) ensures the continuity of business processes in catastrophe or disaster situations, building organizational resilience and mitigating risks. Theoretically, BCP covers all the roles throughout the company, and identifies a blueprint of all key functions and processes with the objective of maintaining or restoring critical operations. However, due to poor documentation and misinterpretation of the complex business processes between the stakeholders, pinpointing and documenting all the key functions and processes is still a challenging task. This paper studies and presents a new approach to complement the management of the BCP, which is being held by a case study in an insurance company, and contributes with outcome learnings from the practice. The aim is to complement and leverage enterprise's domain knowledge about key business processes and functional needs. Design & Engineering Methodology for Organization is used to represent the business processes, and therefore, aid managers in implementing and maintaining BCP.

Keywords: Business continuity · Business transactions · DEMO · Business impact analysis

1 Introduction

The concept of business continuity (BC) is quite recently introduced in the industry. It began in the sixties as IT *"disaster recovery"*, embedded with the need to protect the high investments done in computer systems, and exists today as a result of both the evolution and the conjunction of a set of distinct roles [15].

Events like September 11 2001 and hurricane Katrina in 2005 showed the vulnerability that companies that are technology dependent such as those in the finance, bank & insurance and telecommunications industry have. More recently, with the latest wave of terrorist attacks and due to this leverage risk, this theme

© Springer International Publishing AG 2016
R. Pergl et al. (Eds.): EOMAS 2016, LNBIP 272, pp. 154–171, 2016.
DOI: 10.1007/978-3-319-49454-8_11

is now discussed on a regular basis in boardrooms across the global corporate landscape as BC preparedness can mean the difference between life and death for a company.

A BCP establishes the strategies, procedures and critical actions needed to respond and manage a crisis situation [19] and expresses an organization condition to responds to unexpected disasters, disruptions or sudden business changes [4].

The British Standards Institution defines BC as the *"capability of the organization to continue the delivery of products or services at acceptable predefined levels following a disruptive event"*, also it defines business continuity management (BCM) as *"is a holistic management process that identifies potential threats to an organization and the impacts to business operations those threats, if realized, might cause, and which provides a framework for building organizational resilience with the capability for an effective response that safeguards the interests of its key stakeholders, reputation, brand and value-creating activities"* [14].

Furthermore, The British Continuity Institute [1] states that the aim of BC is to provide a documented framework and processes to allow the organization to resume all of its business processes within its recovery time objective after a disruptive incident. Creating resilience to manage unpredictable changes within the IT and business ecosystems is fundamental to empower the business in returning to the original state in the presence of a Severe Business Disruption (SBD) occurs.

With these goals in mind it is fundamental to have an enterprise wide view and a tangible and consistent plan that ensures a covering blueprint of all the areas throughout the company in order to achieve the completeness of the organization's mission and a strategy to ensure the continuity of the operation. For that it is necessary to create a full map of all critical and non-critical processes in order to predict the consequences of disruption of a business function or process. Consequently, if necessary, the organization could be replicated in a different environment using deputies and understudies. In these emergency events, the previous mapped processes are resumed in order to reconstruct the vital operations and ensure the resumption of time-sensitive operations and services. Usually, a business impact analysis (BIA) includes the gathering of information to develop these recovery strategies.

Therefore, outline all critical processes and determine which actors are needed to perform these tasks is essential to ensure that the BC plan establishes organizational resilience [13]. One of the main challenges to implement an internal BCP is to establish the necessary knowledge about all key resources, key activities, key actors and all the interactions between them. Additionally, after a SBD an organization every so often needs to adapt their business to new realities and for that it needs to redesign and re-engineering their processes. Hence, it is important to have a methodology that allows an organization to change/adapt their processes, allowing the operation to continue working with the resources available.

In this line of reasoning, the DEMO theory and methodology [7] are used in a BC ecosystem to assess the understanding, designing and engineering implementation of a BC solution under an intellectual manageability needed: insight and overview over the most complex tasks. DEMO theory and methodology captures business oriented transactions, allowing the understanding of the essence of an organization [7]. The traditional approaches used for BCM can this way obtain some improvements if they are based on the essential model.

To summarize, this paper contributes with an integration between BC best practices and the DEMO concepts, to allow the construction of new models that enhance and serve as foundational knowledge to help building a BC Plan. The integration of these two disciplines can allow a company to have a clearer view of the business and have a shared language that can be more easily understood by all involved stakeholders. Additionally it can allow to establish an easier way to redesign and re-engineering the business processes in the case of a disaster by supporting the management board dealing with a crisis situation.

1.1 Problem Definition

An enterprise that relies on technology to support its business, often deals with complex business processes that cross multiple departments and disciplines, dealing with both internal and external resources. Managing the challenge of determining and capturing all the processes needed for the BC Plan it is often a very demanding task.

As business continuity practitioner and by collecting over time the insights of key stakeholders and managers involved in the process of the business continuity plan management, key issues to address have been identified in the traditional best practices for creating and managing a business continuity plan.

According to some of the insights from the business key stakeholders and managers, these are the challenges that this paper aims to give an answer:

(i) The BCP needs to have a consensual model representations of the business processes;

(ii) It is necessary to easily validate that the processes are in accordance with what is described in the business plan and verify its integrity and completeness;

(iii) The BCP needs a common driver for the understanding and communication, regardless of context or domain differences, of how to express business flows and activities;

(iv) Tools to provide management an overview of the whole business but at the same time be deep enough, are needed. It is necessary to analyse and decide more easily when is required to approve a BCP;

(v) Reduce the complexity of the representation of complex processes.

The rest of the paper is organized as follows. The next section of the paper, Sect. 2, introduces the ontological approach to BC combined with the concepts of DEMO theory and methodology, where the case study was founded. Afterwards, Sect. 3 present conceptual foundations, particularly about BC concepts and the case study advances. Section 4 explains the research methodology used and in

Sect. 5 the design is presented and the decisions explained. Afterwards, Sect. 6 presents the outcome learnings obtained from the case study and finally, Sect. 7 concludes and presents future work.

2   Background

New solutions to define, implement and manage BCM in the scope of complex organizational business processes [3, 10] have been receiving an increasing interest by the industry, *e.g.*, the TOGAF 9.1 standard [18] that included the principle of BCP within the architecture principles framework. Moreover, some evidences that ontological models are being attempted and tested to fulfil the goals of BCP are found in the literature. In the specific enterprise engineering field, Riege and Aier [17] explore the Enterprise Architecture (EA) contingency factors and the dominating EA application scenarios that are followed in the EA method engineering. The authors point EA models as a realization tool to support the Business Continuity Planning initiatives. Depending on the degree of realization approach followed by an organization, EA is referred as adequate to deliver transparency, *e.g.*, regarding market segments, product catalogues, and business functions of the organization and their interdependencies. At the same time, Winter and Schelp [20] stress the importance of EA when applying to different organizational applications. The context of compliance management, BCP, enterprise governance, risk management, IT service management [2] are pointed as core application examples that can benefit from using EA-based approaches.

2.1   DEMO Theory and Methodology

The ontological design approach presented in this paper follows a separation of business processes (*SoP*) approach founded in the DEMO theory and methodology [7]. From the business processes point of view, DEMO introduce capabilities to deal rigorously with the dynamic aspects of the process-based business transactions using an essential ontology that is compatible with the communication and production, acts and facts that occur between actors in the different layers of the organization. A DEMO business transaction model encompasses two distinct worlds: *(i)* the transition space and *(ii)* the state space.

On the one hand, the DEMO transition space is grounded in a theory named as Ψ-theory (PSI), where the standard pattern of a transaction includes two distinct actor roles: the Initiator and the Executor. Figure 1 depicts this basic transaction pattern. The goal of performing such a transaction pattern is to obtain a new fact. The transactional pattern is performed by a sequence of coordination and production acts that leads to the production of the new fact. In detail, encompasses: *(i)* order phase that involves the acts of request, promise, decline and quit, *(ii)* execution phase that includes the production act of the new fact itself and *(iii)* result phase that includes the acts of state, reject, stop and accept. Firstly, when a Customer desires a new product, he requests it. After the request for the production, a promise to produce the production is

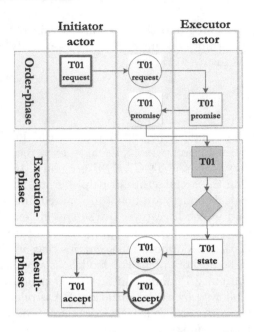

Fig. 1. The DEMO standard pattern of a transaction between two actors with separation between communication and production acts (Adapted from [7]).

delivered by the Producer. Then, after the production, the Producer states that the production is available. Finally, the Customer accepts the new fact produced. DEMO basic transaction pattern aims specifying the transition space of a system that is given by the set of allowable sequences of transitions.

Furthermore, the DEMO state space delivers the model for the business transactions facts, which are products or services, and are obtained by the business transaction successful execution. Throughout the business transaction execution more intermediate facts are required.

Nevertheless, the ontology used here satisfies the following quality requirements (C_4E) [7]: Coherence - composes a whole; Comprehensiveness - all relevant elements are represented; Consistency - it doesn't contain any contradictions or irregularities; Conciseness - as the model only contains the necessary elements and Essence - it is independent of realization and implementation of the enterprise. DEMO-3 allows and representing an organization from an ontological perspective and consists in the integration of four partial models, creating a whole view of an organization. Each one has a specific view of the organization: Construction Model, Action Model, Process Model and Fact Model [6].

The Construction Model (CM), contains all identified transaction kind and the associated actor roles defined from an ontological perspective. It shows the composition, the environment, the interaction structure and the interstriction structure of his elements. It is the most concise model as it has all necessary elements to represent the whole process. The CM of an organization, and specifically for this process, is represented in an Organization Construction Diagram

(OCD), a Transaction Product Table, and a Bank Contents Table (BCT). The Action Model (AM) sets the action rules that will base the actors while dealing with their appointments, specifying the production and/or coordination acts that should be fulfilled. The Process Model (PM) details the coordination event kinds and the applicable rules, including the cardinality of the events and contains only the event rules between transaction processes, represented by links between process steps. It is represented by the Process Structure Diagram (PSD) and as an option by a Transaction Pattern Diagram (TPD) to complement the model. The Fact Model (FM) explicits the ontological model of the state space and the transition space of its production world and is represented in an Object Fact Diagram (OFD).

3   Organizational Requirements

The aim of this section is to provide important information to assist the understanding of the organization's needs and constraints, while building a BC strategy.

To support the company's value chain, a series of activities interact within the company [16], some of which have a direct and indirect interaction with the customers and suppliers - Primary Activities [5], albeit its performance is dependent on several other processes - support activities. Following a SBD, it matters to recover straightway the primary activities and the essential support activities towards that goal.

All interaction generated around these activities, customers, suppliers, distributors and other internal and external stakeholders are accomplished by organizational processes. These processes are very important pieces for BC because they generate the flows of information.

BCM allows an organization to build resilience to threats [12], but to build it, first, there is a need to understand the organization, the organization's commitments and value added. What are its products, services, activities and associated resources, which are the essence to ensure the continuity of its critical activities at an appropriate level [9,11].

With the requirements to implement and maintain a BCP, an organization must identify organization's activities, functions, services, products, partnerships, supply chains, relationships with interested parties, and the potential impact related to a disruptive incident [8]. Additionally, its links between the BC policy and the organizations objectives and other policies, including its overall risk management strategy, must also be included [14].

ISO 22301:2012 is the international standard for Business Continuity Management Systems (BCMS), and replaced the BS 25999-2, which was withdraw in 2012. This standard provides a framework for managing business continuity in an organization regardless her type or size. Organizations that want to establish, implement, maintain and improve a BCMS, ISO 22301 applies. His structure focuses on specific key areas which are crucial for business continuity planning, clause four of the standard is particular interesting for this study, because is focused on the context of the organization to determining external and internal issues that could have an impact on the organization. This part stresses the potential impact that a SBD can have on the expected results on the overall of the organization's activities.

The BIA and Risk Assessment are present on ISO 22301 and are important steps in a business continuity plan. The BIA is focused on the results of the interruption of critical business functions and attempts to quantify the financial and non-financial costs associated with a DI. Whereas risk assessment explores all possible loss scenarios that must be taken into account, a BIA predicts the effects of a disruption for critical business functions and process, gathering information required to develop the best recovery strategy.

This impact assessment should focus on the most critical areas of the business, particularly in areas like security, finance, marketing, business reputation, legal compliance and quality assurance, and should take into account all possible failures and related costs. Therefore, and if possible, all impacts should be expressed financially and compared with the costs of possible recovery strategies.

The BIA is part of the base for the BCP and a vital piece of the process in a comprehensive Business Continuity Program. ISO 22301 stresses the importance of concluding four distinct steps to determine and assess the potential effects of an interruption to critical business operations. Figure 2 shows and highlights the overall steps to accomplish the BIA process.

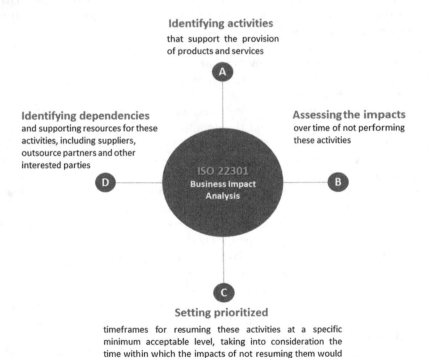

Fig. 2. Business impact analysis (Adapted from ISO 22301 (2012)) [14, p. 15].

The goal of BIA is to detect and classify which business units/departments and processes are essential to the survival of the company. Identifying correctly all business processes will help evaluating the impact of disasters on business, providing the basis for investment in recovery strategies as well as grant the correct investment in prevention and mitigation strategies. After perform the BIA, critical business processes and dependencies are identified, which will allow the organization to prioritize resources and focus on the most critical processes first, when doing planning or actual business process recovery during an SBD.

For protection and mitigation purpose, measures for each critical business process, which may be affected by a DI, should be proactively explored. The study of an alternative implementation, shall be assessed according to the organization's risk appetite and possible SBD's.

3.1 Insights from Stakeholders and Managers

During the normal BC program life cycle, represented in Fig. 3, some important tests/exercises are to be completed every year:

  (i) Project Management;
 (ii) Risk Analysis and Review;
(iii) BIA;
 (iv) BC Strategy;
  (v) Plan Development;

Fig. 3. The business continuity life cycle (Adapted from the BCM institute).

(vi) Testing and Exercising (BC test with the designated area team members; Disaster Recovery test with IT members; Tabletop exercises with area managers; Call tree exercise with all company members and key suppliers; Structured walkthrough with management and area members);

(vii) Program Management.

Regarding some of the designated points, they show up as a challenge to be created and maintained. Managers and area members often consider it confusing, challenging and very demanding. BIAs and the structured walkthrough are the topmost complains on this list. The BIA from one side is very demanding regarding all the details needed to establish the impact that a specific process can have on each business unit and to the organization as a whole, but on the other hand also need to have a vision of the inside and an overview of the organization to validate if they are coherent and consistent with what is described in the processes in which they were grounded. Based on the existing processes the analysis done to them will provide information on the short and long term effects of a disaster.

The structured walkthrough exercise is done with management and team members to identify and correct weaknesses of the plan. Involves management and representatives from each of the functional areas coming together to review the plan and to decide if the plan connected to their area is accurate and comprehensive and can be executed when required. Assess the documentation for errors, missing information and inconsistencies across the plan can be identified. Reviewing a plan that sometimes has a significant numbers of pages of information is quite grievous and time consuming. Top management quite often reinforces that although they need to guarantee that the plan is concise and consistent with the company requirements they need a more easy way to establish a coherent understanding of the company regarding business systems, information related to them, communication and organization.

3.2   The Case Study Description

This case study is implemented on a corporate company that offers insurance solutions products through several channels: agents, third-party distributors such as brokers and banks and also by using direct marketing channels. A global BCP has been developed and is maintained and adapted by each country individually, which has the responsibility to adjust their BCP to local laws and regulators requirements. A formal process that includes a continuous review of internal controls is in place to enforce the corporate policy on continuity. The implemented BC program must follow internal rules to fulfil with the organization's BC principles.

The documentation process is a procedure that is in line with the internal requisites to have all local processes described, documented and reviewed as needed. All processes must be described in a way that the organization can easily understand them. All the tasks that compose the process must define how it works and how individuals from different groups work together to achieve the business goal for the described process.

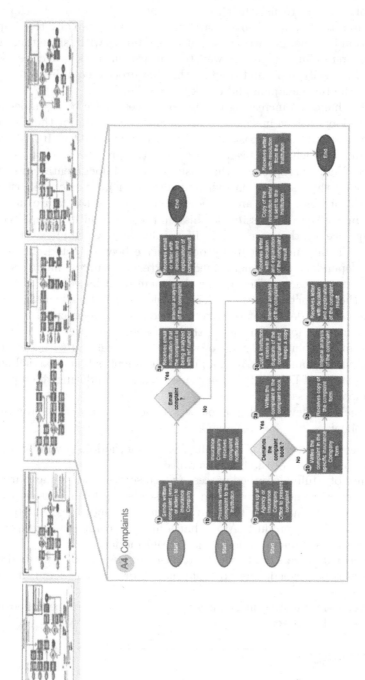

Fig. 4. Original full customer service life cycle process representation

The method to capture business processes is a arduous assignment to accomplish. Stakeholders tend to use their natural "language" very much related to their specific area to describe their internal processes. Occasionally this implies misinterpretation by other departments that they interact with, since there isn't a common understanding about the way to capture business processes. Managers also need to easily audit and validate that the process complies with what is described at the business plan and check its completeness.

On the other hand, an increasing number of processes are being undertaken by external providers, which in some cases, the documentation for these specific processes, sometimes does not exist or have poor documentation. It also exists the need to validate if what has been requested to the provider is what is really being delivered. Figure 4, represents the existing original documentation (obfuscated on purpose) that is based on rich text files (RTF), for the full customer service life-cycle process. It has an augmentation of one of the figures and has been adapted in a way to be possible for his full presentation in a single view.

By consequence of the normal BC life cycle, and as result of the last BIA assessment, some undocumented processes have been detected. These new processes are dependent on, or performed by external sources, having several dependencies between them. The existing documentation based on RTF is not clear and lack the interaction between all stakeholders. Taking advantage of fact that exists the need to document these new processes, it was decided to launch and test a new method for documenting these missing processes.

In order to find a solution to some of the constrains related with the implementation and maintenance of a BCP, a pilot experiment is being carried out to analyse the relevance of DEMO in helping management validating the representation of business processes.

The approach to develop this pilot was done by using the procedures, described as follow:

- In the absence of a described process the DEMO methodology will be used to produce the description of the business process;
- In the absence of a fully described process (which serves a particular purpose), but still there are some data from the process-related documents, it will be complemented with data from the related structured activities that produce that specific service or product. After that a full and complete description of the entire process will be done using the DEMO models;
- When a described process exists, then a reverse engineering of described business processes is performed. The existent schemas or flowcharts and the result will be compared;
- Tasks and activities involved in IT-heavy operations for all processes covering critical areas, will be described.

4   Methodology

This section explains the research methodology used to gather information related to the challenge for assessing and designing business continuity processes, presented at this paper.

The research methodology used was based on five steps:

(i) Identification of the problem - it was based on the feedback given from the BC participants and from managers, and consists in defining a method to evaluate the consistency and completeness of business processes. They need to ensure that each process is recorded in a correct, consistent and suitable way. The method also needs to ensure that the BC plan addresses all processes, activities and interdependencies between all stakeholders. Moreover, some exercises that support the BC life-cycle (structured walkthrough and checklists), were identified as areas for improvement as the existing documentation that supports these activities is often referred as poor or excessively complex. A common language between all stakeholders is needed when representing business processes to avoid misinterpretation.

(ii) Defining objectives - they were defined based on business needs and by reviewing literature, in order to identify the possible solutions for the problem. In addition, the BIA needs to identify activities that support the provision of products and services as well as identifying dependencies and supporting resources for these activities. It was necessary to establish connection points for all requirements to test possible solutions.

(iii) Designing and developing the solution - DEMO was identified as a possible solution for the aspects raised above. During the research, DEMO reveal key aspect to help mitigating the problems found. DEMO is focused on business processes and defines mechanisms to assess their consistency and has conversation-based techniques focused on specifying collaboration patterns.

(iv) Collecting information to build the DEMO models - the information to generate the ATD model presented at this case study was based on the existing documentation collected from RTFs related to the business process and also with one-on-one interviews with the stakeholders of the process.

(v) Present the solution found - the new methodology was presented and explained to the process owner and other stakeholders. It was necessary to perform several interactions to the first model before being able to present the final version of the ATD model.

5   Design

This section briefly explains and characterizes the case study regarding the solution achieved for the design of the model presented here.

Foremost and in order to understand the whole process that was assessed, it was necessary to collect all transactions, identify actors and their respective roles on each transactions and all action rules related to them. Then it was necessary to link all the information together to build a complete view of the business process in place. Figure 5 exhibits the new representation for the full process of the customer service life-cycle by using the DEMO ATD model supported by Table 1. It represent the whole process in a single view in opposition to the original representation of the process that had six figures.

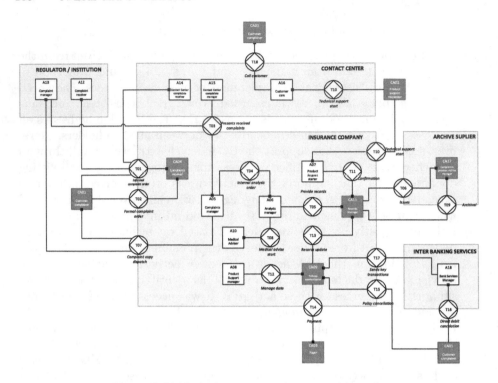

Fig. 5. DEMO ATD - customer's service life-cycle

It was necessary to perform several interactions to the ATD model to eliminate some of the redundant transactions and expressly identify all necessary actors. At the end, the information gained at the presented model by having a full view of the whole process, plus subsequent DEMO models, will be used for a better and easier identification of key business processes and help on prioritization of his principal components of the recovery process.

5.1 Delivered Artifacts

The ontological design presented here has been created using all designated rules and conventions found in the original requisites, contains the minimum possible entities needed to complete the process and all his correspondent relationships. Some of that actors share common transactions due to the regulator specification or due to the transaction specification. T01, T03 and T07 are examples of shared transactions that in some cases are executed or initiated by one of the actors, depending the origin of the complaint, but needed some abstraction of its representation. The developed model is easier to modify even when there is a change in the business or a request change done by the local regulator.

Table 1. Transaction result table - Customer care.

Transaction type	Result type	Initiator	Executor
T01 - Informal complaint order	R01 - Insurance company IC receives complaint C	CA01	CA04
T01 - Informal complaint order	R01 - Complaint C is received by the regulator	CA01	A12
T01 - Informal complaint order	R01 - Contact center receives the complaint C	CA01	A14
T02 - Formal complaint Order	R02 - Complaint C is registered at complaint book CB	CA01	CA04
T03 - Presents received complaints to insurance	R03 - Receives list of complaints C from the contact center	A15	CA05
T03 - Presents received complaints to insurance	R03 - Receives list of complaints C from the regulator	A13	CA05
T04 - Internal analysis order	R04 - Complaint analyses starts CA	CA05	CA05
T05 - Provide records	R05 - Records R are supplied	A06	A11
T06 - Issues stored records	R06 - Record R is consulted	CA11	CA05
T07 - Complaint copy dispatch	R07 - Sends copy C to Client	CA05	CA01
T07 - Complaint copy dispatch	R07 - Sends copy C to Regulator	CA05	A13
T08 - Medical advise start	R08 - Technical advice TA is given	CA06	A10
T09 - Archival	R09 - Compliance C blueprint is archived	A11	A17
T10 - Product support start	R10 - DM product support DMPS is provided	CA02	A16
T10 - Product support start	R10 - F2F product support F2FPS is provided	CA02	A08
T11 - Confirmation	R11 - PII data PD is confirmed	A07	A11
T12 - Manage data	R12 - Customer data CD are updated at the insurance policies	A08	A09
T13 - Records update	R13 - Customer records R are updated	A08	A09
T14 - Policies Payment	R14 - Receives a payment P	A09	CA03
T15 - Policy cancellation	R15 - Cancellation request CR is received	CA01	CA09
T16 - Direct Debit cancellation	R16 - Direct Debit DD is cancelled	CA01	A18
T17 - Sends key transactions	R17 - Information of Non-payment NP by the customer is received	A18	CA09
T18 - Calls customer	R18 - Client receives a retention call RC	A16	CA01

6   Outcome Learnings

Regarding the problems addressed at the beginning of the article and referring to the challenges raised by the key stakeholders and managers, we attain the following outcomes:

(i) The BCP needs to have a consensual model representations of the business processes - Regarding to this, it was identified that the new method caught the attention of managers and stakeholders as it provides an easier way to describe the overall process, dependencies between departments and provides a common driver to express business flows and activities. It will mitigate the misinterpretation among departments that interact to accomplish a shared processes.

(ii) Managers need to easily validate if processes comply with what is described at the business plan and check its completeness - Concerning to this issue, the DEMO ATD model was able to represent the processes in a more complete and comprehensive way. The result here was the combination of a correct business requirements assessment, completed with the ATD model which allowed to add additional information from a new group of stakeholders. These new representations were not present at the existing original RTF of the process and were captured during the interviews done with the stakeholders. In this aspect, this was a good enhancement comparing to the original representation as permitted to bring new facts for new artifacts and by consequence allowing them to be accountable for the business continuity program.

(iii) The BCP needs a common driver for the understanding and communication, regardless of context or domain differences, of how to express business flows and activities - The case study permitted to introduce the EE discipline and DEMO methodologies and guided their evolution inside the organization. According to Jan Dietz, only through of an ontology of the company, which is the understanding of the construction and operation of a business, in a way that is independent of the realization and implementation, can substantial strategic changes of enterprises be made intellectually manageable. The integration with BCP permits at the same time, capture and preserve knowledge (essential to mitigate risk), allowing the organization to share it more easily, because will have a common language among all the stakeholders. Simultaneously it can allow them to discuss design issues and optimization opportunities during the process.

(iv) Tools to provide management an overview of the whole business but at the same time be deep enough, are needed. It is necessary to analyse and decide more easily when is required to approve a BCP - It was identified that these new representations and semantics used reinforced a better understanding of the entire process as a whole and provided an overview of the entire business by extending this methodology.

(v) Reduce the complexity of the representation of complex processes - The use of an enterprise ontology to understand the essence of the organization will help managers to better deal with complex processes. The division of the organization into its three aspect organizations (Business, Informational and Documental), provides the means to reduce the complexity of the organization and its business process models. The business process used for the case study is far from being a very complex process, nevertheless it was possible to reduce its complexity and highlight key aspects of the process, providing the means to future work.

Figure 6 was used to highlight the areas where DEMO can be useful on the BCP. The use of a DEMO model in the area Testing and Exercising", which is resumed and explained on Fig. 7, allows management to have a wide and simplified view of all business processes, empowering them to better evaluate the plans consistency, verify if it addresses all necessary activities to support business processes and if it is correctly constructed. Using the ATD model in conjunction with the available descriptions of each process, it is easier to audit and confirm if the plans are consistent and accurate.

In the area corresponding to the Business Impact Analysis, where are represented steps A, B, C and D (bottom part of the figure), is also highlighted the

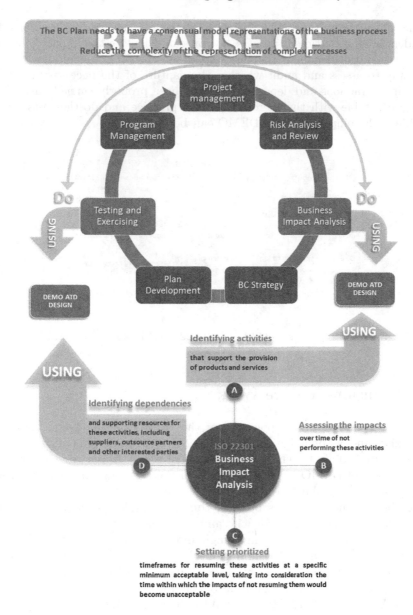

Fig. 6. Represents Figs. 2 and 3, adapted to show where DEMO is relevant

ATD Model in order to underline where DEMO leverage the BIA. It will effectively permit the identification of all activities related to products and services that support the business processes and all dependencies related to the processes of all stakeholders (phase A & D) by using this design model. It will turn phases B and C easier to accomplish as all activities are more accurately done.

The BIA process thoroughly needs to detect all possible interactions and dependencies of a particular process, so you can calculate the impact of a SBD in business and determine if they are impacted. The ATD model allows for an easier way to assess and audit whether the capture of the necessary resources and their interactions and dependencies have been properly carried out.

Figure 7, table with the exercises used to practice and do the tests for the BCP life-cycle, pinpoints where DEMO can be used.

Exercise Type	What is it?	Benefit	DEMO
Checklist	Distribute plans for review	Ensures plan addresses all activities	Using ATD Design
Structured Walkthrough	Thorough look at each step of the BCP	Ensures planned activities are accurately described in the BCP	Using ATD Design
Simlation	Scenario to enact recovery procedures	Practice session	N/A
Parallel	Full test, but primary processing does not stop	Ensures high level of reliability without interrupting normal operations	N/A
Full Interruption	Disaster is replicated to the point of ceasing normal operations	Most reliable test of BCP	N/A
Call Tree	A structured (system) that enables a list of persons, roles and/or organizations to be contacted	Tests the respond to an emergency	N/A

Fig. 7. "Exercises type" - adapted from ISO 22301 Whitepapper (2012) [14, p. 6].

7   Conclusions/Future Work

This research illustrates the potential of the DEMO methodology: knowledge which exists and is applied at the business ecosystem to design and model business processes and aid to remedy organizational issues. In our research, we consider the used of DEMO in conjunction with the BC program to be beneficial to complement and validate the BC Plan.

For the presented business process, the ATD model permitted to identify organization's activities, dependencies and relationships with interested parties, showing all possible interactions in a single model. By using DEMO ATD design in conjugation with the BC Planning methodology allowed to validate if the process fulfilled all the requirements in a single view. It also permitted to illustrate some new representation of iterations and key actors not previously represented (CA11 - T13; CA17 - T07/T09; A10 - T08 as examples). The representation of all actors of the process all together permitted to detected missing flows undetected at the traditional representations. The methodology and language used allowed the understanding between the various stakeholders and encouraged the dialogue among parties. Moreover, using an ontology model instead of an implementation model, permitted to reduce and simplify all the links between entities and actors, contributing to decrease the complexity of the process.

DEMO ATD permits representing realistically all accountable aspects of a business process and empowers BIA to reflect a more accurate calculation of the impact of a SBD at the business.

Future work will cover more areas in order to leverage knowledge and empower management on decision making while validating a BC Plan.

References

1. BCI, C.: Risk and business continuity management guide. Business Continuity Institute (2009)
2. Braun, C., Winter, R.: Integration of it service management into enterprise architecture. In: Proceedings of the 2007 ACM Symposium on Applied Computing, pp. 1215–1219. ACM (2007)
3. Cerullo, V., Cerullo, M.J.: Business continuity planning: a comprehensive approach. Inf. Syst. Manage. **21**(3), 70–78 (2004)
4. COBIT: Cobit 5 for Assurance. ISACA (2013). https://books.google.pt/books?id=FDdbAwAAQBAJ&lpg=PA1&dq=cobit
5. Daft, R.: Organization Theory and Design. Cengage Learning, Boston (2015). https://books.google.pt/books?id=yPq5BwAAQBAJ
6. Dietz, J.L.: Demo-3, Models and Representations. Enterprise Engineering Institute, Utrecht (2014). http://www.demo.nl/publications/doc_download/237-demo-models-and-representations-37
7. Dietz, J.: Enterprise Ontology: Theory and Methodology. Springer, Heidelberg (2006)
8. Drewitt, T.: A Manager's Guide to ISO22301: A Practical Guide to Developing and Implementing a Business Continuity Management System. IT Governance Ltd., Ely (2013)
9. Drucker, P.F.: Concept of the Corporation. Transaction Publishers, Piscataway (1993)
10. Elliott, D., Swartz, E., Herbane, B.: Business Continuity Management: A Crisis Management Approach, 2nd edn. Routledge, Abingdon (2010)
11. Engemann, K.J., Henderson, D.M.: Business Continuity and Risk Management. Rothstien Association Inc., Brookfield (2011). www.rothstien.com
12. Gallagher, M.: Business continuity management. Accountancy Irel. **35**(4), 15–16 (2003)
13. Hiles, A.: The Definitive Handbook of Business Continuity Management. Wiley, Hoboken (2010)
14. ISO22301: Business Continuity Management. British Standards Institution (2012)
15. McCrackan, A.: Practical Guide to Business Continuity Assurance. Artech House Technology Management Library. Artech House, Norwood (2005). https://books.google.pt/books?id=vjKEQgAACAAJ
16. Porter, M.: Competitive Advantage: Creating and Sustaining Superior Performance. Free Press, New York (1985). https://books.google.pt/books?id=o1y1AAAAIAAJ
17. Riege, C., Aier, S.: A contingency approach to enterprise architecture method engineering. In: Feuerlicht, G., Lamersdorf, W. (eds.) ICSOC 2008. LNCS, vol. 5472, pp. 388–399. Springer, Heidelberg (2009). doi:10.1007/978-3-642-01247-1_39
18. TOGAF: TOGAF Version 9.1. Open Group Standard (2011)
19. Tucker, E.: Business Continuity from Preparedness to Recovery: A Standards-Based Approach. Elsevier, Amsterdam (2014). https://books.google.pt/books?id=v95FBAAAQBAJ
20. Winter, R., Schelp, J.: Enterprise architecture governance: the need for a business-to-it approach. In: Proceedings of the 2008 ACM Symposium on Applied Computing, pp. 548–552. ACM (2008)

Educational Business Process Model Skills Improvement

Josef Pavlicek[1](✉), Radek Hronza[2], and Petra Pavlickova[3]

[1] Faculty of Economics and Management,
Prague Department of Information Engineering,
Czech University of Life Sciences,
Kamycka 959, Prague 165 00, Czech Republic
pavlicek@pef.czu.cz
[2] Faculty of Electrical Engineering, CTU,
Zikova 4, Prague 6 – Dejvice, 166 27 Prague, Czech Republic
hronzrad@fel.cvut.cz
[3] Faculty of Information Technology, CTU,
Zikova 4, Prague 6 - Dejvice, 166 27 Prague, Czech Republic
Petra.Pavlickova@fit.cvut.cz

Abstract. We found fundamental problems with the quality of business process models designed by students during education. Their design very often miss particular quality (from the business point of view). To ensure high quality of the designed process models opportunity should be given in order to use the mathematical expression's qualitative characteristic of the process model (i.e. quality measures of the process model). To improve their knowledge, we are trying to find metrics for quality process measurement. These metrics must be able to influent the quality of the model. This quality is affected by the experiences and knowledge of the process designer, mainly students. That's why the process creation is immediately followed by the quality control. The quality control shows if the modelled process models are created according to the expected quality. We develop the software to an educative tool to support a quality of designed process model. This tool serves as a very important educative tool for the teaching of the process modelling and to get feedback from students works. The goal of this paper is to describe how to improve the business process model educative skills, using quality measures of the process model.

Keywords: Education process improvement · Business process model · BPMN · Measures of quality of process models

1 Introduction

During our work on the process models designed by students for the university environment, we gained a lot of mistakes in the business process model. These mistakes were due to poor knowledge of the process designers (students). These designers are primarily students in informatics science. These designers are leaving the universities without deep process modelling knowledge and this knowledge gap influents real

R. Pergl et al. (Eds.): EOMAS 2016, LNBIP 272, pp. 172–184, 2016.
DOI: 10.1007/978-3-319-49454-8_12

business environment. To solve this problem we decided to find answers to these research questions presented at the chapter: 'Research questions'.

The beginning of the process modelling reaches the beginning of the 20th century as one of the tools for the organization description and for the description of the key activities [1]. Nowadays, it is used also in software engineering for the development of the information systems and for the key processes digitalization.

The principle of the description and documentation of the organization key processes is based on the idea, that if the particular organization needs increase "effectivity", it needs to update organization business processes too. It is suitable to use the process modelling and through it describe all the business process in the organization. The key output of the process modelling is to create the business process documentation of the organization (etc. according to the ISO 9000) that serves for:

- Familiarization with the process running and all the details:
  a. For example the time of entrance to employment, audits, outsourcing, etc.
- Materials for process running and determination of the necessary steps in process redesign due to outdated methods, legacy, new technologies, department reorganization, improving of efficiency and effectiveness, etc.
  a. Recently it is not possible to manage organization as it was formerly and it leads losing the competitive advantage.
- Materials for specification and monitoring of the key parameters in the define parts of the process organization, showing possible to use for the objective determination of measure or improvements in process running.

The principles mentioned above are the basic parts of the process management (known as business process management see Fig. 1) that, nowadays, is well known. Students from CTU Prague participate in all the projects within the fellowship in the

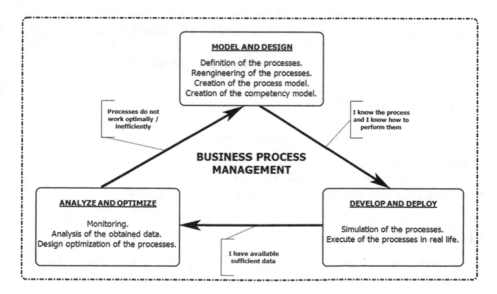

Fig. 1. Business process management, 2016 execution of the process

Centre of knowledge management. One of the goals of the Centre (CKM) is students' growth and possibility to gain experience and practice already during their studies.

During the process model creation, the main requirement is to fix as many errors as possible (thanks the process quality measures this process can be automatized as jUnit test in the programming approaches etc.). As long as errors are not being detected, plenty of work will be required finding and eliminating them. Moreover, if the design of process models is done by non-experienced persons, especially students in the role of consultants, detecting errors is more critical and requires a lot of time for the regressive control of the process models.

2 Research Questions

The general question of the research team is: "If it exists a mathematical description of the connection between something relative as "quality of the process" and how is it possible to quantify and then affect it". The research team earlier demonstrated that the mentioned issue was investigated [2]. The goal of this paper is to continue in above mentioned issue, extending the issue and finding out answers to the following questions:

1. Are these found out quality measures applicable to the process models designed in BPMN notation?
2. If not, is it possible to prepare the set of quality measures only for process models designed in BPMN notation?
3. How can these measures affect the final quality of the process models in BPMN notation and help to educate new process consultants (students)?
4. Is it possible to design the teaching tools based on the mathematical expression qualitative characteristic of the process model?

Generally, it leads to summarize the results in the field of process measures and successive recommendation and how it is possible to affect the design of quality process models in BPMN notation with the goal of detecting the errors in the process models, especially designed by non-experienced process consultants.

3 Materials and Methods

Firstly it is convenient to explain following terms:

- process model,
- model language for designing the process model,
- existing possibilities to affect the quality of the process models.

3.1 The Process Model

The process model is structured in graphic order of the information about the process running (see Fig. 2), or about the relation among more processes. Thereby, it is "for the

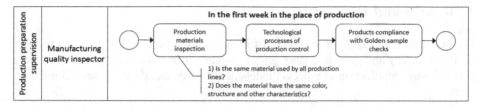

Fig. 2. Example of the process model in BPMN notation, 2016

process model reader" allowed to understand all activities and connections between them and the sources connected in the given process.

We suggest the list of more important characteristics of the process models:

- brevity,
- clarity,
- accuracy,
- graphical quality,
- model adequacy.

The final form of the process model is the result of the work of process consultant and the work is hardly affected by the subjective perception. And that is why the design of the process models is a nondeterministic activity. Therefore, it is necessary to deal with the activities that provide acceptable level of the intersubjectivity and keep the parameters mentioned above.

3.2   The Model Languages for the Process Model Design

A lot of model languages exist for the process model design (graphic presentation of the processes). These are for example:

- Unified Modeling Language (UML) [3]
- Business Process Model & Notation (BPMN) [4]
- Event-driven Process Chain (EPC) [5]
- Petri nets [6]
- Finite State Machine (FSM) [7]
- Subject Oriented Business Process Management (S-BPM) [8]
- ARIS [9]
- Yet Another Workflow Language (YAWL) [10]

Each model language is different and the final process models have different characteristics. As it was said in the introduction, in this paper we limit only for the BPMN language. And if it will not be told differently, but always with the term "process model" we will keep mind the process model designed in BMPN notation for the following text.

4 Results and Discussion

The best model language or tool by itself is not enough for the design of the brevity, clarity, accuracy and graphic quality process models. It is necessary to deal with more possible ways of affection of process models quality. For this purpose, several methods exist:

- SEQUAL Framework [11].
- UAL Framework [11].
- The Guidelines of Modeling (GoM) [12].
- Quality Framework for conceptual modeling [ISO 9126 standard for software quality].
- Seven Process Modeling Guidelines (7PMG) [13].
- Quality Measures of the Process Models [2].

Further familiarization with these methods (especially 7PMG), will lead the research team to the fact that the affection of the process model quality is needed to split into two parts:

1. **The process model design:**
   - The junior process consultant during the design at first comes out of the rules/principles/recommendations for the process modelling. It should be structured as methodological instruction.
2. **Verification of the quality model:**
   - The senior process consultant verifies the final quality after the process model design and decides about the changes that lead to the quality result.

The research team applied a lot of principles of the process modelling in the field of education at the Universities (Czech University of Life Science, Czech Technical University and University of West Bohemia), and also in the commercial sphere. During this practice and studying principles and process model quality verification, it was found out a coming up to extensively omitting certain recommendations and principles. Therefore, it was decided to create the system (its absence also affected the research team) for quality verification with providing feedback regarding possible process model changes to the students (and also to the professional process consultants). An appropriate tool measures recently mentioned process model quality.

4.1 The Process Model Quality Measures

As it was mentioned in previous chapter, from the available research outputs, it is obvious that the key parameters of the process models (i.e. brevity, clarity, accuracy and graphic quality) may possibly influence, thanks to the process model quality measures.

In this chapter we get to know with the existing process model quality measures and measures made out by the research team, especially the reason of affecting the quality of process models designed in BPMN model language.

4.2   Existing Process Models Measures

The research team worked in the past upon the identification of the quality measures of the process models and identified a lot of them [2, 14] - Fig. 3.

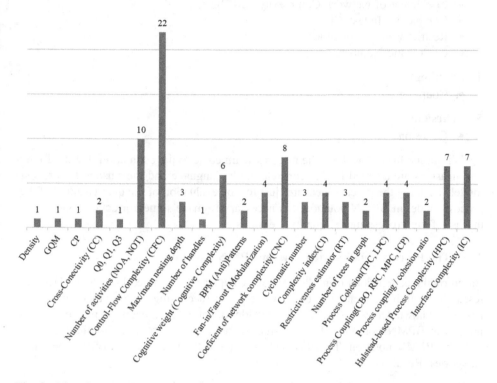

Fig. 3. List of suggested measures defined for BPM and listed in the relevant resources (WoS and SCOPUS etc.) and their frequency during the interval of the years: 2001–2014 [14].

A list (see below) of the measures was created, sorted to the appropriate categories, according to the complexity of the process model.

1. **Size:**
   - Number of Activities (NOA).
   - Number of Activities and Control-flow elements (NOAC).
   - Number of Activities, Joins, and Splits (NOAJS).

2. **Modularity:**
   - Fan-in/Fan-out (Modularization).
   - Maximum nesting depth.
   - Mean nesting depth.
   - Interface Complexity (IC).

3. **Complexity:**
   - Cognitive weight metric.
   - Control-flow Complexity (CFC).
   - Halstead-based Process Complexity.
   - Coefficient of Network Complexity (CNC).
   - Complexity Index (CI).
   - Restrictiveness estimator.
   - Cyclomatic Number.

4. **Coupling:**
   - Coupling.

5. **Cohesion:**
   - Cohesion.

Within the further analysis the research team came to the estimation that the found out measures are adapted for the concrete model language and their usage for process model. To apply the process measures just for the evaluation of the quality grade of the process model in BPMN notation it is necessary to make some corrections and create the list of the process model quality measures.

4.3   The Process Quality Measures in BPMN Notation

Based on the conclusions from the previous Chapter and obtained knowledge [15] our research team implemented specific corrections (according to the theoretical and practical knowledge with the design and identification of the errors in the process models in BPMN notation). The research team creates the new list of the measures right for BPMN notation. Together with it came to the reassessment of the measures categories. Result is:

1. **Size of the model** – this type of measures expresses the size of the model. This is the basic type of the measures; these basic values are used for the calculation of the more complex measures. We can assume that the size of the process right influence its complexity. It also confirms one of the recommendation for the design of the intelligible process models according [13].
   a. Number of Elements:
      - Number of pools
      - Number of swimlanes (in other words Number of participants)
      - Number of activities:
        1. Number of tasks.
        2. Number of subprocesses.
        3. Number of call activities.
        4. Number of event. subprocesses.
        5. Number of transactions.
      - Number of events:
        1. Number of start events.
        2. Number of intermediate events.
        3. Number of end events.

- Number of gateways:
  1. Number of Exclusive gateway.
  2. Number of Inclusive gateway.
  3. Number of Parallel gateway.
  4. Number of Event gateway.
- Number of data:
  1. Number of data objects.
  2. Number of data stores.
- Number of artefacts:
  1. Number of text annotation.
  2. Number of groups.
- Number of message flows.

   b. Process depth (i.e. how many levels of the subprocesses is the process compose with):

- Maximal process depth.
- Average process depth.

2. **Complexity of the model** – this type of measures expresses the complexity of the process.

   a. Control Flow Complexity (CFC).
   b. Halstead-based Process Complexity (HPC).

3. **Structure of the model** – this type of the measure expresses the quality of the design of the internal element's structure that affect the process passing.

   b. Nesting depth:

- Maximum nesting depth.
- Mean nesting depth.

   c. Interface complexity:
   d. Number of end events within swimlines:

- Maximum number of end events within swimlines.
- Mean number of end events within swimlines.

   e. Multiple decision making (cascade of "if "consecutive).
   f. Cycles number.
   g. Duplicate display of the model elements (especially participants, events and activities).

4. **Comprehensiveness of the model** – this type of the measure expresses the severity of the model understanding from the side of the user/reader:

   a. Cognitive weight (CW).
   b. Coefficient of network complexity (CNC).
   c. Anti-patterns.
   d. Assigned owner for the model.
   e. Assigned responsible person for the model.

5. **Modularization of the model** – this type of the measures expresses the level of the modularity of the process design:

   a. Fan_in.
   b. Fan_out.

6. **Modularization (Fan_in/Fan out).**

4.4   Metrics Calculation Software

All above discussed metrics are supported by Metrics calculation software. This software is based on the research team results [2, 15–17] and on the diploma research of Richard Mach [14] leaded by J. Pavlíček. This software is running on the Czech university of Life Sciences application server Athena.pef.czu.cz (http://athena.pef.czu. cz:8080/BpmMeasuresWebClient/). The main purpose of this software is to support business process models of the student, who tries to be deeply experienced in this subject. Software calculates discussed metrics values based on XPDL file standard and it is free for use for anybody.

Metrics Calculation Software Layers. As the Fig. 4 shows the conceptual structure of Metrics calculation software, we can split it into 4 layers:

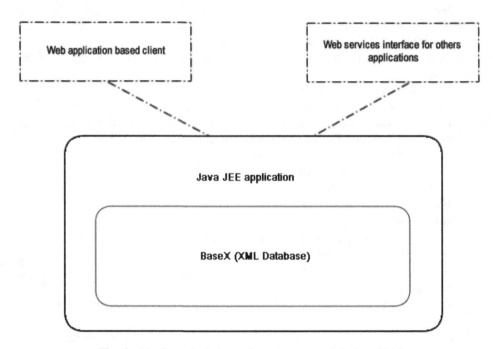

Fig. 4. Metrics calculation software conceptual design, 2016

1. **BaseX (XML) database** - This is open source XML database used for storing XPDL data file. XML database supports XPATH and XQUERY queries useful for metrics calculation.
2. **JEE JavaBean application** – this is application running on the GlassFish 4.x application server. This application contains Web client graphical interface. This interface allows users to calculate metrics by uploading XPDL file.

3. **Web application** - this is part of JEE application running on the GlassFish. It was developped in Vaadin framework. Vaadin generates java script files, which are presented at the users' side browser (Fig. 5).
4. **Web Services interface** – this interface is not yet developped. We suppose to support REST WebServices. This service will be available upon future request.

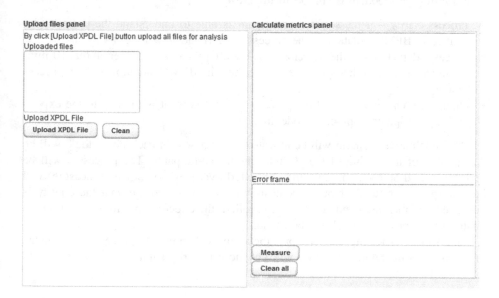

Fig. 5. Metrics calculation software current design, 2016

5   Discussion

The research team used the knowledge of the existing measures of the process model quality, added other attributes affected their quality (for example role metamorphosis, fuzzy responsibility) [15]. All the knowledge was verified with the students' cooperation, either leadership of the final thesis or during their fellowship. On the basis of these procedures we primary focused on the design of the appropriate set of the process measures for the BPMN reason. Together with that were created measures suitable for educative purposes in the process of model design. In this phase of the research it is only theoretical draft that is necessary to check in practice.

The verification will be done in cooperation with the general public and students of the subject Human Computer Interaction (CULS Prague, KII, Gestor J. Pavlíček) and the verification and identification will be done especially:

- As to the usability of the identified measures in practice.
- Finding the allowable intervals of the resultant quality measures BPMN process models.
- As to values correlation between the key measures and the key parameters of the process models.
- Finding if some combination of the measures can lead to the creation of new ones.

The selected method of the verification is the qualitative usability test it the CULS lab. To the study participants we introduce BPMN process models. We will identify the users' reactions and perception of the key features of the process models (brevity, clarity, accuracy and graphic quality). We will correlate that with the results of the designed quality measures of the process models in BPMN notation.

The qualitative scenario is spread to the study:

- Process clarity – if the selected participant is able to understand the process (described in BPMN notation of the process model) and how long it will take.
- Process adaptation – if the participant is able after the concrete interval (ca. 10 min) to understand the other processes (described in BPMN notation of the process model).
- Qualitative characteristics of the processes – that is what is missing to the experienced participants in process modelling.

This qualitative scenario will be repeated in 3 phases. In each phase there will be the running of the testing of the 10 independent participants. The processes will be reviewed based on each phase so, that the stated hypothesis (i.e. quality measure) will be confirmed or refuted. If our hypothesis will be confirmed, i.e. that the quality is possible to be measured and also to be controlled, the effective tool for controlling the quality of the process model will be found.

Apart from answering the questions, the study will spread the students' knowledge of the process modelling. Thus we will get more material suitable for our study and usable in teaching.

6   Conclusions

As it was said above, the key output of the process modelling is the creation of the subsidiary/descriptive documentation of the processes. This documentation should perform the educational purpose (CULS Prague and CTU Prague students).

The procedure of the process models design is needed to normalise, i.e. to establish the rules for the modelling. Setting the control mechanisms will discover the poor quality of process models and provide the necessary information to their correction. The suitable example can be the principles of ISO 9001 [18].

The goal of this paper was to find the answers to the three questions defined above. Now we can summarize finding out the hypothetical answers. We have to say hypothesis, because all answers have not been completely verified yet. But we can promise, the research is going ahead and during the conference time we will be presenting new results recorded at the CULS Usability Lab with the eye tracking system.

1. **Are these found quality measures in process modelling suitable for the process models in BPMN notation?**

In particular, yes. The problem is, that the found measures are sometimes specific for the concrete model language and the BPMN notation is not possible to be applied directly (without corrections). The BPMN notation together exhibits a lot of specifics that fundamentally affect the quality of the process models.

2. If not, is it possible to create the set of the quality measures for the process models in BPMN notation?

It is possible to create the required set of the measures. It this Paper, the research team suggested the list of the measures just for the BPMN notation. It is needed to mention, that it takes only about the first draft that was not checked in practice. That is why the research team recommend the final list of the measures checks in practice through the qualitative research in the usability lab CULS and CTU according to the above described procedure. If it will be possible, the draft of the project classes should be done and also the appropriate recommendation, which quality measures to be used for which class.

3. How can these measures affect the final quality of the designed models in BPMN notation and help in the process of education of the new process consultants (i.e. students)?

The measures can affect the quality directly and indirectly. The strength of the influence is dependent upon the many factors. During the usability test it is needed to track the direct effects (for example the effort of the smallest process nesting). Their impact to the quality of the process is needed to register and the results consulted with the designers of the processes and if needed re-verify in the usability lab. The indirect effect will be studied by the interview after the study termination in the lab. Every "participant" (the person that cooperates in the research as a process designer) will discuss about the problems during the process design. The participant will indicate the most important problems that should be solved. This discussion will lead to understand if setting of some measure will not lead to the useless stress of the process designers. This stress can affect the final design by its simplification. This phenomenon is negative and should be eliminated. During the test the participant will do a lot of acts that can be retroactively projected from the study record. The test and also the record of the test are very useful educational material.

4. Is it possible to design the teaching tools based on the mathematical expression qualitative characteristic of the process model?

Yes, it is possible. We developed "Metrics calculation software" which is helping students to improve their process models skills. This software is described above.

The results of the measurement of the quality measures are leading to the finalization of the list of the process quality measures in BPMN notation. After this finalization of the list it will be possible to create the advanced automated tool, that can control the quality of the process model after the creation. This tool is giving to the author (student) feedback/recommendation how the process model should be changed. It can be based on the Metrics calculation software developed and tested now. It has to support the documentation and can be effectively used for quick quality check of designed processes.

This study can change by the time to the special educational workshop. This workshop can help the teaching of the process modelling thanks to the usability lab. This can lead to the standardize procedure of teaching of the process modelling. This will highly reflect the knowledge of the process consultants and finally the designed company processes.

References

1. Mendling, J.: Metrics for Process Models: Empirical Foundations of Verification, Error Prediction, and Guidelines for Correctness, 1st edn. Springer, Heidelberg (2008). http://www.amazon.com/Metrics-Process-Models-Foundations-Verification/dp/3540892230
2. Hronza, R. et al.: Míry kvality v procesním modelování. *Acta Informatica Pragensia*, **4**(1), 18–29 (2015). http://aip.vse.cz/index.php/aip/article/view/93
3. OMG: Unified Modeling Language (UML) (2008). http://www.uml.org
4. OMG: Business Process Model & Notation (BPMN) (2014). http://www.omg.org/bpmn/index.htm
5. Scheer, A.W., Oliver, T., Otmar, A.: Process modeling using event- driven process chains. Process-Aware Inf. Syst. 119–146 (2005). http://books.google.com/books?hl=en&lr=&id=ZENNdQq8p74C&oi=fnd&pg=PA119&dq=Process+Modeling+Using+Event-+Driven+Process+Chains&ots=ZfXNZRJ_8I&sig=G1ajjHWo5DHl_I1wvJQtp6OiFoo#v=onepage&q=EEPC&f=false
6. Ajmone Marsan, M., et al.: Modelling with Generalized Stochastic Petri Nets, 1st edn. Wiley, New York (1994)
7. Wright, D.R.: Finite State Machines (2005). http://www4.ncsu.edu/~drwrigh3/docs/courses/csc216/fsm-notes.pdf
8. Fleischmann, A., et al.: Subject-Oriented Business Process Management. Springer, Heidelberg (2012)
9. ZČU:Metodika ARIS (2015). http://home.zcu.cz/~mjanuska/html/metodika_aris.html
10. Ter Hofstede, A.H.M., et al.: Modern business process automation: YAWL and its support environment (2010). http://www.yawlfoundation.org/yawlbook/index.html
11. Krogstie, J., Sindre, G., Jørgensen, H.: Process models representing knowledge for action: a revised quality framework. Eur. J. Inf. Syst. **15**(1), 91–102 (2006)
12. Becker, J., Rosemann, M.C., Uthmann, C.: Guidelines of business process modeling. In: Business Process Management, pp. 30–49. Springer, Heidelberg (2000)
13. Mendling, J., Reijers, H.A., van der Aalst, W.M.P.: Seven process modeling guidelines (7PMG). Inf. Softw. Technol. **52**(2), 127–136 (2010)
14. Mach, R.: Návrh a tvorba nástroje pro optimalizaci procesů na základě analýzy BPM modelů. Fakulta informačních technologií (2015)
15. Pavlíček, J.:Odhad manažerských charakteristik vývoje IS v etapě specifikace požadavků. Česká zemědělská univerzita v Praze (2006)
16. Hronza, R., Špeta, M.: Business process center of excellence at the faculty of electrical engineering at the Czech Technical University in Prague. In: 2013 IEEE 15th Conference on Business Informatics, pp. 346–349. IEEE, Prague (2013). http://ieeexplore.ieee.org/lpdocs/epic03/wrapper.htm?arnumber=6642898
17. Náplava, P., et al.: How to successfully start the transformation of an academic institution. case study on the process mapping project at the Czech Technical University. In: Complementary Proceedings of the 8th Workshop on Transformation & Engineering of Enterprises (TEE 2014), and the 1st International Workshop on Capability-oriented Business Informatics (CoBI 2014) Co-located with the 16th IEEE International Conference on B, pp. 1–15, RWTH Aachen University, Prague (2014)
18. ISO :ISO 9001 Quality Management Systems - revision., 1996(353) (2015). http://www.iso.org/iso/iso9001_revision

Author Index

Printed in the United States
By Bookmasters